IN CASE YOU GET HIT BY A BUS

T0028966

How to Organize Your Life Now for When You're Not Around Later

ABBY SCHNEIDERMAN AND **ADAM SEIFER**
FOUNDERS OF EVERPLANS
WITH **GENE NEWMAN**

WORKMAN PUBLISHING • NEW YORK

■ ■ ■

DEDICATED TO DOUG, JOAN, ALDO,
AND SO MANY MORE WHO LEFT US TOO SOON
AND PROVIDED THE INSPIRATION THAT MADE
THIS BOOK A REALITY

■ ■ ■

Library of Congress Cataloging-in-Publication Data is available.

ISBN: 978-1-5235-1047-4

Cover and interior design by Lisa Hollander
Illustrations by Nancy Butterworth and Caitlin O'Neill

Workman books are available at special discounts when purchased in
bulk for premiums and sales promotions as well as for fundraising or
educational use. Special editions or book excerpts can also be created to
specification. For details, please contact special.markets@hbgusa.com.

Workman Publishing Co., Inc., a subsidiary of Hachette Book Group, Inc.
1290 Avenue of the Americas
New York, NY 10104
workman.com

WORKMAN is a registered trademark of Workman Publishing Co., Inc.,
a subsidiary of Hachette Book Group, Inc.

Printed in the United States of America on responsibly sourced paper.
First printing November 2020

10 9 8 7 6 5 4

CONTENTS

■ ■ ■

PLANNING IS IMPORTANT

■ ■ ■

For more than ten years, we have been obsessed with helping people get their lives organized in case "something unexpected happens." By far the most difficult part of our mission used to be convincing people that the "unexpected" actually happens. And that unexpected things *could* happen at any time, like getting hit by a bus, as our not-so-subtle title suggests. Then, at the beginning of 2020, the entire world was hit by a bus in the form of a pandemic. The unexpected, the very thing our company was built around, became reality for just about everyone on the planet.

Life as we knew it ground to a halt. Those families that could, hunkered down to minimize the impact, and most everyone feared the worst. Mostly, that fear was around catching COVID-19 and having it take us, like it has far too many others. We feared for our children and how to keep them safe, calm, and educated. We feared for our parents, some with existing health conditions, who would have to fend for themselves during a time when they needed us most. It seemed like everything was falling apart with a shocking quickness. The economy crumbled, leaving millions unemployed and wondering how they'd pay their rent or even afford essential items. Adding to the insidiousness was not being able to physically interact with so many people we loved, because doing so would risk everyone's health.

But there were undeniable bright spots too: a warm text from a friend you lost touch with years ago; a post on social media from someone on the road to recovery; a former coworker checking in to see if you were okay. Group video calls with family members became the norm, a chance at least to see each other's smiling faces (and poke fun at parents who spent half the call trying to figure out how to turn on their cameras or microphones). Birthdays, holidays, and graduations were celebrated remotely, but we could still be "together." These were the moments that made us forget how tough everything had become and focus on what's really important—the hope and strength we get from those we love, who themselves take strength from us in return.

The feelings of hope and despair that arise during a crisis can often motivate us to make lasting positive life changes. But as memories fade and normal routines return, that feeling of hope and purpose can diminish. This book is intended to help you renew, reinforce, and remind yourself of that hope for the rest of your life. *We believe planning for your family and loved ones is the key.* Our mission has always been to help as many people as possible prepare for the unexpected. That mission—to help people ensure that their family isn't left unprepared when the "unexpected" strikes—has taken on an even greater, more solemn importance now. But really, it was always that way for us.

Everplans was born when Abby Schneiderman, one of our cofounders, was planning her wedding back in 2010. She used online sites like the The Knot (theknot.com) to keep everything in order, as so many do, when her brain switched from marriage to death for some reason. She wondered: "What's next? What other big life stages are there, and what other resources are there to guide people through them?" Abby began researching and found plenty of resources to help people plan for the birth of a child, buy a home, send kids to school, and plan their finances and retirement. But after retirement planning, that was it. There was a big hole—death—not addressed. It didn't seem right that the *only* unavoidable life stage, and the most scary and overwhelming one, didn't have any helpful, down-to-earth resources or tools to guide people.

Abby, a repeat tech entrepreneur, got to thinking. She mentioned the idea to her friend and colleague, Adam Seifer, another tech veteran in New York. Together, we spent about a year researching the idea and were shocked at how little was available to help us prepare ourselves for the so-called worst. We got our friend and colleague Sarah Whitman-Salkin on board and began researching and writing about every aspect of end-of-life planning we could find.

Everplans was the result. And it grew quickly.

Then a tragedy occurred, one that would change the trajectory of Abby's family, and the company, forever. Her fifty-one-year-old brother was killed in a head-on collision by an impaired driver. Everything changed in an instant. Abby and her family were thrust into a position many families experience: They were shocked, heartbroken, and unsure what to do next. Her brother had made some financial arrangements, but her family had no idea what he would have wanted. And suddenly, they had to make all sorts of stressful (and expensive) decisions in an incredibly short amount of time.

A stark realization set in about Everplans, one that had been an elephant in the room for some time: In order to really make a difference for people at their time of greatest need, we had to help people get a plan in place *ahead* of time. That way, if a tragedy or emergency struck, their families would have easy access to everything they needed. We needed to create a digital platform to store information and guide people on how to organize the right things, create

the right documents, and share them with the right people. That's when we found Gene Newman, a longtime editor and writer who gave us the final thing we needed: an approachable and sometimes even funny voice unlike any other covering these tough topics.

Years later, Adam was put to the test when his mother received a tragic terminal diagnosis. Having a clear picture of what needed to be done, he helped her get everything organized and was able to make rapid, guilt-free decisions about her care. Most important, it afforded him more quality time with her at the end, and low-stress, reflective time with his dad and brother after her passing because all those loose ends had been tied up.

Over time, as more and more people started using Everplans, we realized the site wasn't about death—it was about life. Because getting everything organized lets you live to the fullest, knowing you're prepared for anything, having done your very best for those you love. And that's what you'll find in this book: a plan to do just that. It's easier than you think.

PLANNING IS NOT THAT HARD

■ ■ ■

One of the greatest frustrations of life is not knowing what you're going to need or when you're going to need it. We all have a general idea, but it's almost impossible to keep everything straight. Now imagine a family member stepping in and trying to take over for you when they don't even know where to start.

This book will walk you through all the things you need to know and do and what decisions you have to make when you or those who will survive you need it most. The idea is for the crucial aspects of yours or a loved one's life to be in complete and clear order, so no one is left with a stressful mess to untangle.

Like most things unknown to us, this may seem overwhelming at first, even time-consuming and difficult. But impossible? Hardly. Like most everything in life, knowing where to start is the tricky part. But once you get going, it becomes more manageable, and then, almost imperceptibly, it becomes automatic.

Now that we're all friends, let's get to work and gauge where you are now on a basic planning scale: novice, intermediate, or expert. For those honest enough to admit you're a novice,

you're our type of person. This means you recognize the need to get in gear and are ready to take action. We feel the same way about intermediates, who've done some planning—like creating a Will or buying Life Insurance—but realize there's much more to be done. As for the experts, it's time for a reality check. Even people who think they've covered all the bases still often leave inadvertent complications behind for their family.

Abby's dad fancied himself an expert planner when he said, "All my legal documents and important plans are with our estate attorney." Then her mom interrupted, asking, "But wait, Milton, who's our estate attorney?" You might have a folder with legal documents and instructions, or a fat file with an attorney, but our lives are made up of so much more.

PLANNING IS LIBERATING

. . .

Would you file your taxes every year if it were optional? Right. If taxes were a mere suggestion, few people would pay them. From our perspective, it would be nice if getting the details of your life in order were also compulsory. But there's no threat of fines or legal action if you don't create a Will, name a Health Care Proxy, or refuse to share the unlock code for your phone with someone you trust. Our advice throughout this book helps you manage your life better now, but more importantly, it helps your family avoid what we call "defaults" later. Defaults are the excruciating ordeals they'll be forced to face if you choose to do nothing.

We know organizing every aspect of your life isn't like a five-day juice cleanse, getting a new hairdo, or going full Marie Kondo on your closet and dresser. The results aren't immediate, and you might not be around to enjoy many of the benefits. We all love instant gratification, but this type of planning forces you to look beyond your own personal gain and know your family has a well-lit path forward if you're not around.

The good news is that you don't have to do it all at once. We'll help you focus on the most important stuff, with tips and tricks along the way to keep you motivated, as well as guide you through the stickiest parts.

Since everyone's life is filled with different priorities, it's obvious that everyone's plan is different. We're totally flexible about this, especially with our "Side Missions" scattered throughout each Level, which may or may not apply to your life. But here's a good question to consider as you get started: What's important to you?

Most people simply say "family." But we want you to go deeper than that. What's *really* important to you? It doesn't have to be one thing. Our lives aren't that simple. It might be something that hurts a little or even makes you uncomfortable to think about, because being challenged can spring us into action.

We all have different motivations. Maybe you witnessed the chaos a friend experienced after the death of a family member and don't want your own family to suffer the same fate. A parent might be terrified at the prospect of their young children being raised by an unfit guardian, or worse, in foster care. Money is often the cause of most issues, and perhaps you don't want your family going to war over what you leave behind. Or maybe it's as simple as you waking up in the middle of the night completely wrought at a pandemic that went from a story on the news to a new reality.

Once you have a clear vision of your purpose, think of it as a picture-in-picture box on a TV screen following you around throughout this entire book. That picture might have an image of your kids, your spouse or partner, your siblings, your puppy, or a person you loved who is now gone. When you get discouraged or overwhelmed, take a second and visualize that image in your head, then repeat this mantra: *This* is why I plan!

A last piece of advice before we get started: Don't let your mind go crazy or freak out about how you're going to get all of this stuff organized. We'll cover that in due time with our "Plans of Attack" that accompany each section. For now, we want you to let all of this information wash over you. So pens and pencils down (at least for now), take a deep breath, and get ready for an exhilarating ride.

■ ■ ■

LEVEL 1

START WITH YOUR STUFF

Passwords, People, Money, and Your Abode

HERE'S WHAT YOU'LL HAVE
WHEN YOU'RE FINISHED WITH THIS LEVEL:

- A system for managing all your passwords and secret codes

- Your money and assets organized so that you don't have a panic attack

- An instruction manual for your home and vehicles

- A decluttered address book where your most useful contacts rise to the top

ACCESS GRANTED
PASSWORDS & CODES

■ ■ ■

The typical person has an average of 130 different accounts, according to a password manager platform called Dashlane. How is anyone supposed to remember 130 passwords? Let's not forget why you need passwords in the first place—because of identity thieves and hackers. So now you don't just have to remember a code, you have to make it complicated enough so it can't be easily figured out. And then if any of your accounts are compromised, you have to frantically create and remember new passwords.

When we think of passwords, we're not just focusing on your email, social media, and Amazon accounts. We're talking about *everything* you use to protect any of your assets, property, and information. That means PIN numbers, combinations, unlock codes, online passwords, usernames, and don't forget the always-fun answers to secret questions.

Even if you don't fancy yourself a digital person, you still have passwords—maybe to access a health care portal, or receive benefits, or open your garage door. How do you remember them all? People typically keep track in a number

of common ways. They download and maintain all their passwords in a convenient (and often free) password manager app on their phone or computer. They keep them on a digital note or an actual piece of paper. Or they try to keep them all in their head.

Guess which is the most popular method? Take your time. OK, we'll spill it: According to a Pew Research Center study, 65 percent of people say the method they use most often is to "memorize them in their heads." The worst possible method is also the most popular, because of course it is. The next most popular method is writing them on a piece of paper (18 percent), which isn't ideal but is much better than relying on memory.

The reason these numbers hit so close to home for us is that we are maniacally obsessive about security protocols. We wouldn't have started a business and built an entire platform that protects people's most personal information if it wasn't always on our mind. This puts us on the paranoid, protect-everything-at-all-costs end of the spectrum. You don't have to be crazy like us, but it really helps.

We understand that passwords are a hassle. We wish the world was a place where people weren't required to institute such complicated measures to ward off devious marauders. But the truth is, no one thinks passwords matter until they get hacked. The same way no one cares about calamine lotion until they get assaulted by mosquitos.

Before we get into password storage methods, there's one thing

PASSWORD MANAGERS: OUR LIST

- **1Password (1password.com): $36–$60 annually**

- **Dashlane (dashlane.com): Free version for up to fifty passwords; between $60 and $90 annually if you choose premium or family**

- **LastPass (lastpass.com): Free version for one user, $36–$48 annually for premium**

For a more up-to-date list along with links, hit up this page on the web to get more info: incasethebook.com /password-manager.

you need to focus on before you do anything else—deal with the modern-day appendage otherwise known as your phone.

SHARING YOUR PHONE PASSWORD

In an emergency, how could someone you trust access your phone?

This handheld computer, which connects you with the rest of the world, holds the keys to your life. Because of this, sharing your unlock code might make you nervous. This is understandable, because no one should be snooping around your private matters unless you grant permission. That said, you can't take a time-out from an emergency—or death—to share the unlock code, so you have to take a leap of faith.

Even with all the new biometric tech around fingerprints and facial recognition, accessing your phone still comes down to a four- or six-digit code, which needs to be entered when restarting a device or after a long lockdown period. You might be clever enough to have a family member register their fingerprint or face on your phone, but they'll still need the code.

How should you communicate the code in a way that makes you feel comfortable? Here are some options:

Smart and Secure

Keep it in one of the password-storing methods we recommend later in this section. We don't want to jump ahead, but your unlock code should be front and center, since it's a source of vital information and access.

Good, but Problematic

Write the code down and store it with important documents. Please keep it updated or else you will drive the person who needs to access it crazy. "The good news: She shared her code! The bad news: She must have changed it at some point, because it doesn't work, and now her phone is going into a blender."

Side Mission:
CAN WE SEE SOME ID?

In a world that's becoming overwhelmingly digital, some of the most important and official things we own are still printed on paper or require some sort of physical ID. Although a few are ornamental certificates meant to be displayed (like a college degree), others are extremely crucial when you need them.

The challenge: How long would it take you to locate the following list of things?

BASIC RULES

You've got a ten-minute limit. If you don't have or need the ID or document listed, skip to the next item on the list. You must physically find the official document or ID, so if you can't search for it right now but still want to play you must know with absolute certainty where it is. (We're operating on the honor system, so play fair.)

Set the timer on your watch or phone right now. Ready, set, GO!

THINGS TO FIND

- Birth certificate
- Citizenship documentation/green card/visa
- Driver's license/nondriver's ID
- Military ID
- Passport
- Social Security card
- Work ID
- High school diploma
- College/university diplomas (bachelor's, master's, doctorate, etc.)
- Religious confirmation certificate
- Professional or trade certifications or designations
- Adoption papers
- Marriage certificate
- Divorce decree
- Military discharge papers

How'd you do? Could you find all the things you needed? Are you out of breath from running all over the house? Take a minute, get some water, and cool down.

The point of this is to make you realize how many forms of ID and official documents we accumulate throughout our lives. Although some are ceremonial, others are vital in day-to-day life (driver's license) or in providing benefits to your family if they need them. (Did you know you can't get a death certificate without a Social Security number?)

Terrible for Security, Great for Access

Don't lock your phone. A Pew survey found that more than a quarter of smartphone owners don't lock it. Perhaps you don't care who accesses your phone. You really should. Apple released a commercial about privacy that said, "There's more information on your phone than in your home." If you lose it, someone else will have way too many personal details about you and everyone you know. You don't have to create a code that's impossible to remember, but always have some kind of code, just in case.

Please Don't Do This!

Store the unlock code in a note-taking app or document that's accessible *only* on your phone. How would someone access your phone to access your phone? This might seem like an obvious "duh" because it is. We'd sooner you put the code on a sticky note taped to the bottom of your desk with a list of clues directing a code-worthy person to the location than risk getting locked out. Because once you're locked out, it's usually for good.

You may have seen stories of families that could no longer access Grandma's iPad because they didn't know the password, or even law enforcement unable to get the code to unlock a suspected criminal's phone. There's a reason for this, and Apple and Google aren't entirely to blame. It's about security.

Accidents and death don't play by the rules, so sometimes you have to find a work-around to suit the situation.

PASSWORDS: The Next Level

Those people who want even more security can put in the extra effort with the following measures. They may add a modicum of hassle to your life and the lives of those people who may have to access your accounts in the future, but they won't be nearly as much trouble as having everything about you stolen and sold on the dark web.

Two-Step Verification (or Two-Factor Authentication)

This is when a string of numbers is sent to your phone after you've entered your password, allowing you to complete the login process. It's sometimes mandatory for sites with sensitive information, like banks or email. You don't have to enter the code every time, only after a set period of time (like every thirty days) or when accessing that site from an unfamiliar computer or phone.

The security upside is that a person would need to have your password *and* phone to gain access to that account. The downsides are that you could lose your phone or not have your phone readily available, and you would be unable to log in until the phone is back in your hand. Hackers can also intercept the codes since they are sent via SMS. It's still an effective layer of protection, but there's another option if you want more security.

Authenticator Apps

This is another form of two-step verification, but you access the codes through an app on your phone. The codes are constantly being generated, and it makes you feel like a superspy since they have a timer always counting down to their expiration. We're partial to the no-frills Google Authenticator, but there are others available, such as Microsoft Authenticator and Authy, all of which are free and can easily be found in the iPhone or Android app stores.

Backup Codes

Whenever you enable two-step verification, either via SMS or using an authenticator app on your phone, you should always ask yourself, *What happens if I lose my phone or change my phone number? How will I get back into the site where I just enabled two-step verification?*

The answer: That's what backup codes are for!

After turning on two-step verification, you'll almost always be given a code—usually a long string of numbers that you can use *one time* in place of the SMS code or the authenticator app. You should always write this number down or take a screenshot and put it in a safe place where you keep other important documents or files. You can even copy it and add it to the notes field for that specific account in your password manager. Most sites will let you enter that code by clicking a link on the page where the two-step verification code is usually entered (it's sometimes called a recovery code). Frequently using this code will disable two-step verification, so you'll need to turn it back on again.

(continued on page 10)

PASSWORD STORAGE METHODS

We just made our case for sharing access to your phone; now apply the same logic to your computer, tablet, and any other device, since those can matter just as much. Now, on to the four methods people use to store passwords.

	OLD SCHOOL: Pen-to-Paper	**NEWER OLD SCHOOL:** Digital Documents
Method	You write them in a notebook, on a well-worn piece of paper, or possibly on a series of sticky notes that have lost their stick. Then you refer to them whenever a password is required.	You keep them in a Word document, Google Doc, or some sort of note-taking app (such as Google Keep or Apple Notes).
Upside	It's familiar and reliable and proves you have some system in place. It's not in the cloud, so it can't be hacked—someone would need to literally break into your home to access it.	You have a tried-and-true way to access all your passwords in one place and can do it on the go if the document is in the cloud and accessible on your phone. If you're not sure where a password is in the document, you can easily search for it.
Downside	Anyone with eyes who comes across it will have access to all your accounts. Unless you always update it after you change a password, it quickly becomes outdated. Many sites force you to refresh passwords frequently or after a security breach, so if you don't have that piece of paper with you when you need it, you'll have to reset the password.	Keeping it updated is a hassle. It's not as bad as a piece of paper, but close. If you don't keep it in the cloud, you can accidentally delete it. If it's labeled "passwords," anyone who uses your computer could find it. If you give it a secret name, anyone could access it with a simple search for the word *PayPal*, *Venmo*, or *Citibank*.
Bottom Line	We admire how you like to keep your password management quaint, like an old black book or Rolodex, but this is not an ideal solution.	This isn't a terrible way to keep track of your passwords. If you do this, you're on the right track but still have trust issues. If this is your preference, we won't make you feel bad. Just promise to keep it updated somewhere safe but still accessible if your family needs it.

---→ *The Good, the Bad & the Ugly*

THE "WRONGEST" WAY: In Your Head	THE SOLUTION: A Password Manager
You don't have passwords written down anywhere but instead either use the same easy password for every site or try your best to recall them from memory whenever you're accessing a site or service. When you fail, you simply click "Forgot Password" and reset it each time.	You download software like Dashlane, LastPass, 1Password, or another offering that stores all your passwords. These services also generate random secure passwords on the fly, make sure you don't reuse passwords, and allow you to safely and securely share passwords. You have to remember only a single master password to access them all.
There's little upside here. It's true, no one can hack your brain. You think you gamed the system with the forgot password trick, forcing each site to serve you every time you need to access it.	Password managers allow you to seamlessly use them via extensions and plug-ins on your computer and app integrations on your phone. By generating unique passwords for all your accounts, you won't even know (or care) what the passwords are anymore. If any of your accounts are compromised, you can fix the problem within seconds. If you need to find a password, you know exactly where to look and can find it quickly. You can also include all sorts of other codes and passwords from your life, as well as credit card info.
"Forgot password" isn't a sustainable method—if you have multiple email accounts, your family will be completely in the dark if they need to access any of your accounts.	How many times have you read about seemingly impenetrable systems being hacked? Way too often, which makes this a hard sell. Also, if you forget the master password and don't use any secondary security methods, you're toast. And although many password managers offer the majority of their services for free, almost all charge a monthly or annual fee to use the more advanced features.
Nope! We already mentioned the survey that said this is the way most people keep track of their passwords, but you're not "most people." You're much better than that.	Password managers make life easier and are a gift for your family. We were super skeptical of these services at first. But once you take the leap, you'll wonder how you ever survived without them. You should also know that these companies live and die by security, so the smallest breach in trust will destroy them.

(continued from page 7)

AUTOSAVE?

All browsers and most phones allow you to save passwords automatically. For us, this method doesn't allow for a complete password picture, is confusing to navigate, and assumes you don't use any other browser or access passwords only on your phone. Using one of these options is a good start—and you can easily import all of them into a proper one-stop-shop password manager—but lacks the flexibility of one.

This isn't the only place where backup codes will come in handy when you're accessing a protected device or service. For example, when you encrypt the hard drive on your PC or Mac, which means a person would need your password or encryption key to gain access to your hard drive, you'll be given a backup code that you can use in case you forget the password for your machine. Think of it as a second "key" to get in the door of your machine, but one you would use only in an emergency.

Yet Another Reason to Share Your Phone Password

If you currently lock down your devices and accounts using any of these advanced methods, your family needs to be aware of it. You could share all the passwords you have, but if they don't have access to your phone and email, they won't be able to get into any of your accounts. The point of these extra security measures is to keep bad people out and allow good people to get in when needed.

KEYS TO THE KINGDOM:
Your Most Important Passwords

Not all of your accounts are created equal—some stand well above the rest. If you were stranded on an island and could bring only five passwords, which would you choose? Here are some examples to get you prepped for island living.

Google

For millions of people, Google is the mothership. It includes email (Gmail), documents (Drive), photo backups (Google Photos), contacts, calendar, phone info (Android), video (YouTube), and home automation (Google Home). It might also be the account you use to sign into other accounts across the internet. It's a little frightening how deeply Google reaches into our lives, which also makes it an ideal pick for the top five.

If you rely on another platform for your primary email, like Outlook or Yahoo (or AOL, if that's still a thing by the time you're reading this), then that should make your list.

Apple

Apple, like Google, traps you in its digital tentacles, though the tentacles are far sleeker and more expensive. Your Apple ID and password should provide the works to whoever will need it.

Amazon

Amazon is simply massive, to the point where you probably don't realize how often you use its services. Perhaps you have Amazon Prime for free shipping and entertainment (movies, TV, and music), books on a Kindle, photo storage, and an Echo device listening and responding to you in your home right now. It might seem like it's just a shopping site, but if your life is this intertwined with a company, then perhaps it's something your family would need to access.

Speaking of shopping, any account with a credit card associated with it should receive extra attention. The last thing you want is one of those being compromised.

Facebook

There are now more than a billion people on Facebook. It has become a communications platform as much as a place to share photos of dogs, meals, and impulsive opinions. Like Google, Facebook has become a way for many people to log in to the majority of their other accounts and apps.

Banking & Benefits

Anything you use to pay bills, check balances, or receive any kind of benefits (like health care or insurance) should be considered. We go deeper into this later (see page 17), but for now pick one that you consider the most important, whether it's a service that aggregates all your accounts or the place where you keep most of your money.

Cloud-Based Storage

We devote a section to digital photos much later in the book (see page 165), but for now you should consider including any cloud-based service you use as a backup. It could be Dropbox, Microsoft OneDrive, or another paid or free storage service that isn't one of the major accounts you're already sharing (such as Google, Amazon, or Apple).

Perhaps after reading our suggestions you'll realize you have more than five major passwords worth sharing, or maybe you have only two and the rest don't matter. Regardless, for now the limit is five that would provide the most

value to your family if you actually disappeared to an island.

By the way, if you had a password manager, then you'd need to share only one password. Just saying . . .

Cryptocurrency

Cryptocurrency lives in a digital online wallet. If you lose access to it because you forget your password or misplace the security dongle used to log in, these funds will be lost forever. Seriously. Forever.

OFF-LINE TIME

Most of this section has been devoted to storing and managing digital passwords, but what about the codes you use that aren't directly tied to an online service (or get you online)?

PINs

ATM/banking codes, the last four digits of your SSN, or other codes that prove you are who you say you are on the phone.

Lock Combinations

A safe or a padlock with a tricky combo.

Home Security System

High-quality home security systems have become easy to obtain, but they're still confusing for people without a bit

of technical know-how when it comes to installing and operating them. Some rely on Wi-Fi, which can be a problem if there's an outage. We all know that once an alarm starts blasting, it's panic time. To prevent others in your household—and visitors who need access—from having a heart attack, don't forget to share the keypad master password and the safe word or phrase you use to cancel a false alarm.

More Keypad Codes

There are even more keypad codes lurking in your life: car doors, garage doors, offices, storage facilities, Batcaves (yes, even Batman needs codes). Perhaps this is how you open a home safe if you upgraded from a combination lock.

Plan of Attack

PASSWORDS & CODES

Here's what you need to do to get it done:

USING A PASSWORD MANAGER

TIME: One to two hours to import and organize all your existing passwords (manually and automatically if you use an assortment of browser or phone password storage programs). Then let the program do all the work from here on out.

COST: Free for some, upward of $30–$120 a year for others we listed on page 3.

CREATING A DIGITAL OR HANDWRITTEN DOCUMENT

TIME: Three to four hours to organize all your existing passwords so others can understand them—and a solemn pledge to keep it regularly updated for the rest of your life.

Safe Words & Phrases

Apart from turning off a false alarm, you may need to use a phrase like a PIN when calling customer service. For example, if you want to cancel your cell phone service, they may require a four-digit code or an answer to a secret question. It's these types of things that will drive a person crazy if they don't have the answer.

Final Sweep

Take some time to look around your own home and life and see if any other passwords or codes are lurking about (like on a suitcase). Be mindful of the type of access you, and *only you*, have. It might seem obvious that the combination to the safe is the month and year you moved into your house, but who else would know that?

It can be daunting to put all your passwords and codes in one place, but it's no longer a concern once you get it done. Speaking of which, do you have your Wi-Fi password handy? See what we did there? You just went on an entire password journey and we never even mentioned one of the most important passwords in your home: the one for your Wi-Fi. Or the password for the router where you set up the Wi-Fi password in the first place. That's how sneaky passwords can be.

■ ■ ■

ALL YOUR MONEY
EVERYWHERE IT LIVES

■ ■ ■

You likely have lots of money in different forms scattered all over the place. Some is liquid, like the money in your bank accounts, investment portfolios, and possibly hidden in a box at the back of your sock drawer. Other assets are part of your net worth, including retirement accounts, real estate, possessions, and perhaps a Life Insurance policy. These are the things you know have value (and often represent the majority of your wealth), but turning them into cash isn't always simple.

There are severe penalties if you dip into a 401(k) or IRA before you're allowed to do so, and high-value items rely on the current state of the market. A home worth $300,000 twenty years ago could be worth triple that today, or much less if the housing market tanks. If you have a Life Insurance policy, you usually have to—um, how do we put this gently?—die for it to pay off . . . and you won't be doing any of the spending.

Right now, ignore the real or perceived value of everything you currently have. Your net worth might be important for your own sense of security, a financial advisor, the IRS, or your heirs hoping to inherit a fortune, but it doesn't help you get everything organized. We want you to focus only on what you have. That's the interesting thing about our method of planning, especially when it comes to money.

For years people have told us they've avoided planning because they don't want all their sensitive information in one place where others can easily find it. What they don't realize is that the amount of money they have doesn't matter. What matters is letting

HOW THIS HELPS AFTER YOU'RE GONE
(Assembling your assets)

- It provides a clear picture of your financial universe so nothing goes unaccounted for or missing.

- It allows your family to apply for and claim benefits.

- It can make the probate process, where a court validates a Will, go more smoothly. We cover this in Level 2 (see page 84), and yes, it's as exciting as it sounds.

- The right people can close bank accounts and transfer assets, mainly to beneficiaries.

- They'll have a better handle on paying any final expenses and taxes.

- None of your assets will go "unclaimed" because no one knows about them, which happens. All the time.

someone know the name of their bank, or the place where they keep investments, and that's not sensitive information.

When preparing your financial overview, don't worry if you leave a few things out. The goal is to identify the really important assets; the rest will fall into place eventually. You don't have to get too granular. We know those adorable pig-shaped salt and pepper shakers might fetch $12 on eBay, but be realistic. Those might be a sentimental heirloom; this section is all about cold hard cash.

The only ways your family can find out how much money you have is if they're authorized to access your accounts, you tell them, or they get the information without your approval, which is underhanded and possibly illegal. A stranger who works

at the bank has access to all your balances, and they could be much shadier than your family members, and you don't freak out about that. We've learned that the reason people play the "I'm worried about my personal information becoming public" card is that it's another excuse to avoid getting a plan in place. Sharing the basic stuff won't put your information in peril.

Also, it's easy to lose or misplace money. According to the National Association of Unclaimed Property Administrators, states are collectively holding more than $41 billion in unclaimed assets, including dormant bank accounts, stock splits, Life Insurance payouts, gift cards, and uncashed payroll checks. The reason: Their beneficiaries are completely unaware of them.

YOUR FINANCIAL BLUEPRINT

 It's time to dive into your pile of cash and swim around like Scrooge McDuck. We've separated possible assets into four different buckets, each with a varying degree of liquidity.

LIQUID:
Money you can access immediately

Checking/savings accounts

Investments (including online-only accounts like E-Trade or Betterment)

Hidden stash

Paycheck

Annuities

Pension/disability

Unemployment

Social Security

Alimony and child support (unless you're the one paying)

Royalties

Substantial amount of gift cards or unclaimed refunds

SLUSH:
Money that's tied up but can still be accessed under the right circumstances

Your home (if owned)

Vehicles (if owned)

Money market account

Business interests

Stock options

Trust fund

Money people owe you

RESERVE:
Money that's tied up and will incur penalties if you withdraw it too soon

401(k)

403(b) (a retirement account often available to employees of tax-exempt organizations and public-school workers)

IRA

Roth IRA

Bonds

529/college savings

Certificates of deposit (CDs)

Future benefits (Social Security, pension, certain Life Insurance policies and annuities)

ICE:
Money that isn't money yet but could be made liquid under the right circumstances

Life Insurance policy value

Tangible assets (land, business, equipment)

Valuable assets (jewelry, collections)

Intellectual property

Patents

Copyrights/trademarks

Rewards and miles (these are often closely tied to credit cards, which we cover in Level 2; see page 97)

Cryptocurrency

QUESTIONS FOR EACH FINANCIAL ACCOUNT

Don't feel the need to be a completist when it comes to the following details:

Where is the money?

This could be as simple as listing the bank name or investment house, especially if you don't want anyone accessing your money while you're still alive. If your account is only online, or you access it primarily online, the login information should be included with your passwords. If it's a Trust, then you're way ahead of the game and can breeze through the rest of this section.

After you're gone, there's a legal process that needs to be followed, and it's not as easy as a family member waltzing into the bank or logging in to a site and emptying your accounts. This is why your family, or the person in charge of handling your estate (your executor), will need to know where these assets are. If they know you have a savings account at Chase, they'll contact the bank and say you've passed away, and the bank will help set the process in motion.

Sharing the account or PIN number?

This is more for the person you name as your Power of Attorney (POA), which entails permission to manage your finances (see page 66). If you're worried someone other than your POA would use your PIN number with bad intentions, don't share it. If you think it won't cause any harm, safely share it. You make the call.

A personal contact?

If you use a broker or advisor, that person is a wealth of information (pun very much intended). Their info will appear in your contacts, which is covered later in this Level. If you have a faceless bank or a site holding your money, you need to provide only the name of the institution.

Any relevant paperwork?

Think of each account and asset. Most are probably online, which means a trustworthy person in your life can access past statements if you provide them with a username and password.

WHEN THE PROOF IS IN THE PAPER

Owning real, tangible things is a little more complicated than having money in an account. Aside from the fluctuating value (usually up for a house and down for a car), there may be other strings attached (like a mortgage). Again, at this point, value doesn't matter; concern yourself only with proof of ownership.

Here are some examples:

❑ Deed to a house

❑ Title for a vehicle

❑ Receipts (for high-ticket items)

❑ Court orders (divorce decree, settlement document)

❑ Contracts (sale of property, bill of work)

❑ Certificates (authenticity for artwork, collectibles, or rare items)

As digital as the world has become, some things still need to be on paper, and possibly also notarized. Transferring ownership can be complicated—or expensive in terms of fees or taxes—if you don't make preparations in advance. But those are later problems. The issue at hand is, where do you keep all this documentation? Is it in a locked drawer? An unlocked drawer? On file with your attorney? In a safe in your home or at a bank? Did our asking you this question send you into a bit of a panic because you forgot where it is?

You'll want to find the documents, take digital pictures, keep them somewhere safe, and then make a note of where they're stored. A driving principle behind the Everplans platform is based on consolidating all this information and making sure it's safe and accessible for when it's needed. We get very upset knowing how many easily attainable assets can disappear into a void when they're sorely needed in a time of despair.

LIST YOUR ASSETS

If an asset is not cash or a big-ticket item like a home or car, ask yourself the following questions before considering it something of value:

What is it?

Is it something that would make the folks on *Antiques Roadshow* flip out? Is it an expensive piece of jewelry, a rare baseball card collection, or an authentic seventeenth-century Persian carpet?

(continued on page 23)

Side Mission:
MAKING SURE THE KIDS ARE ALRIGHT

Since you're well on your way to getting a plan in place, including information about your underage kids should be a snap, because they don't have as much baggage as adults. They carry cute little luggage, and the rest of their life is snugly packed into yours.

The following information can help communicate required and helpful details about your kids, whether you're planning a weekend trip or are on a one-way passage to "Never Neverland," as Abby's late ninety-eight-year-old grandmother-in-law called it.

CONTACTS FIRST

Doctors & Medical Pros
Who's your kids' general practitioner or primary physician, and what's the name of the practice? Ditto for their dentists and any specialists they see (eye doctors, allergists, dermatologists, and so on).

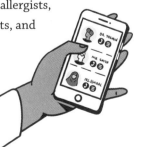

When we cover organizing your health-care contacts (see page 51), you'll want to do the same for your kids. If you have young kids, you probably already have this information hung up on your refrigerator or readily accessible to anyone who would need it in case of emergency.

Another smart number to include is Poison Control (1-800-222-1222) in case a child comes in contact with something dangerous but isn't symptomatic. Call 911 if the child is having a medical emergency because of poisoning (not breathing or unresponsive).

SCHOOLING

Teachers come and go, so adding all of them into your contacts will junk up the works. Unless there's a designated contact, the name of the school and one primary contact should suffice.

FRIENDS

Keep a current list of your kids' best friends and how you can contact the parents. Perhaps you connect with them via Facebook, but that might

➞

not help someone else who is suddenly tasked with the responsibility of caring for your child. Print out a list of only the most important numbers or write them on a kitchen wipe-away board, and keep them updated. Also include other contacts, such as members of the family who live close by and trustworthy neighbors.

DOCUMENTATION & FORMS

IDs

The good thing about young kids is they don't have many forms of identification to fill their little wallets (which they tend to lose). There's the birth certificate and a Social Security card if you requested one when they were born. Other possible documents: passport, adoption papers, and proof of citizenship.

Medical Records

Gather up all the medical records you have on file for your kids, which includes annual physical reports (tracking things like weight and height percentile if they're younger), vaccinations, surgeries, and major illnesses. And, of course, spell out

> # IF YOU HAVE CHILDREN, IT'S EASIEST TO GATHER THEIR MEDICAL INFO WHILE YOU'RE ALSO DOING IT FOR YOURSELF.

any and all special medical issues like life-threatening allergies and chronic illnesses. Even if your kid(s) has an unusual birthmark you get checked every year, it should be noted. In Level 2 (see page 116), we show you how to organize all of your medical data and paperwork about any health conditions. (If you have children, it's easiest to gather their medical info while you're also doing it for yourself.)

School & Activities

Keep all of the following things in the same place: application and permission forms, report cards, correspondence or alerts sent from the school, list of teachers, and class pictures from each school year.

You can also include extracurricular activities outside the classroom (sports, arts, camp), which can be tough to manage if you have multiple children with varied interests.

It's common to have this information spread across your email and phone, with more of it stashed in a drawer in the kitchen or home office, making it a scavenger hunt for anyone lending a hand. One way to keep the digital aspects organized and accessible is to create a shared folder in the cloud, like Google Drive. Each kid should have their own folder, and within each folder there should be a subfolder for each year. When a new school year begins, simply create a new folder.

For the physical stuff, you can do as Abby's mom did and keep a box for every year with graded tests, papers and stories she wrote, and artwork. She still keeps them in a basement storage room, and Abby loves to go through them with her kids when they visit.

AGE-BASED VARIABLES

Keeping up with a child's personality, and their diverse world of needs at a particular moment, is forever a challenge. Sometimes it's easy to track, like when they're a baby and you're in full control. But as they develop into more fully formed humans, things can get, well, complicated. This makes the next bunch of things solely dependent on what makes your child unique. Some may never change over the years; others may change by the hour. As your children age, this information transitions from being vital for babysitters and possible guardians to becoming more of a journal of memories they can appreciate if they have kids of their own one day.

BEHAVIOR & QUIRKS

If a child has a diagnosed condition, it should be included among medical issues. But this is also about overall demeanor. Are they outgoing or shy? Easygoing or particular? Are there any bedtime rituals, concentration tricks for homework, or warning signs when they're on the edge of a tantrum? Parents inherently know these things; possible guardians might not.

DIET

This can change frequently and without warning. A child who eats only chicken nuggets for a full year may one day switch to an all-spaghetti diet . . . until they rediscover their love of pizza four months later. And a love of pizza lasts a lifetime. The easy way to keep track of this is to focus on allergies (unless they're life threatening, which belong in your medical records) or extreme dislikes ("She'd sooner eat roadkill than shrimp").

GENERAL LIKES/DISLIKES

This is like food, but doesn't include food. Does your child love the water? Are they happier playing outside or reading a book? Do they have a favorite sweatshirt or pair of flip-flops they would wear every day if they could? Make little notes about these things so the memories don't get lost.

EXPENSES

You can breathe easy, for now, because the big expenses for your kids don't go here. Those go in "Money You Owe" coming up in Level 2 (see page 96). You can list allowance, money they get from the Tooth Fairy, or other minor expenses, since they're temporary—and also quite cute.

SPECIAL NEEDS

If your child has special needs and requires extra care, you already know the effort required to keep things running. But if something were to happen to you, where would that leave your child? Are you keeping a journal to track all of the above? Are there any things a possible guardian or caretaker needs to know? The same way many people keep passwords in their heads (and you know how we feel about that), they may keep caretaking routines in there too.

Your child's care is always the priority, so organizing the details can't be something you say you'll do when you get around to it. We're completely sympathetic, but being overwhelmed comes with being a parent, which includes making sure your kids are taken care of if something happens to you. Early in this book we told you to visualize your purpose when things get tough. Now is one of those times.

(continued from page 18)

If so, you don't want it to accidentally end up in a donation bin. Especially since one of those Persian carpets sold at a Sotheby's auction for $33 million in 2019.

Where is it?

This could be another easy answer. You don't have to provide the exact longitude and latitude, but don't turn it into a scavenger hunt either. "In my dresser," "locked in a home safe," or "surrounded by a moat of fire in a puzzle box that requires the answer to three riddles" is fine. (Just don't forget to share the combination, key location, and riddle hints.)

What is it worth?

Ideally, if it's that valuable, you might have had the item insured with a "floater" policy, which is for expensive things, like wedding rings, that are easy to lose or have stolen. If you don't have any coverage, you most likely have a receipt or bill of sale somewhere on file. If it was a gift or inheritance, Google the item and get an approximation of value.

LIFE WITH BENEFITS

The following are different types of revenue streams that flow from a range of sources. Odds are you qualify for at least one, but possibly more.

Pension

Are you currently receiving, or due, a pension?

Social Security

You worked your entire life putting into the system, so it's only fair that you get what you're owed. Spouses or family members are often eligible for Social Security benefits, in the form either of an ongoing payment or a one-time death benefit. (Fun fact: This string of nine numbers is important for many reasons. For example, you can't get a death certificate without it.)

Disability

If you've suffered some sort of misfortune that qualifies you for disability, how do you collect? It could be from the government (public), an employer (private), or an insurance policy. There may also be a death benefit for survivors you leave behind.

Unemployment

If you lost your job through no fault of your own, you and your family earned this money to stay on your feet. If you're collecting—benefits used to last for as long as twenty-six weeks in most states before the pandemic—include your Department of Labor login details among your passwords and note how you receive the money. In some instances, the spouse of a person who died may be able to collect any money owed. But before you do anything, it's best to check with your state's DOL and know the rules, since pretending a person is still alive to collect benefits will get you in trouble.

A DIGITAL HAND WITH YOUR FINANCES

Put aside the old-timey bankbook and confusing Excel spreadsheets, and try out one of these financial aggregation tools, which can help you gather all your finances in one place without having to log in to each of the specific sites separately.

All these platforms work in pretty much the same way: You create an account and connect all the accounts and assets you want to track (savings, checking, investment, property, vehicles, benefits, and so on), and they compile the data in a nice, clean dashboard. They're secure, often have built-in budgeting tools to help you get your finances in shape, and allow you to keep on top of the money coming in and going out without having to do any work.

If you already manage your finances and assets this way, great job! For people new to this game, here are some popular options. You can also check out incasethebook.com/financial-tools for more in-depth reviews and links.

MINT.COM: A solid free offering, Mint connects to almost every US financial institution. If they don't list your account type, you can email their support team with suggestions. It's easy to sort and search transactions, and there are decent budgeting tools if you're willing to put in the effort.

CLARITY MONEY (claritymoney.com): Similar to Mint when it comes to aggregation, Clarity has a nifty feature that combs through all your transactions and

WARNING!

These sites and apps can be addictive. It's very easy to waste way too much time checking balances and toying with budgets like it's a game. If you think of these as a way to keep on top of all your accounts without having to go to multiple sites, they're helpful. Plus, you can add the login details to your list of passwords and rest easy, knowing everything is truly in one place.

Annuity or Longevity Insurance

If you don't know what Longevity Insurance is, you will when you hit page 110. For those who are hazy on annuities, they're fixed sums of money paid to a person annually, usually for the rest of their lives.

It's like receiving a paycheck for money you've already invested, or lottery winnings on a payment schedule as opposed to a lump sum.

Alimony or Child Support

Keep the location of the divorce decree or court documents detailing

suggests canceling subscriptions if you don't use them often (multiple entertainment streaming services, the gym, etc.).

PERSONAL CAPITAL (personalcapital.com): Operating primarily as an online financial advisor and personal wealth management company, Personal Capital has its fee structure based on a percentage of the amount of assets they manage for you. They also offer aggregation tools to link your accounts.

TRIM (asktrim.com): Another free budgeting app, with optional paid features, that helps you cut (or "trim") the expenses you don't need, Trim also helps you gain a better understanding of where your money is going and how to spend less of it.

YOU NEED A BUDGET (YNAB.com): This service offers a free monthlong trial and costs $84 a year. It's a bit intensive and mostly centered on creating a budget and saving you

money (it claims to save people an average of $600 over their first two months).

QUICKEN: If you're looking for software, you can use this oldie but goodie. Options include $35–$45 a year to see all your accounts in one place, categorize expenses, create budgets, track debts, and pay online bills, depending on which subscription tier you choose.

eMONEY ADVISOR: The only way to gain access to this platform is if you get it through your financial advisor (if they offer it). It's not as flashy as the others, but it has the basics and shares all the info with your advisor so they can help you manage everything, if you want.

ASSET-MAP: This is another platform you need to get through a financial professional. It provides a graphical layout of all your assets that's easy to understand, while highlighting the accounts or assets that need attention, so you can reach any goals you've set.

the support arrangement handy. Also be aware that if an ex-spouse responsible for paying support dies, support dies with them. This is why the payee might have to create a Will (see page 70) and leave a percentage of their estate in lieu of future payments, or buy a Term Life Insurance policy (see page 108) and name the ex as a beneficiary if the child is underage. Of course, it's a bit more complicated than that, but so is divorce.

Lottery or Prize

Congrats on being lucky! If you received a lump sum, then this cash is already included in one of the accounts we mentioned earlier. If the prize pays out over a series of years or was a "Win $1,000 a Day for Life!" scratch-off, you'll want to provide information about how you get paid and the state where you won (in case the lottery commission needs to be contacted). You'll also want to stay alive as long as possible.

Reverse Mortgage

We've seen enough late-night TV commercials to know these exist, and we've done enough research to know you'll want to keep track of the company that gave you this mortgage loan and the location of the settlement documents.

MILITARY HONORS

These are for veterans who put their lives on the line for their country, or for the survivors they leave behind. Share your Department of Defense identification information. Service members are due a military burial, which requires the necessary documents, namely the discharge papers (DD 214/Separation Documents) for the funeral home to provide benefits. This properly honors the deceased and can save the family a bundle.

According to the National Cemetery Administration, benefits may include a gravesite at any one of their 142 national cemeteries, the opening and closing of the grave, perpetual care, a headstone or marker, and a burial flag. Even if the veteran opts for cremation, their ashes can be buried in a national cemetery and receive the same honors as those buried in a casket. When we get around to discussing funerals (see page 198), keep this in mind if you or someone you love has earned these benefits.

BENEFITS: DON'T FORGET TO INCLUDE...

DETAILS ABOUT IT.	If it's a complicated arrangement, like a settlement that pays out over time, you may need to provide an explanation or associated paperwork. If it's painfully obvious, like a monthly Social Security check, you don't have to waste your time. Still, providing an account number never hurts.
HOW AND WHERE YOU GET PAID.	Do you receive a check in the mail or direct deposit? Since you already have your bank accounts organized, this'll be easy to trace.
A CONTACT.	Does a specific person help out, like a pension administrator, or should they just call a main number and hope for a pleasant phone rep?
ONLINE DETAILS.	Almost everything happens online, so once you get your passwords sorted properly (like we already covered on page 2), these details will be safely tucked away among those accounts.

WHY YOU (REALLY) NEED JOINT ACCOUNTS

If you're married or have a longtime partner, you need to grasp the importance of joint bank accounts. A dear family friend of Abby's (who generously agreed to share her story with us after her husband's tragic suicide) told us her husband's accounts were frozen the day after his death, leaving her with only $400 in her checking account. "He paid all the bills and I knew nothing," she told us. All of a sudden, while in shock and grief, she was hit with late fees and overdue notices and had no idea what to do. It took a lot of work and was an unnecessary burden during a terribly difficult time. (If you or someone you know is thinking about suicide, please get help by visiting suicidepreventionlifeline.org.)

> **TIP:** To avoid unnecessary complications, set up your primary spending accounts as joint tenants with rights of survivorship (JTWROS), which allows the surviving member to continue to access that account and pay bills until the estate is settled.

MONEY YOU HAVE

PULLING IT ALL TOGETHER

TIME: Two hours to identify and list all your sources of money and valuable assets; less than one hour to connect your accounts to a financial aggregation app or software.

COST: The majority of the apps we suggested (see page 24) are free because they make money by suggesting offers and services.

If you choose a paid option, it should be less than $100 a year. Software like Quicken should be less than $50 a year. If you don't want to use a digital solution and require an accountant or financial advisor, cost depends on whether they're fee-based or commission-based. You'll need to give yourself two weeks to set up meetings with prospective money pros and see what best fits your budget.

"SAFE" DEPOSIT BOXES

We're going to ask a question of those who have a safe deposit box, but please don't take it the wrong way: Why do you still have a safe deposit box? (Also, fun fact: It's called a "safe deposit box," not a "safety deposit box.")

And the reasons not to have one are numerous. For starters, they're not convenient at all. You might think they're supersafe, but a *New York Times* article titled "Safe Deposit Boxes Aren't Safe" explains how these boxes are a lot less reliable and secure than we've

been led to believe. For example, there are no federal laws in place to protect them or the owners from theft or misplaced items, and most banks don't even install them in new branches anymore because they're such a pain.

But if you're still set on keeping the box, or getting one someday, let us suggest some ground rules.

What to Put in It

It's fine to store *some* important documents, like the deed to your house, the title to your car, a Life Insurance policy (even though it's mostly done online now), and some valuable items like heirlooms and jewelry. Maybe even letters to your family you want handed out after you're gone.

What Not to Put in It

Don't store things that need to be accessed quickly during an emergency or after a death. We're talking about your Will, Power of Attorney, or Advance Directive, all of which we'll cover in Level 2. The reason: Emergencies don't keep banking hours. These documents serve a purpose and need to be accessible.

You also shouldn't load it up with cash, fake passports, or illegal weapons, like we've seen in movies. Each box isn't its own sovereign nation. Just because it's fancier, shinier, and smells better than a typical storage facility doesn't mean it's above the law. A court order or a search warrant can be used to access the box in many cases. If you stop paying for the box, or the bank closes, there's no guarantee items won't go missing, never to be seen again. The *New York Times* claimed a man lost an estimated $10 million in watches, coins, and other items when his box was relocated and items disappeared.

Grant Access to Someone

If you still want to fill the box to the brim, this part is imperative: You have to let someone you trust— your spouse, at least one adult child, a sibling who doesn't drive you crazy—know it exists and have authorization to access it. Otherwise they'll have to get a court order, which takes time and isn't a fun process. To grant access, visit the bank branch where you're renting a box and name a designee, authorized user, or whatever they might refer to this person as.

Then tell that person the bank location, the account and box number, and where you keep the key if you don't want to give them a copy.

TIP: The details for each account or asset you have often vary, so simply pointing a person you trust in the right direction—like telling them the name of your financial advisor (see page 52), giving them access to an aggregation tool, or sharing your list of accounts once you compile them—will (kinda) show them the money!

■ ■ ■

YOUR PAD
AN OPERATING SYSTEM

. . .

Remember instruction manuals? We're talking about the really thick ones that took up half the box of the product they came with. Then they got thinner. Now you're lucky to get a quick-start guide with a few schematics, a warranty card, and some safety information. And yet there seem to be more and more pieces with each new thing that comes into our lives.

That includes our homes, vehicles, and other aspects of our lives that require care and maintenance after we've so carefully put them all together. So how do you create something your family can refer to and understand without it turning into an Ikea furniture fiasco?

If you're in charge of all the moving parts, what would everyone else do without you? If someone else handles the house or apartment stuff, what would *you* do?

It helps to start by thinking of household stuff like this: Will the things and services you manage

HOW THIS HELPS AFTER YOU'RE GONE
(or if You're Just Away for a Bit)

- Another family member can step up and seamlessly keep the home running.

- They'll know who to call if something breaks or needs fixing.

- Your vehicles will get the care they need without losing value

or making your property look like a junkyard.

- Those little unnoticed things you do to keep your home safe, like cleaning filters and changing smoke detectors, won't go unnoticed anymore.

(or rely on) still be needed in the event of, well, an event? If the answer is yes, you'll want to make sure you or your family can continue their lives uninterrupted. If you live alone, it's just as important (if not more so), because you're the only person with any of this knowledge.

When it comes to your home, it's all about keeping things operational. Think of all the time, effort, and

money you poured into your place to get it to where it is today. That wisdom was hard won—it deserves to be passed on far less painlessly than it was learned.

POOL YOUR KNOWLEDGE

Whether you're the person who manages the Wi-Fi and thermostat, the washing machine but not the dehumidifier or the lawn mower, but definitely the area that always floods in the basement, it's important to record what you know. Just because something doesn't interest you or you've never dealt with it doesn't mean you shouldn't care, because you use that thing too, and you'd be bummed if you suddenly couldn't. That includes the Wi-Fi, heat, and clean air. (HEPA filters don't change themselves, you know?)

To make sure you're fully prepared, we're going to visualize each part of your home, and later you'll take an actual tour of your own place to do this for real. Try

not to focus on anything outside your control. There's no need to sift through your contacts for people who might be needed during an emergency, like if a pipe bursts or you have a termite infestation.

WHAT IF YOU RENT?

Here's the best part of renting a home or apartment: If something breaks, it's not your problem. The not-so-great part: Chasing down your landlord or super to get something fixed can be harder than finding Bigfoot. This is why it's vital to include them in the list of contacts you pull together as the final step of Level 1 (see page 53).

But renting doesn't mean you should skip over the walk-through; you still need to explain how your rented space operates. You still have the same rooms as a homeowner. There might be fewer of them, along with less square footage, but it's still your home.

(continued on page 35)

YOUR HOME MATRIX

Before we send you to your first room, consider the many things that permeate your home like the scent of cookies straight from the oven. They may be located in common areas, hung on walls, and keeping you safe, warm, or well lit.

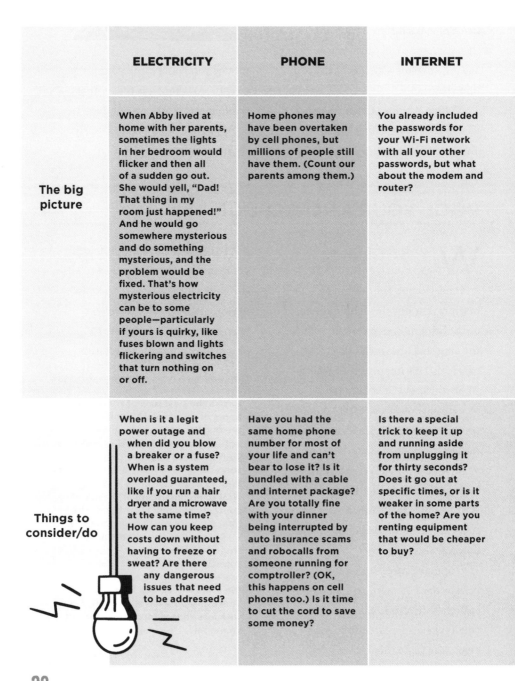

	ELECTRICITY	PHONE	INTERNET
The big picture	When Abby lived at home with her parents, sometimes the lights in her bedroom would flicker and then all of a sudden go out. She would yell, "Dad! That thing in my room just happened!" And he would go somewhere mysterious and do something mysterious, and the problem would be fixed. That's how mysterious electricity can be to some people—particularly if yours is quirky, like fuses blown and lights flickering and switches that turn nothing on or off.	Home phones may have been overtaken by cell phones, but millions of people still have them. (Count our parents among them.)	You already included the passwords for your Wi-Fi network with all your other passwords, but what about the modem and router?
Things to consider/do	When is it a legit power outage and when did you blow a breaker or a fuse? When is a system overload guaranteed, like if you run a hair dryer and a microwave at the same time? How can you keep costs down without having to freeze or sweat? Are there any dangerous issues that need to be addressed?	Have you had the same home phone number for most of your life and can't bear to lose it? Is it bundled with a cable and internet package? Are you totally fine with your dinner being interrupted by auto insurance scams and robocalls from someone running for comptroller? (OK, this happens on cell phones too.) Is it time to cut the cord to save some money?	Is there a special trick to keep it up and running aside from unplugging it for thirty seconds? Does it go out at specific times, or is it weaker in some parts of the home? Are you renting equipment that would be cheaper to buy?

FURNISHINGS & DECOR

Do you keep track of things like paint colors, carpet, tiles, drapes, and furniture details in case things need to be replaced or reordered? It's a bonus if the person who scratched a wall or broke a tile knows where this info is kept.

Make a list of this info so things can be replaced without hassle. For example, one of the coauthors of this book (we won't say who), "accidentally" knocked a hole in the wall of his childhood bathroom (we won't say how). Luckily, his mom still had extra wallpaper swatches that matched. (OK, it was Gene.)

SECURING THE PERIMETER:
New School

High-tech home security systems like we mentioned earlier (see page 12) are quite common now that they're more affordable and (somewhat) easy to self-install.

Put together an easy-to-understand guide for the people in your family who genuinely don't care about how cool the system is. We'll consider professional monitoring systems later (see page 53). For now, focus on troubleshooting. How are the system settings accessed, including the password for the app? Whom do you call if it's not working correctly? What's the system name if you have to replace a component when a rogue squirrel takes a camera? If you have a panic button, how does it work? Do you have lights set on timers to give the appearance that you're still home when you're away?

SECURING THE PERIMETER:
Old School

Not all security systems are digital and fancy. Most of us still use keys, though some of those are going digital too. Assuming you're still part of the majority of the world who stick a piece of metal into a slab of wood, start with thinking about where you keep the extra key. (If you say, "Under the mat," we might give you a hug. Sure, it's completely insane, but it's still adorable.)

Are there instructions for entering or leaving the house? Does a neighbor have an extra key? What happens if you need access to a door *inside* the house that's locked?

⊢──────→

	HOME AUTOMATION	SMOKE & CARBON MONOXIDE DETECTORS	FIREPLACE
The big picture	Let's start with the Amazon Echo, Google Home, or any other voice-controlled AI plug-and-play device that does everything from stream music, movies, and news into your home to control its lights and temperature. (You might also like to scream at a robot voice that doesn't scream back—we won't judge.)	The devices that can save the lives of everyone in your home also tend to be the most neglected. According to the National Fire Protection Association, an average of 1,450 fire deaths occur every year in homes with missing or nonfunctioning smoke alarms.	A cozy hearth can often be the spiritual center of a home, the place where memories are made. It also needs maintenance, or it can become dangerous.
Things to consider/do	What devices are you using? Your answer will likely reveal all you need to know to access the software and settings. Good thing you're sharing that info along with your passwords. (See how it all comes together?) Are there any special instructions, tips, or preferences? Do you use other devices for other specific purposes—maybe like connecting your Echo Dot to a high-end speaker for better sound?	Smoke detectors need to be changed every ten years, a task made slightly easier because each has the date it was manufactured on the back. Most contemporary models will chirp or beep when they start to malfunction or the battery needs changing. You also don't have to wait until it begins to chirp to take action. We suggest checking each smoke/carbon monoxide detector in your house twice a year when resetting your clocks for daylight saving time.	Provide tips or advice on safe usage, including cleaning or routine maintenance. When was the last time the flue was cleaned? Where do you get wood, and how big do you build the fires?

(continued from page 31)

Focus only on the stuff you oversee personally and want to keep in the family, particularly if it prevents unnecessary expenses.

As we glide through each area of the home, identify and consider what information needs to get passed along. We'll be your tour guides, but it's your home—only you know where you keep the special grill lighter to relight the pilot on the water heater when it craps out on a cold morning in January.

BASEMENT

Unless it's been converted into a playroom or entertainment center, or their laundry machines live there, people usually avoid basements unless something requires maintenance or they need to store something out of sight. (Plus, 78 percent of basements are haunted! We're kidding; it's really only around 37 percent.)

HVAC (Heating, Ventilation, and Air-Conditioning)

These are the lungs and circulatory system of your home. What keeps them up and running? How often do you get your system serviced? Do you change filters on your own or do you have a service agreement? If you have warranty or important service-related paperwork, where does it live? If it's temperamental, what are the troubleshooting steps to take before making a service call?

Include the average temperature settings per season and whether your thermostat is controlled by Nest or another home automation system or you set it manually. Can you explain it so an eight-year-old could operate it? (Note: This includes sharing the password along with all the others.) What are the settings if you're traveling and the house will be unoccupied for a few weeks or months? Is there an automatic hold at a specific temperature?

Water

Maintaining a basic water source and keeping the toilets, showers, and washing machines running is the priority. Is it not much more than paying a water bill? Are there recurring problem areas? Is the main water shut-off valve properly marked and easy to operate? This is important if you're away during the cold months, when the pipes can freeze and burst if you don't run

the heat when you're away. Is the water ever discolored? Why? Maybe you have a well or a septic system problem your family needs to know about.

Laundry Machines

We're throwing this in the basement category despite the fact that you might have a laundry room. Unlike a laundromat with easy-to-follow instructions, many of these fancy machines are more complicated than a space shuttle. How would you explain the best way to operate the washer/dryer to a house sitter or a guest who rarely does laundry, so they don't ruin any clothes or the machine?

Mold, Floods, and Musty Smells

Funky things can grow in dark, damp basements. Are there any areas in yours that are darker and damper than the rest? Do you have flooding problems during big storms or when large amounts of snow melt? If dealing with water is a regular thing,

when does a mop-up suffice and when should you call someone with a sump pump and plumbing license to deal with it?

Infestations

Things that move also live in dark, damp basements, such as insects, rodents, and creepy-crawlies you probably don't want to think about. It can happen anywhere in your place, but basements are usually ground zero. Which areas attract the most disturbing vermin? What types of traps do you use, if any? How often should you spray or get inspected by a pest control company?

Final Sweep

Visualize your basement. What else do you have going on down there? Any foundation problems? Something that needs to be monitored closely? A storm drain or sewer line that backs up? A dehumidifier to keep the moisture level low?

MAIN FLOOR

On to the areas where we eat, drink, and be merry—and then pass out in front of the TV afterward.

Kitchen

Rather than get overly specific, you want to concentrate on function.

We'll talk more about the reasons you love your kitchen in Level 3 (see page 172), but for now think about your major appliances—refrigerator, oven, stove/gas, dishwasher, garbage disposal. Do they require any special instructions? If one conks out, is it still under warranty? Should it be repaired, or does it make more sense to upgrade?

You may not want to bother with the small appliances—microwave, blender, slow cooker, toaster, steamers, mixers, coffeemaker, juicer—and that's OK. They are typically easier to replace unless there's an active warranty or you went super high-end. (Most normal people don't toss away a classic espresso machine because the froth isn't frothy enough, for example.)

The same goes for cooking and serving accoutrements. A cheap set of pans you bought on sale at Target probably doesn't need to be recorded. But a serving bowl that was handed down from your great-grandmother should make the list (see page 177).

The kitchen is also a place where you can have an immediate effect by just doing a walk-through. If there are things you haven't used in a long time—we're looking at you, egg cooker—consider donating it. We collect a lot of stuff we think we might use one day, but when it looks like that day isn't coming, it might be time to make space for things you actually use.

Living Room/Den

Also known as the place where you kick back and relax when you're not worrying about things growing and skittering around in the basement, the living room or den is the entertainment nerve center of the home. It's also the place where things can get complicated and messy.

Start out simple: Imagine explaining how to watch your TV to a ninety-year-old grandpa. Do you have cable or satellite? Have you cut all the cords and started using an Apple TV, Roku, Chromecast, or a gaming console (Xbox or PlayStation) or other set-top box to access your shows and movies? Is the sound through the TV, or do you have a separate surround sound system? What is your remote situation? Are you the type of family that plays remote roulette, with a stack of them on the coffee table? Or have you consolidated your system with a universal remote?

If you're the keeper of a complex system, it's up to you to make it simple. And maybe that means printing out a piece of paper with easy-to-read instructions. An example can be found on the next page.

See how easy it can be to understand? We had a system like this in our office written on our whiteboard walls to explain how to use different inputs on our TVs for meetings. This helps with troubleshooting because it slyly gives all the details that have been

TO WATCH CABLE:

1. Press Cable on the main remote.

2. Set the TV to Input 2 (Input button on TV remote).

3. Set the surround sound to SAT/CABLE (or leave it off and watch TV like a caveman).

TO WATCH APPLE TV:

1. Press Apple TV on.

2. Set the TV to Input 4.

3. Set the surround sound to Device 1.

programmed into the remote. If people go to watch cable, and the screen is blank, they can look at the sheet, notice the TV input isn't correct, and fix it without having to hassle a nerd.

Don't fret about the actual streaming services. We're saving those for your "digital world" in Level 2 (see page 146). For now, pay attention only to the hardware. It might not be as interesting as bingeing season one of *Ozark*, but it allows everyone to watch what they want at all times without any tech hassles.

UPSTAIRS

If you live in a ranch-style home or a one-floor apartment or condo, you're out of luck. We joke. Use your imagination and consider where you sleep, do your business (small office), or do your other business (bathroom).

We have good news. Unless you require that the bed be made a certain way (even after you're gone), these rooms don't really have much going on. Does the mattress need to be flipped? Explain it. Is there a

(continued on page 42)

Side Mission:
ANIMAL INSTINCTS

For many of us, our pets are integral parts of the family that have very particular operating instructions.

When it comes to dogs, America is verging on a belly-rub crisis. Or, in the case of cats, that spot right above their tail that makes them like you for a few precious seconds. According to the American Pet Products Association, only 9 percent of people with Wills have made provisions for their pets. Although it's incredibly sad to think of our pets without us, the best thing for them is to do just that.

Because, strange and unjust as it is, *the law sees pets as property*. And since you can't leave property to your property, you need to name a guardian and make financial arrangements for your pets.

THREE WAYS TO START A PET PLAN

1. ESTIMATE KIBBLE COSTS: Put together a simple budget that includes food and treats, veterinary care, and other recurring expenses (grooming, training, walkers, and so on).

2. NAME A PET GUARDIAN: This is a person whom you want to take care of your pets if you cannot. Try to pick someone who will be happy to love them as much as you did—even though that's not possible.

3. SPECIAL INSTRUCTIONS: To help your guardian ease your pets into their new life, write down instructions about feeding habits, medical history and conditions, favorite toys and activities, and special quirks.

LET'S NOT MAKE THIS A RUFF EXPERIENCE

Although the basics about your pet may seem obvious, sharing them could make a world of difference for your furry (or not-so-furry) friend.

Before you start to get sad, know that this doesn't have to be about you leaving this world. What if you had to go away on an unexpected trip and your usual caretaker (besides a spouse or kids) was not around? Your pet's world revolves around you, so it's not easy for them either. Having all this info readily available creates a smooth transition regardless of the scenario. Let's dig into what details to share:

→

- Breed | Birthday: estimate if you're not sure; this could also be the adoption date.

- Feeding habits: portion sizes, dietary restrictions (allergies), special treats

- Veterinarian: contact info and medical records

- Medical conditions/medications: most recent vaccinations (along with the frequency), heartworm meds, flea/tick prevention, bone/joint/muscle issues, skin irritations

- Pet insurance: company, account number, online login info, and how to file a claim (these details should also be included with your passwords)

- Favorite toys: lacrosse balls, squeaky duck, laser pointer

- Favorite activities: swimming, long hikes, agility training, watching nature documentaries and *Dr. Phil* . . .

- Quirks: scared of thunder, doesn't like to be picked up, won't use the litter box if you're watching

- Other pertinent details: microchip info, grooming tips, pedigree papers

This should be enough to get you started, but feel free to get as specific as you like. You can even create a little memory scrapbook to overwhelm someone with cuteness. Plus, if you're one of those owners who has a social media account loaded with pet photos

and stories (Gene is totally guilty of this), be sure and share that info too.

NAMING A PET GUARDIAN

Quite simply, who would you want to take care of your pets if you couldn't?

Start with temporary situations, like when you go on vacation or are recovering from surgery or an accident. Next, think of the extreme: What if you suddenly weren't here anymore? Would it be the same person or people? A neighbor down the hall or block might be able to watch Barky Bark Wahlberg for a few days but might not be willing or able to take him in forever.

Once you identify new possible pet parents, talk about it with them to be sure they'll happily take your little (or big) lovebug into their lives. This is not something that should come as a surprise to either the new owners or your pet. They should know, and preferably like, each other already.

Since you can't leave money directly to your pets—remember the whole "pets are property" thing—you can stipulate that the person caring for your pet will have access to some four-legged funds. You'll need to include a provision in your Will naming a person to care for them, or you can create a Trust (details on both appear in Level 2 starting on page 66).

This isn't as unreasonable as it sounds. For example, Majel Barrett-Roddenberry, the widow of *Star Trek* creator Gene Roddenberry, set up a $4 million trust for their dogs, plus an additional $1 million for a domestic employee to care for them. If you're leaving behind millions for your lucky dog or cat (or snake or lizard), you don't want the new owners to go too crazy. In the more likely event that you're leaving a few thousand, you want it to last. Either way, you don't want your guardian to be too money focused or you've chosen the wrong person.

If there's any money remaining once your pet finally takes that peaceful stroll across the rainbow bridge, you can stipulate that the caretakers get the leftover balance or donate it to a predetermined charity. And although you should include your pet in your Will, the primary drawback is the legal system, which moves slower than a sloth on Valium. What happens to your pet in the meantime? Solution: A Trust kicks in right away.

ANIMAL PLANET

Dogs and cats aren't the only pets that need a just-in-case plan—lots of other animals like fish, snakes, or spiders require our care too. A financial advisor we spoke with set up a Trust for his horse. Did you know that some parrots can live up to 50 years and get extremely attached to their owners? And turtles can live a whopping 80 to 150 years, so they can outlive us all.

ONE LAST TREAT FOR THE ROAD

To avoid any transition stress, provide your designated pet guardian with access to copies of any official documents they might need, as well as a house key in the event of an emergency. If your pet will be relocating to live with someone far away—preferably near a beach and long hiking trails—perhaps a neighbor or friend can care for your pet until the big trip?

Finally, congrats on being a pet hero! You've earned a lap sit from your cat or a shortened walk with your dog the next time it rains.

(*continued from page 38*)

CPAP machine, or other equipment, that might need to be returned? You'll want to include information about any medical devices in your Personal Medical Journal (see page 116), but it's good to be mindful of them now.

Bathrooms are also routine—unless something leaks, a toilet handle requires jiggling, or a showerhead regularly pops off and sprays wildly all over the room. There could also be a mold problem, or maybe a system you have when it comes to cleaning out the medicine cabinet and replenishing toiletries.

If you have a home office, it can get tricky. Do you use it for an actual moneymaking venture or is it where you get work done outside the office? If it's part of a small business, even if it's occasionally selling stuff on eBay, we cover all that in a Side Mission later (see page 74). If it's

a place used to handle household management, this becomes the central nerve center for another family member to keep everything running smoothly if you're not around. Make that clear.

Think of all the equipment and how it works. Does the computer need to be explained because it's not used by anyone else in the household? Then there are printers, backup drives, perhaps even the home for the Wi-Fi modem and router. Do you have a shredder? What does it eat? Is this where you have a safe or locked file cabinet where all the important household documents live, including deed, warranties, and mortgage paperwork? What about the checkbooks?

We'll leave the cleaning and sorting to Marie Kondo and HGTV, but a little organization in this space goes a long way.

THE GREAT OUTDOORS

What about your place that's not really *in* your place?

Is your garage where you keep your car, or is it a de facto storage space? Do you have a system for organizing tools and other maintenance supplies? Are there toxic chemicals stored there that

your family should know about? Do the holiday decorations live there? If those items aren't in the garage, maybe they're in a shed, attic, or hallway closet?

If you have a garage door opener, how do you keep it operational, since those things always seem to break? If it has a code, that goes with passwords. If you have extra remotes, where do you keep them?

What about your landscape situation? Do you take pride in keeping a lawn or garden looking tip-top? Do you have special flowers or vegetables you plant each year, perennials that need tending? Which plants always grow best where, and what are your secrets? If you hire someone to help, that'll go in your contacts. But if you mow, fertilize, and tend to your yard yourself, lay it all out so it doesn't turn into a messy, overgrown jungle. The same goes for leaf and snow removal and tending to dangerous trees that overhang the home and could be a threat during a storm. Do you have a roof and gutter maintenance schedule, or any property issues related to your neighbors? If there's a pool, do you care for it personally or use an outside vendor (which naturally should be included in your contacts)?

When it comes to outdoor lighting, what's your setup? Is it on an automated schedule? Is it part of a larger home automation system? How would someone reprogram it? A widow told us that after her husband passed away, she didn't know how to control the porch lights, since they were connected to an automated system only he knew how to operate.

In terms of scheduling, what about the garbage and recycling pickup? These are the types of things that should be on a calendar on the fridge. Same goes for how to suspend mail service if you're away for a time. What about newspaper delivery? Or those coupon circulars in plastic bags always wet with dew that appear out of nowhere? Since you have no control over these, do you tell a neighbor when you're away on

THE WRITING ON THE WALL

Here's a funny story about a garage. A former coworker of ours was visiting her father's house, and he took her to the garage and moved a few boxes to reveal a safe. When he couldn't remember the combination, he told her to wait, walked across the garage, and looked at the wall where he'd written the combination in pen. He then walked back to the safe and opened it. Inside were the titles to his three cars. The point: If he'd never showed her (on a whim!) that the combination was *written on a wall* (*in pen!?*), she would have had no idea what to do if she'd found the safe or wanted to sell the cars.

vacation to throw 'em out so people don't know you're away?

At this point you're thinking of going away on vacation, which isn't a bad idea since *we just covered your entire home*. Now that your mind is swimming with all the information locked in there and yearning to be set free, maybe you're starting to see the factors you tend to take for granted. Running a home is like a second job, but instead of receiving a monthly paycheck and a gold watch after thirty years, you and your family receive comfort, safety, and ideally lots of money if you keep it in shape and sell it one day, all of which is why you take the time and effort to maintain it.

JUST PUT IT IN STORAGE

Too much stuff? Not ready to get rid of it? In the process of moving or downsizing? So many of us have uttered that familiar phrase: "Just put it in storage."

Self-storage is an enormous business in the United States, with close to 10 percent of households renting storage units that amount to about 1.7 billion square feet of space, according to industry blog *SpareFoot*. Blame it on people running out of room in their homes, nomadic lifestyles, reality auction shows, and every serial offender on *Law and Order: SVU*. Storage is here to stay, even long after we're gone.

So what happens to a storage unit when someone dies? Here are the possibilities.

Shared Access

This is the ideal situation. If the renter has already shared the location, unit number, keys, and/or keypad access code to the unit with someone, then it's smooth sailing. Just go to the place and empty it out and vacate.

No Access

Monthly fees still need to be paid by the estate's executor to avoid foreclosure. If the unit is set up to autopay by credit card, that account needs to remain active. If payment was made by check, the executor of the estate (see Level 2, page 79) will need to write a check from his or her own account until the unit can be legally accessed. Next, the executor

Plan of Attack

HOME OPERATING SYSTEM

DOING THE WALK-AROUND

TIME: Three one-hour shifts of walking around every room in your house, and the surrounding perimeter, with your phone and taking photos and notes; two hours to transcribe those notes and photos into a worthy instruction manual/troubleshooting guide, as well as gathering up related paperwork (warranty info, actual instruction manuals). Add an extra three to five hours if you want to make a fancy book and include the photos and documents (books can take a while to create . . . trust us). It's nice to have a printed version, but make a digital copy as well so it's always somewhere safe, accessible, and easy to update.

COST: This should take up only your time, and maybe $15 to $30 in supplies if you create an actual book.

---

needs to get documentation that proves they have the legal right to access the unit, which can happen fast or take up to sixty days. Once the necessary paperwork is obtained, the facility manager will grant access to the unit. From there, it's a matter of emptying it out and closing it down.

Surprise!
There's a Storage Unit

If a storage unit was never mentioned, here's how you'll probably find out it exists:

A call: The person listed as an emergency contact will receive a call from a storage facility manager.

A letter: A certified letter will arrive at the last known address for the renter before the unit gets foreclosed on, although many states have relaxed this requirement.

A charge: Payments for the unit will appear on a credit card or bank statement, indicating a monthly or annual charge. Generally, you'll want to make sure the unit is cleaned out as soon as possible to avoid paying fees, or worse, forgetting about it until you start seeing strangely familiar items on *Storage Wars*.

But if you just can't give up your storage space now that you're aware of the hassle that awaits those who don't know about or can't access a storage facility, here's what to share if you have one: the name and location of the storage facility, the unit number, the key or lock combination, and the monthly or annual fee.

HITTING THE ROAD

et's assume you have a car. Maybe even two. Perhaps you have other vehicles, such as a boat, RV, or motorcycle. For some people, these vehicles are how they get to work or around town, but for others, they're metallic members of the family.

Regardless of your relationship with these machines, your family and loved ones will need to know what to do with them after you're gone. To keep this as simple as possible, start with the most basic of basics: What type of vehicles do you have? Car, truck, motorcycle? Snowmobile, tractor, airplane?

Next, what can you easily recall off-hand? The make, model, year, color? And where do you keep them? This is obvious if your car is parked in the garage or driveway, but it's more complicated if you live in a city and use a parking lot or have your boat moored in a harbor full of boats.

Now it's time to drill down on the details. Quick: What's your license plate number? See! (Kudos to those who actually knew the answer.) Also, note the registration number and state of registration (and when it's due for renewal) as well as the VIN number/serial number/hull number.

Finally, treat your car or other vehicle like you did your home and think of all the things no one else would know. You're already aware of including the keypad code with your passwords (if your car has one). What about where the extra keys live? Does the vehicle require extra care (as in: never wax my Corvette)? Are you paying for a roadside assistance service or amenities like satellite radio or in-car wireless data? Are there any quirks that make your car run better (or at all?), like, "If it starts clanging, add a quart of oil" or other tips that could save a new owner time and money?

Finally, do you have a special connection to the vehicle? Was it your grandpa's boat and you learned to fish on it? Did your uncle help you rebuild the engine just before he died? Although this is more about the emotional side of planning (see Level 3, page 177), your child may think twice about junking that sweet Trans Am with the eagle on the hood after learning it's where they were conceived. Though that may also be a good reason for them to sell it immediately—but you see what we're getting at.

■ ■ ■

MAKING
FIRST CONTACT

• • •

Throughout Level 1 we've remained laser focused on your passwords and codes, assets, home, and vehicles. We kept telling you to think about how the people in your life would manage what you manage if you couldn't anymore. Now we need to consider the people themselves.

Remember the little black book? (Note to millennials: Skip the next few paragraphs or read on and don't judge—you'll be there someday too.) Your version of a little black book was undoubtedly battle worn, creased, and a complete mishmash of everything: family, friends, doctors, repair contacts, food-delivery services, and more. It was supposed to be alphabetical, which made it a game each time you wanted to enter or retrieve a number. "My old buddy Carrie. Did I put her under C? Or her last name, which changed?"

Updating it was fun too. If it was in pencil, you'd erase and write over it until you created a hole in the page. If it was in pen, you crossed it out and wrote it near the original number wherever you could find

space. If you wanted to start a new book, you usually had to transcribe it by hand. This was how we kept track

HOW THIS HELPS AFTER YOU'RE GONE
(Listing contacts)

■ **A way to reach important contacts your family will need to settle your estate (example: estate attorney, financial advisor).**

■ **The network of professionals and associates you built over a lifetime won't go to waste.**

■ **Personal contacts your family may not know about can be contacted with news of your passing and funeral information.**

of contacts before phones started to get a little smarter, but you'd still have to input the numbers and names by hand. Then the process became automated, allowing you to save numbers when you got a call. This presented a new problem of how to categorize people who were peripheral in your life and work. But now that phones control our lives, no one needs to remember anyone's number because they're all right there in your contacts. Some people probably don't even know their own number. And although smartphones may have robbed us of our need to remember numbers, they've done good things too. They've made it so we can get in touch with anyone at any time. They've turned our address book into something that's easy to update, even when it becomes a complete mess.

That mess usually comes from automatic imports carried over from old phone after old phone, plus other sources. Like when you synced it with your Gmail, Outlook, or Facebook contacts and ended up with tons of people you do your best to avoid. But their numbers are right there on your phone next to people who really matter.

So you'll want to get your contacts organized in a way that cuts all the excess and puts people right where you need them. To do this, you'll need to put aside your feelings and focus on the people who serve a function in your life. It might sound cold, but it'll provide clarity and allow the most important of those very people to view your contacts with absolute certainty—and not wonder who that Brandon guy in your contacts is.

YOUR TOP FIVE CONTACTS

Similar to your most important passwords (see page 10), you'll want to identify your most important contacts. Instead of focusing on the people you contact the most often, think about situations—because that's when dormant numbers become the most important numbers. A plumber doesn't matter, for example, until a plumber is *all* that matters.

Why aren't we focusing on your spouse, kids, siblings, and close friends first? Because that's not helpful. Pay attention to the numbers *those* people need to know (because they already know their own numbers).

How many "pros" do you know? From doctors to financial experts to lawyers, it's probably quite a few. But

To get you thinking about your most important contacts, here are the types of emergency situations when a lesser-known contact is needed:

MEDICAL	A primary care physician, or other doctor managing a specific condition, who can also call in necessary medication or point you in the right direction if another specialist is required.
HOME	When a pipe bursts and water is pouring through the floors, when an infestation is suddenly active (and gross), when something important breaks (think water heater, HVAC system, the roof) that you can't fix.
FINANCIAL	If you get a letter from the IRS and/or a personal financial crisis is looming, and you need guidance.
LEGAL	If the cops show up at your door or if your family needs a copy of your Will or other legal documents.
WORK	Who's the one person at your job, or former job if you still collect benefits, who won't give your family the runaround?

does your family know who these professionals are and what they do? You might think that a financial advisor, a gastroenterologist, or, in Abby's dad's case, an estate attorney would be obviously known to the people closest to you, but there's a decent chance you're wrong.

We're all familiar with naming an emergency contact if something happens, but not all emergencies are the same. We just presented five categories above—designate a main contact for each. The people you name might not have all the answers, but ideally they know enough to either help in a pinch or refer you to someone who can. This is what a network is all about—contacting the right people until you find a solution.

Once you've identified your emergency point people, here are some rules to keep in mind when creating a contact.

Include a first and last name.

This might seem like a "duh," but need we remind you about Brandon? He did that thing that time? No, we don't know who he is either. If you don't know their last name, see the next page.

Include a title or the function.

You can also make the title their name. Examples: Landscaper Billy, Casino Host Barbara, Foot Doctor Frank, Dog Walker Roger.

Include an email.

If you don't list a contact's full name or title, an email address can be very telling. If it's a work email (kelsey@financialmoneycompany.com), it's easy to research and identify the purpose this person serves, whereas a personal email (stan@hotmail.com) usually means that person is or was a friend.

Always use the Notes or Description Field.

This works best while that person is still fresh in your head. It may seem like a hassle when you just need to cram a number into your phone, but take a minute to include something about the person. You (and those who survive you) will be happy you did it. Think of it like a mini Yelp review set to private: "Dr. Cho is a Zen master of root canals"; "Caroline helped me figure out my property tax bill"; "Kevin always plows the driveway before I even call him."

THE REFERRAL ZEN MASTER

People are always looking for the best professionals across every field, and usually at a sensitive moment. By keeping your contacts organized and annotated, you'll be the go-to referral hero for your friends, family, and coworkers. Need a chiropractor who also happens to be a miracle worker? A proven financial advisor you can trust? An attorney to look over a contract? By keeping on top of your contacts, you'll eventually have a name for every situation instantly at your fingertips—and so will friends and family who inherit your contacts. As a bonus, since word of mouth is also the biggest driver of business, you might get preferential treatment from the pros you recommend. Not a bad perk for a Zen master.

One last thing: Don't feel the need to load up your phone for the sake of it, but don't be shy either—include as many numbers as you'd like. Just try to add the info we suggested.

WHAT'S UP, DOC?

The older we get, the more doctors we collect. Unless you're managing a condition that requires regular care from a specific provider, your main medical contact is often your primary care physician. Then there are all of your other doctors, specialists, caretakers, and medical pros to round out your roster. Mentally circle all the ones you have:

❏ Likely main contact: primary care

❏ Allergist

❏ Cardiologist

❏ Dentist

❏ Dermatologist

❏ Endocrinologist

❏ Gastroenterologist

❏ Gynecologist

❏ Hematologist

❏ Immunologist

❏ Infectious disease specialist

❏ Internist

❏ Neurologist

❏ Obstetrician

❏ Oncologist

❏ Ophthalmologist

❏ Orthopedic surgeon

❏ Orthopedist

❏ Otolaryngologist (ear, nose, throat)

❏ Pediatrician

❏ Pharmacist
(or drugstore you use)

❏ Physiatrist (physical medicine and rehabilitation)

❏ Plastic surgeon

❏ Podiatrist

❏ Psychiatrist/therapist

❏ Rheumatologist

❏ Urologist

❏ Vascular specialist

Perhaps you're suffering from a condition and haven't taken the time to find a specialist and make an appointment? Quit putting it off and reach out to your network to get whatever ails you taken care of. Or hit up Zocdoc, a helpful digital medical network where you can find a local doctor with good reviews.

MONEY FOLKS

Identify the people in your life who have their mind on your money (in a professional capacity, of course).

❑ Likely main contact for money management: financial advisor/accountant

❑ Likely main contact for employment: HR rep/union rep/helpful coworker

❑ Financial planner

❑ Insurance agent or advisor

❑ Investment manager

❑ Tax preparer

If you like to manage your money all on your own, or if you rely on robo-advisors instead of humans, include those details among your assets discussed in the "Your Financial Blueprint" section (see page 16).

If you don't have a specific point of contact for every one of these services—maybe you bought insurance from a big company and don't have a designated agent—include the company name along with a helpful description (for example: "Transamerica, main number; they sold me Life Insurance"). This way your family will know to call the main number and inquire about the policy if they can't do it online.

LAW ABIDING

Identify the attorneys and legal professionals who help keep you on the right side of the law.

❑ Likely main contact: general legal counsel

❑ Corporate law

❑ Criminal defense

❑ Employment

❑ Estate planning

❑ Family/divorce

❑ Personal injury

❑ Property law/real estate

You may not require frequent legal help, or maybe you're in trouble all the time (we're not here to, um, judge). But if you enlisted the help of an attorney twenty years ago to create a contract or your Will, it's important for your family to be able to get in touch with that person if they have questions. Speaking of which, if you created a Will twenty years ago and haven't thought about it since, you need to look into it immediately. (Well, not "immediately," but when you hit Level 2, see page 70.)

AN UNBROKEN HOME

You're now fully able to create a Home Operating System, so you and your family know how to handle solvable problems without making a call. When that problem grows beyond your control, however, it's time to know your limitations and call in an expert if necessary.

The "expert" doesn't need to be a person; it can be a big company too. If the power is out, wouldn't it be much easier to grab your phone and know the number to call (along with your account number in the description) than to angrily search for the number while fumbling around in the dark looking for an old bill?

RENTERS HAVE IT EASY

The best part of renting is that if something breaks (on its own), you have one number to call. You should still skim that list again to see if any of them apply, like a cleaning service or handyman/woman. Other than that, here are the main three:

- Landlord or management company
- Building superintendent (or "super" since no one calls them superintendent)
- Doorman/woman or security amenity (if applicable)

It might be tough to identify one primary contact since homes present a variety of possible issues. This is why you should include all the contacts a person would need, be it a family member, a home sitter, or a babysitter. The list of things that could go wrong tends to be longer than we think. Start by considering the following:

- ❑ Cable/internet/home phone
- ❑ Cleaning service
- ❑ Electrician
- ❑ Exterminator and pest control (termites included)
- ❑ Garbage and waste removal
- ❑ Handyman/woman
- ❑ HVAC cleaning and repair
- ❑ Landscaping
- ❑ Mail/local post office
- ❑ Mold remediation/air-quality control
- ❑ Plumber
- ❑ Pool care
- ❑ Roofing contractors and repair
- ❑ Security amenity (example: number to the front gate if it applies)
- ❑ Security system: name of the security company and account number
- ❑ Septic service technician
- ❑ Snow removal

When we compiled this list, we couldn't help but notice that it's full of "sleepers," or contacts who don't seem important until a crisis hits. One way to make some of the more unusual contacts useful is to break one of our rules and include them in an "Emergency Contacts" section of your Home Operating System. This prevents your phone from getting junked up with too many sleepers but keeps them easily accessible if someone needs a number. Get creative and imagine unexpected situations while you're at it:

- ❏ If the roof caves in

- ❏ When the basement floods

- ❏ If a tree is menacing your house

- ❏ If spirits from another dimension try to escape from the basement (because that's breaking the deal you cut with them!)

Side Mission:
PARENTAL GUIDANCE

The parent-child role reversal is real—and it can be tough.

Think about how your parents felt when you reached adulthood and moved out of the house. A part of them may have rejoiced that they'd done their job to prepare you for the world (and they could start walking around the house naked again), but part of it was surely sad for them because their baby no longer needed them like you once did.

However, when the roles reverse and you become a caregiver to a parent, it's a much different experience. Watching a parent's health or faculties decline is extremely difficult. If you want to make it through without having a breakdown, you have to take a lot of deep breaths and focus on what you can control.

Start with an overarching health assessment to find out what you're up against. Is it a chronic and ongoing issue that needs to be managed or is it an acute or terminal illness where time is limited?

In either instance, you need a plan that starts by gathering the following information.

DOCTORS AND CAREGIVERS

You know how to organize your own doctors in your contacts; now you'll want to do the same for your parents, but with a twist. Managing each doctor can be complicated—some of them may overlap—but the goal is to keep them from running your parent around in circles. For example, you want to be sure that one doctor doesn't order tests that another doctor has already run.

Create a list that can be managed by you and shared with anyone else offering care. If it's a technically savvy crew, it can be a shared electronic document, but paper is fine in this instance since the contacts should be limited to only the most essential people.

Along with doctors, are there any home, nursing, or assisted-living contacts? What about an ambulatory service or a driver (who's not you)? These people need to go on the list too.

MEDICATIONS AND TREATMENTS

People are prescribed a lot of drugs these days, and seemingly more and more as they age. According to a study cited by the *Washington Post*, 25 percent of people in the latter half of their sixties take at least five prescription drugs. That number increases to 46 percent for people in their seventies. Managing prescriptions for another person can easily feel like a part-time job, albeit a necessary one, since the wrong dosage could have adverse consequences. To confirm that the right meds are taken at the right time, and to keep everyone on the same page, you need to be organized. Here's how to do it:

- Make a list of every medication that needs to be taken, even if it's over the counter.

- Include the name of the pharmacy or service that delivers the drugs.

- Add the name of the prescribing doctor, who should also be on the contact list.

- Give directions for taking them, including frequency, timing, with or without food, and any other requirements.

- Also give instructions for when to refill them so your parent doesn't run out.

We suggest doing all of this in a digital document, because a handwritten piece of paper is a pain to update, is potentially hard for others to read, and could get lost between multiple caregivers.

If you're in charge of filling the pill case with the daily, weekly, or monthly dosages, set reminders on your phone or try out a medication app. If someone else needs to pitch in because you have other obligations—and you will—print out instructions and be confident they won't mess it up.

There may also be a matter of equipment or specialized care, which should go in the same document. It could also include instructions for following a specific diet, any exercises or physical therapy program, when to test insulin, or more extreme measures like catheter cleaning or regularly turning a bedridden loved one to avoid sores.

TIP: Dispose of obsolete medication quickly so it doesn't cause confusion and accidentally reenter the routine.

MAKING APPOINTMENTS

Appointments can be the most disruptive part of caring for an aging relative, since you're working around other people's schedules. The recurring ones, like monthly checkups or dialysis, are the easiest to anticipate; the ones that pop up or get rescheduled need more attention, particularly if they're with a specialist with a perpetually packed schedule. You don't want your loved one to miss an important appointment or find out the doctor they need to see is booked for months and end up in the emergency room to treat something that might not be an emergency.

Managing their entire appointment schedule is rarely realistic. Being aware of the most important appointments or the ones that cause your parents the most stress, and maybe even tagging along to offer support, could be more reasonable. If that's too much of a stretch, try your best to check in regularly after an appointment to stay current on their condition and state of mind.

THE MONEY FACTOR

Let's keep this short, because talking about health insurance can make even the healthiest person feel sick:

- **What type of primary insurance do they have (Medicare, Medicaid, private)?**
- **Do they have any supplemental insurance policies?**
- **Is medication included as part of these policies or is it separate?**
- **How do they get reimbursements?**

It's never easy to stay on top of all the bills, but it's necessary, especially if your parents are on a fixed income. Often, you may think something is covered, only to find out later it wasn't, forcing you to waste time and mental energy on the phone disputing the charges. Ease this management burden slightly by at least adding the information about how to access your parent's various health-related accounts online to your own password-keeping method.

CLASH OF PERSONALITIES

Those of you dealing with a parent or loved one in need of care probably read everything we wrote and thought, *This is all well and good, but my parents can drive me absolutely crazy! They don't listen to my advice, won't follow the diet, constantly complain about every doctor, never want to take their meds . . .*

We get it. On paper this seems much easier, but personal idiosyncrasies can derail the best of plans. This is why you need to take a breath and stick to the things you

⊢———▶

can control. No matter how frustrating it may get, remember that people in need of care are also frustrated. Just because your parents might not be as spry and spunky as they once were doesn't mean they're children, and they might lash out if you treat them as such. Unless they're suffering from a horrible disease that greatly reduces their faculties, they should be playing an active role in their own care.

Even though you might want to punch a pillow every time they test your patience on the smallest details, try to remember why you're doing this. You think they enjoyed

> **THEY CARED FOR YOU WHEN YOU NEEDED IT. NOW IT'S THEIR TURN.**

getting no sleep for the first few years of your life or freaking out when you missed curfew by an hour? They cared for you when you needed it. Now it's their turn.

PAPERWORK

Those with some experience in caring for aging parents may be wondering why we didn't mention anything about medical directives, such as Living Wills or Health Care Proxies. That's because it's coming up in Level 2 (see page 120), and we have a Side Mission (see page 192) devoted to more specific medical documents when the end is imminent.

HITTING THE ROAD (or Water)

For issues with cars and other vehicles, the main contact might simply be AAA (which should be in your passwords, FYI). For others, provide the following details: vehicle service center, mechanic, and dealership (if applicable). If you have a boat—otherwise known as "a hole in the water into which you throw money"—share the dock, dry dock, or marina details, Captain.

YOUR PERSONAL VIPS

Medical professionals, service people, and other vendors play a part in your life when you need them, but a host of other people play different roles and might be harder to categorize. These are the people who might be able to provide guidance or assistance during a difficult situation, which sadly can involve an accident that puts you temporarily or permanently out of commission. On a more upbeat note, your family will know who to invite if they ever plan a surprise party for you.

Friends

Your family knows them by name, but do they know how to reach them? Facebook has solved this for the most part, but not everyone is down with social networks. What about those friends with whom you've lost touch but still love like crazy? It could be a college buddy from many years ago or someone you've played mah-jongg with for ages. (From a less cheery, and blunter, perspective: Who would you want to be at your funeral that your family has no idea exists?)

Coworkers

It's crazy how you can see someone every weekday for twenty years and still not necessarily be friends, but a bond is formed. That's how jobs go. Sometimes former coworkers morph into close personal friends, sometimes they're well-regarded acquaintances. Include how you know them in the contact description, since your family might not even know them.

Neighbors

The extent of the relationship your family has with your neighbors might just be a friendly wave when driving by, or something deeper. Anyone who's lived in the same place for a long time knows that neighbors can be lifesavers in an emergency. All they need is a call and they're always ready to help out.

Religious Organizations

If faith plays an important part in your life, this is a must. Include the main contact for your church, synagogue, mosque, temple, or wherever you go to pray. Your family may attend services with you, but there's always a chance you'll need a priest, rabbi, imam, shaman, or person of faith in an emergency.

Other Organizations

Do you belong to any groups (support or otherwise), veterans' associations, clubs, or alumni associations? It's easy to let these slip through the cracks.

Charities and Volunteer Work

Giving to charity is great, as is devoting your time to a cause. If you've done work to help others, whether it's regularly volunteering for events, being a big brother or sister, or manning a phone for a telethon, these are the contacts that could inspire others to pick up where you left off.

Plan of Attack

ORGANIZING CONTACTS

ROUNDING THEM UP

TIME: Initial skim, sort, and pruning of your existing contacts: thirty minutes. Adding or updating the contacts we suggested, which includes researching people and professionals you may not have seen in a while (doctors, mainly): three to five hours. Then get in the habit of including the pertinent details listed on page 49—full name, title, email, short description—every time you add a new contact to your roster.

SHOW THEM THE WAY

Remember the main purpose of bringing order to your contacts: You're making it as easy as possible for your family or loved ones—as well as yourself—to get in touch with all the people who play some part in your life.

Feel free to make the contact info as basic or comprehensive as you like, but the goal is to point your family and loved ones in the right direction. If they have to spend an afternoon doing random Google searches and making a half-dozen phone calls to get in touch with the person who does your taxes or cuts your lawn, you're doing it wrong.

WHAT ABOUT FAMILY?

Don't worry, we'll get to them eventually and in a much bigger way. They're in an entirely different Level because you need to do more for them than simply list out a name, number, email, and description. Plus, haven't we given you enough people to think about for now?

■ ■ ■

Break Time

Life's Milestones and Pit Stops

Your plan is now alive! Think of it like a beautiful, low-maintenance houseplant. When placed in the perfect spot in your home, it requires only a bit of care to keep it from wilting. It needs to be significantly updated only when your life changes, like when these things happen.

A WALK DOWN THE AISLE

Newlyweds, or those getting remarried, have a lot on their plate. Getting all the stuff we mention in order ends up on the back burner in lieu of wedding and honeymoon planning, setting up a home, making out all the time, maybe having some kids, or raising the ones you already have. Still, it's the perfect time to get some routine planning done, whether it's as simple as updating emergency contacts, naming your spouse as a beneficiary for existing health and insurance benefits, or looking into buying Life Insurance (see page 108).

Here's something else to consider: Your money might not automatically go to your spouse when you die, especially if you haven't created or updated your Will (see page 70). Plus, what if you don't want everything to go to your spouse? We're not here to tell you how to distribute your assets, only to let you know your spouse can be the primary beneficiary or one of many beneficiaries, which can be a big factor for blended families. You just need to specify what you want to happen in the event of your death.

SPLITTING UP

Some people completely (and happily) erase exes from their Will, but you may still choose (or be forced) to leave funds to your former spouse. Maybe it's part of a court settlement or for child care. If you get remarried, it's typical for your stuff to go to your current spouse, which could mean children from a prior marriage can end up getting zero if you don't make specific arrangements. A handful of other things you need to update after a divorce: beneficiary designations (Life Insurance and retirement accounts, for example), emergency contacts, shared passwords, Power of Attorney (see page 66), and Health Care Proxy (see page 120).

NEW ADDITIONS TO THE FAMILY

When you have a new baby, everything changes—including your plan. First, you need to name guardians in your Will or get a Will in place if you haven't already. Don't forget to include your bundle of cuteness as a beneficiary (albeit through a guardian). If you have more kids, including those you adopt and/or stepchildren, repeat as necessary.

As your kids transform into full-fledged adults, periodically assess their place in your plans to make sure everything is distributed or split as you see fit. The main goal here is to prevent an all-out sibling war after you're gone.

THE DEPARTED

Sadly, you may outlive some of the people named in your documents. If your Health Care Proxy, your executor, or the person to whom you've granted Power of Attorney dies, you need to name new ones or elevate your alternates to the primary position and name new alternates. If a beneficiary dies, you should reallocate their inheritance to other living heirs or charities close to your heart. Similarly, if the appointed guardian of your children or an adult with special needs passes, it's vital to designate a new one.

It's also common for people who recently lost someone close— or attended a funeral for a family member, friend, or loved one—to become inspired to get a plan in place before it's too late.

IN SICKNESS

It's never pleasant to think about, but this is as real as it gets. If you've been given a diagnosis of a chronic or serious illness, and you're faced with your own mortality, it's best to start planning before becoming physically or mentally disabled.

Start with your Advance Directive, which will be explained in Level 2 (see page 120). Then work your way up to the heavier stuff, which includes talking with your doctors about completing a DNR or POLST, if it's available in your state (see page 192), so you can get the care you want if things take a turn for the worse.

NEW LAWS AND LANDSCAPES

This is when we suggest calling in the pros—financial advisors and estate attorneys—since federal and state laws can change at any time and throw your current plan into chaos. If you move to another state, will your documents still meet the correct requirements? For example, a health care directive from your old state might not hold up in the new one.

MONEY, MONEY, RINSE, REPEAT

Financial situations change over a lifetime, sometimes for good and sometimes temporarily (think postholiday belt tightening, as

in, "I'm eating ramen for the next month").

One of Abby's mentors unexpectedly passed away a few years ago. When we spoke with his wife, a dear friend, she told us that she was required by the terms of her late spouse's Will to give thousands of dollars from his estate to his alma mater. But when they completed their Wills thirty years ago, it was a different time in their lives. She had forgotten about this bequest and wished they had updated their Wills more frequently, because this was something she would've changed.

On the other hand, a big bump in salary or a sudden inheritance windfall, or even a great day at the track, means a big boost to your bank account. Perhaps you didn't think it was important to get a plan in place before, but a trip to a financial advisor or estate attorney is mandatory now that you have finances worth protecting. The same applies when you purchase pricey assets like homes or vehicles, or if you find yourself on the winning side of any lucrative business ventures.

Also, a bigger estate often leads to people willing to fight over it. Look into setting up specific and ironclad asset allocations to your heirs. Once it's in writing, you can rest easy knowing your fortune won't go to waste.

ASSEMBLE THE PIECES

Trusts, Wills, Health Care, and Your Digital Matrix

HERE'S WHAT YOU'LL HAVE ACCOMPLISHED
WHEN YOU'RE FINISHED WITH THIS LEVEL:

- You'll know how to get a Will and Power of Attorney in place, plus Trusts.

- You'll have organized all your bills, debts, and money you owe in a neat, non-depressing pile.

- You'll have composed a Personal Medical Journal and learned about Advance Directives.

- You'll have brought order to every digital account and service you use.

WILLS, TRUSTS, AND POWERS OF ATTORNEY

■ ■ ■

When it comes to traditional estate planning, a Will and Power of Attorney are the two top dogs. Running a close third, though often just as important (and more complicated), are Trusts. Allow us to shatter the mystique of these three cornerstones of planning by explaining them in terms of timing. The easiest way to understand them is to think of when you'll need them: A Power of Attorney is only useful when you're alive; a Will kicks in when you've passed away; and Trusts can work whether you're alive or no longer with us.

WHEN YOU'RE ALIVE: POA

A Power of Attorney, or POA, is something you grant to someone who you choose to speak for you, legally and financially, when you can't speak for yourself. POAs grant great powers over your affairs, but as the saying goes, with great power comes great responsibility. If you're wondering what that looks like, here's what a POA authorizes someone else to do for you.

Pay your bills: It'll be your money, so don't get too excited about this one.

Banking: Make transactions, including deposits, withdrawals, and transfers.

Manage investments: This includes buying and selling securities.

Manage real estate: This includes buying or selling property if you need to relocate, as well as paying the mortgage or rent.

Overseeing insurance: Filing claims or paying premiums.

Taxes: Preparing and filing tax returns.

Even though the power of your finances is in someone else's hands, it's largely clerical bookkeeping work. It's common for people to give their spouse or adult children complete authority over everything. However, if you're concerned about a person's ability to handle your POA responsibilities, you can limit what they can do and name multiple people to take on different tasks. If you have any doubts about a person's ability to act on your behalf, though, you might not want to give them POA privileges at all.

Three Reasons You Need a POA

Bad things happen to everyone. It's an unfortunate truth of life. But even in the direst situations, bills still need to be paid and legal matters addressed. Some possible scenarios for when granting someone POA can save you from additional pain and strife:

1 If you experience an accident, medical emergency, or mental incompetence

2 If you're competent, but still need assistance with routine money-management tasks

(like aging parents who need help with their finances, for example)

3 If you're traveling or unavailable and need someone to act on your behalf, like to sign a contract

HOW LONG DOES A POA LAST?

When you die, the POA dies with you (but not the person you named, of course—that would be horrible). Meaning: The power they have over your finances is no longer in effect after death.

Three Basic POA Types

The main difference between this trio of variations is when they go into effect. It could be today, when you're completely fine (Durable), or if something happens to you and the person you chose is called to action (Non-Durable and Springing).

Durable Power of Attorney:

This is the most typical version and goes into effect the moment the paperwork is signed and stays in effect even if you're deemed mentally incompetent. As long as you're deemed competent, you can change it at any time. If you name your spouse and end up getting divorced, you need to rip it up and pick a new one, since this document will prove to be more durable than your marriage.

Non-Durable Power of Attorney: This is used when you need someone to take care of a specific financial or legal goal and expires if, or when, you're declared mentally incompetent. It comes in handy if, say, you're out of the country and need someone to close on a house or file your tax return. It might not be an everyday occurrence, but at least you now know what it is.

Springing Power of Attorney: This is like the Durable POA, but it kicks in—or "springs" into action—if you become seriously ill, injured, or deemed mentally incompetent. For instance, someone with a Durable POA can go to the bank right now and legally take money out of your account if you're too lazy to make the trip. A Springing POA can legally do it only if you're in a coma.

Who Might Be a Good POA for You?

If you're considering naming someone your POA but aren't sure if they're up for it, have a chat with them to discuss the duties and responsibilities, as well as the scope of your financial and legal affairs. Here's how you know you're picking the right person.

They are responsible: Do they manage their own life and relationships well? Are they detail oriented? If they have trouble managing their own stuff, you probably shouldn't trust them with yours.

They understand the ask: Do they understand what responsibilities come with a POA and are committed to doing it? This is a biggie. We've talked about how giving someone access to your financial world is a tough decision, but handling a POA can be time consuming if they're called to task.

They are good with money: It's a plus if they have a decent understanding of finances and, ideally, business. They don't have to be Warren Buffett, but it'd be nice if they admired someone like him.

They work well with others: The need to collaborate with attorneys, accountants, and others is crucial. This could also include ornery family members who might not be thrilled at the prospect of having to go through this person for cash.

After you talk with someone, you might find out that although you love and trust that person, they'd be terrible at managing your POA. This is your decision to make, so pick someone you truly believe in. It's better to deal with hurt feelings than to have all your property and assets liquidated while you're away on vacation.

How to Get a POA Done

Although the term *Power of Attorney* sounds super-official, getting the actual document completed is quite simple and affordable. If you need something right now, there are a bunch of online legal services that can help you create a standard POA for around $15–$50 (such as Rocket Lawyer or LegalZoom).

Since this offers someone in your life a fair amount of "power"— it's right there in the name of the document—it's always best to consult an estate attorney, who can offer customization, advice about the type of POA you need, and legal witnesses in case it's ever contested. (This goes back to our point about ornery, less-than-thrilled family members.) Plus, the price is usually less than $200, a bargain by most legal-fee standards.

However you decide to create your POA, you'll most likely have to get the final documents notarized, which you can do at a bank, post office, or local government office. If you create it with an attorney, they should have a notary on staff.

WHAT HAPPENS IF . . . YOU DON'T HAVE A POA

If you don't take the time to grant someone a POA and something happens to you, a potential agent may be appointed by the court (either as your guardian or conservator), which can be time consuming, expensive, and stressful. Plus, what if the court names someone you don't trust or even like? We hate to break the mood, but elder abuse is a real and terrible thing. It's also often silent, and people don't realize the extent of the physical or financial abuse until it's too late. You can easily avoid all this unpleasantness by naming the right person now, while you're of sound mind and body.

WHEN YOU'RE DEAD: WILL

Who will raise your kids? Who gets your stuff? To whom will all your millions go? These are the obvious reasons why you need a Will. Here's also why: A Will is vital so your family, friends, and associates don't spend years fighting in court and in person (ideally not with fists). These fights can get even uglier if you have young kids, any type of valuable property, significant financial assets, or all three.

Although the concept of a Will might seem intimidating, its purpose is simply to ensure that your wishes regarding your property, the care of your children or special-needs dependents, and your money are honored. It can be as basic or elaborate as you choose. If you want to keep it simple, you can split your money, assets, property, investments, and anything else you deem valuable evenly between all the people you want to have it (beneficiaries). If you want some people to get more and others to get nothing, this is where you do it. You're in control.

For a very straightforward, no-frills Will, visit one of the many online legal sites, pay a small fee (some are even free), and get started. All you have to do is fill out the parts that apply to you, sign it, and then have two witnesses sign it. Congrats, you now have a Will!

As you can see, the actual Will part isn't all that hard. The bulk of the work is in the decisions you have to make, but even those aren't tough when broken down into manageable pieces.

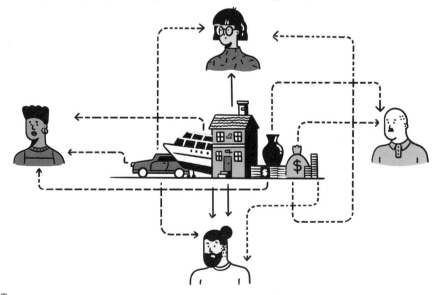

DO AS THE SWEDES DO

The Gentle Art of Swedish Death Cleaning: How to Free Yourself and Your Family from a Lifetime of Clutter by Margareta Magnusson is a fascinating book that created a mini-phenomenon. The general concept is for elderly people to clean and declutter their home while they still have the physical and mental capacity to do so. This includes limiting possessions to what you need and designating items to family members who actually want those things.

You don't have to be near the end of your life to embrace this concept. Perhaps giving away things you're still using is a bit much, but it does make you view some of your personal possessions differently. Are there things that have value only to you and no

one else? A widow we spoke with mentioned how she threw away her late husband's diplomas and degrees. At first it seemed like a big step, but she thought, *What else am I gonna do with them?* She's right. It's not like they're transferable.

Swedish death cleaning is all about removing the obligation your family may feel to hold on to items you owned. Psychologically, the people you leave behind might feel like they're dishonoring your memory by throwing anything away, so they keep things because they feel like they have no other choice. You need to let them know they should take only things they genuinely want. Everything else isn't a memory of you—it's just stuff taking up space.

When you make all these decisions, you can eliminate turmoil before it begins. Isn't it better for family members to be able to blame you for any decisions they don't agree with than for them to take it out on each other? *Family Feud* is a great game show, but it's terrible in real life. (Survey says: Correct!)

Who Gets Your Stuff?

You can leave your assets and belongings to anyone you want. A beneficiary can be a family member or members, friends, pets

> **TIP:** Avoid drama! We're sure your family is incredible, but money, or the prospect of raising your kids, can make people weird. Add in the grief they're experiencing, having lost you forever, and it's common for emotion to overtake rational logic.

(via a human guardian), strangers, organizations, institutions, or dragons (if you believe in such things). By identifying who gets what, you'll relieve some of the stress your family will have to face when settling your estate.

If you don't, a judge who doesn't know you or your family will make these decisions, which is about as appealing as it sounds.

What You *Can* Include in a Will

Actual property: This includes real estate, land, and buildings for which you are the sole owner.

Cash: This means money in the bank, hidden in the ottoman, investments, money market accounts, bitcoin, and so on (basically, all the accounts we covered in the "Your Financial Blueprint" section in Level 1, on page 16).

"Intangible personal property": Stocks, bonds, and other forms of business ownership go here, as well as intellectual property, royalties, patents, and copyrights.

"Unproductive property": This translates as cars you own, artwork, jewelry, and furniture.

Everything else: If you own it, you can give it.

What You *Can't* Include in a Will

Co-owned property: Any property you own equally with someone else (called "joint tenancy"). Example: You can't give away a house you own with your spouse because the property automatically transfers to the surviving owner.

When there's a beneficiary: Any Trusts, retirement plans, or insurance policies that clearly state a beneficiary. If you already determined who's getting it, you can't do it again.

Securities willed to another: Stocks or bonds that are set to transfer to another party upon death, which is just like the example above.

Digital assets: This one is a little tricky, so we'll get into it later (see page 131 if you just can't wait). Let's just say there are gray areas that you can possibly work around. (Just don't tell anyone!)

In short: If you don't own it outright, you can't give it.

More Stuff = More Planning

If you have significant property or assets, particularly elaborate investments or financial arrangements, or property in different states or countries, hire an estate attorney or financial advisor to determine the best way to distribute them. This person can help identify tax-efficient ways so your beneficiaries are taken care of, which may include establishing a post-death Trust (called a Testamentary Trust, which we cover later on page 88) or using other financial and legal expertise.

On the flip side, if you don't have significant or complex assets that require the advice of legal counsel to give away, simply decide who will receive your assets and determine how they'll be distributed, and you're done.

What Happens to the Leftovers?

Who's got time to itemize every single possession in their life? Enter the "residuary estate," which is all the extra stuff you don't think is worth listing out separately. (Examples: stereo system, clothes and shoes, end table, power saw, lamp shaped like a tiger.) For these miscellaneous items you designate a "residuary beneficiary," who takes charge of all the remaining assets you don't include in your Will.

You may want to leave instructions so this person doesn't feel the need to save everything as an eternal shrine to you (unless you're deliciously evil and that's what you demand). Instead, tell them to dole it out to family and friends as they see fit, have an estate sale if they think it can fetch any money, and donate the rest to charity or the local dump.

Before you leave all your possessions to a residuary beneficiary, take a basic inventory of your assets so you're not accidentally including a few gems you want a specific person to have. We're talking about valuable items that might get lost in the shuffle, like expensive furniture, a workshop full of tools, enough designer bags to equal the value of a car, or an actual car that's been in your family for generations. It also might include heirlooms, which are an important part of preserving your family's legacy, which we cover in Level 3 (see page 177).

When it comes to items your family may actually want, put sticky notes or gift tags on the underside of each one with the person's name, letting everyone know that item is claimed. This makes cleaning out your residence after you're gone a sort of scavenger hunt or second Christmas for the family.

Side Mission:
TAKING CARE OF AN ACTUAL BUSINESS

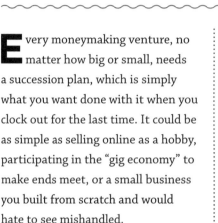

Every moneymaking venture, no matter how big or small, needs a succession plan, which is simply what you want done with it when you clock out for the last time. It could be as simple as selling online as a hobby, participating in the "gig economy" to make ends meet, or a small business you built from scratch and would hate to see mishandled.

A HOBBY WITH BENEFITS

Maybe you sell on eBay or Etsy, sell baked goods at the weekend flea market, drive for Uber, or rent out a spare room on Airbnb. You might also freelance or do contract work. Anything that brings you cash is a plus. Here's a template to open up your enterprise to others:

EXPLAIN YOUR PROCESS. What platforms do you use? How do people contact you? How do you handle transactions?

IS IT A "SIDE HUSTLE" OR A "SIDE GIG"? Is this something you love to do (crafts, baking, photography), or are you supplementing your income by driving (Uber, Lyft), delivering (Amazon, Grubhub), walking dogs (Rover, Wag!), or performing random services (TaskRabbit, Craigslist)?

WHAT ARE THE EXPENSES? How much does it cost? (Be honest.)

HOW MUCH DO YOU MAKE? Where does the money go? Into a separate business account or into your primary checking or savings? (Be even more honest.)

DO YOU REPORT THIS INCOME? (Remember, honest!)

WHERE DO YOU KEEP YOUR PAPERWORK? As well as any relevant permits or tax returns?

WHAT SORT OF DIGITAL SERVICES OR TOOLS DO YOU USE? Think email accounts, web hosting, credit cards linked to payment sites, shipping accounts, and software payments.

FINALLY, WHAT DO YOU WANT DONE WITH ALL THIS IF YOU AREN'T AROUND? Shut it down or pass it to someone else to run?

Whoever is tasked with either closing or taking over your venture needs to be careful when money is involved. For example, if you have $2,000 in your eBay or Amazon seller account, they can't simply take that money as if they'd found it on the street. Your executor needs to include it with the rest of your accounts or valuable assets and pay taxes if any are due.

A SMALL BUSINESS

When does something on the side become a small business? When it starts behaving like one. This includes obtaining an Employer Identification Number (EIN), having separate bank accounts and financial tracking methods, renting a location, hiring employees, and spending all your time making it into something sustainable.

A business has a life of its own and requires a plan of its own. If you've created a succession plan, the same way we did for Everplans, that document serves as the guide. We had to spend months perfecting it with attorneys and accounting for everything, including financial systems, our intellectual properties, and how equity would be transferred, all the way down to the conference

room tables Abby bought off Etsy. (They were one of our first major purchases as a company, and she *really* loves those tables.)

If you have a business and haven't created a succession plan, no matter how basic, then your enterprise can fall into chaos if something happens to you. If you've created a plan and haven't told anyone, then how will your family know what to do? One of our former coworkers told us her father assumed the fate of his business was obvious: His kids would find the documentation he'd created on how to sell it, and then they'd sell it and split the money. In reality, they had no idea where to find this documentation or what they would do with his business. (Luckily, they do now.)

We suggest having a conversation with your heirs, keeping your succession plan among your important papers or, if you went the extra mile, on file with your attorney, who we're betting will be prominently listed among your contacts. (Example: "Herman Adebayo, business attorney, phone number, and email. He knows as much about my business as I do . . . or he should, since I pay him enough.")

Digital Property: Still Not Yours to Give

Although you may consider digital assets like your purchased music, movies, books, apps, games, as well as communications (emails, texts) personal property to do with as you please, the providers of these services have a different stance. Most of them are legally forbidden from disclosing content or granting account access to a third party without the consent of the owner. If the owner dies, the law has generally ruled that the family of the person who owned the accounts *cannot* take full ownership. This is beginning to change, but it's still a murky issue.

Solutions for the Digital Asset Dilemma

To keep this from becoming a really dull diatribe about digital estate legislation, let's just say there are laws in place (depending on where you live), and they're still quite confusing. In the same way that you automatically click "Accept Terms" when presented with an endless scroll of rules and conditions for using a service, no one wants to really dig into dense legislation because we've all got lives to live.

An executor can be granted limited access to a digital account, but if you want a person to have more control, you may have to get a little creative. Some people might include login and password information in their Will in an attempt to transfer digital accounts to heirs. This is a bad idea, because a Will is a public document, and sharing login and password information isn't a secure solution. The internet can be a mean place, and who's to stop some digital hooligan, or identity thief, from combing through Wills and accessing these accounts in hopes of causing all sorts of trouble? Like we said, you have to get more creative than that, which we'll reveal when we dive deep into digital assets at the end of this Level (see page 131).

The Only People Who Get Nothing Are . . .

The people who serve as witnesses to the signing of the Will.

Legally, anyone who signs a Will as a person who witnessed the signing of a Will can't be named as a beneficiary. A witness can be anyone else: friends, associates, a person who happens to be nearby. When a bunch of people at Everplans created their Wills, they used each other as witnesses. Just make sure your adult child or spouse isn't a witness, unless you don't want to give them anything.

Guardians of Your Little Ones

Here's a simple question that rarely has a simple answer: Who would raise your kids, or care for your dependents, if you weren't around to do it? For parents with young kids, or those taking care of an adult with special needs, choosing a guardian is *the most important reason* for creating a Will. We also think it's the toughest decision you'll have to make.

If you're married, it's almost certainly your spouse (if they're still alive, of course). If you're divorced, it's probably your ex-spouse. If you don't have a spouse or your ex-spouse isn't an option, then you've got some thinking to do. Some people have godparents, but that's an honorary title you might give to special people in your life, like best family friends. It doesn't mean you want them to actually raise your kids. Or maybe you already know who you want to serve as guardian but haven't gotten around to making it legal.

But for many, it isn't that easy. Many parents struggle with naming guardians in the event that something happens to both of them. The tension generally comes from having to pick someone on "my side of the family" versus "your side of the family." The way most attorneys get parents to decide this is to have them agree on someone who would make a terrible guardian. Every family has a crazy sister-in-law or completely unreliable brother. The

attorney then explains that if they don't name a guardian, a judge will choose someone from the immediate family and it could very easily be that person. So there must be someone, anyone, who could make a better guardian. This is when most couples need to go away and think about it. And it's also why some people never end up executing their Will, even though everything else is worked out.

How to Pick a Guardian

We already covered the details you need to share with a possible guardian about underage kids in the "Making Sure the Kids Are Alright" Side Mission (see page 19), so refer to that when creating a comprehensive guide to raising or caring for them. As for picking the guardian, here are important factors to consider:

Values: Does the guardian share your beliefs, principles, and philosophy of life?

Personality and lifestyle: What kind of person is the guardian, what kind of life do they live, and is it compatible with your child's personality and interests?

Religious views: Does the guardian share your religious or spiritual views, and will they raise your child accordingly?

Parenting style: If the guardian is already a parent, what is their parenting style like? Is it similar to your own or quite different? Do you think your child would thrive with that type of parenting?

Ability to act as a guardian: Can the guardian handle the responsibilities and duties that come with the job, and do they have the resources necessary to raise your child? Resources may include time, energy, health, financial ability, and emotional wherewithal.

Existing relationship with the child: Do your child and the guardian like each other and have a friendly, healthy relationship?

Location: Does the guardian live near you or far away? Would naming this person require your child to relocate to a new community?

Who Handles Your Kids' Money and Assets?

Typically, the person you name as "guardian of the person" (that's the official, uncomfortable legalese name for "guardian") will also handle the assets left behind for that person. There may be a significant amount of money left behind for your kids, especially if you have Life Insurance, and it's the job of the "guardian of the estate" to manage those finances.

This can be crucial in blended families. Maliciously or not, the surviving parent, or whoever is named as the guardian of the estate, might favor children from a particular marriage over the others. This can happen when a late marriage with a new baby is involved.

We already established that a judge will name a guardian if you don't. That same guardian will most likely also get all the money and assets you've earmarked for your kids. So, if you're having a tough time picking someone to raise your kids, think about whom you'd trust enough to look out for them financially first, and then deal with the emotional stuff second. Or at least think of those sad, lonely piles of money getting into the wrong hands.

Being a Power of Attorney isn't an easy job—and neither is this. Apart from managing the assets, the guardian of the estate also has to make an inventory of the assets for the court and file annual reports detailing the value, income, investments, and estate expenses. Typically, the person you name as guardian of the person will also handle the assets left behind for that person. But you can separate the responsibilities.

When You Trust Someone with Your Kids but Not Your Money

You can choose different people to serve as guardian of a person and guardian of an estate. But why would you?

Let's say your sister is great with kids but horrible with money. And your brother is great with money, but horrible with kids. Suddenly it starts to make sense to split duties.

However, if you opt for different estate/person guardians, they need to be able to work together on the child's behalf. Whenever the person-guardian needs funds for the child, they need to ask the estate-guardian for the money. On paper this makes sense, but you won't be around to manage the personal dynamics if things go south.

Choose wisely and let your separate guardians know beforehand, so it's not a shock. If you sense any tension, choose different people or

find a way to set the person-guardian up for financial success. This can be accomplished by implementing a Trust (see page 86) or helping them learn how to be less crappy with money, which can be tricky.

How Your Will Happens: The Executor

The person tasked with making the decisions you've laid out in your Will a reality is called the executor because they have to "execute" everything. Naturally.

This person is responsible for paying any debts or taxes on behalf of your estate and making sure the people who are supposed to inherit your assets actually get them. An ideal executor is someone with the following skills:

Attention to detail: If an executor screws up, they can be held legally

LEGAL BONUS

Most attorneys will also store the official, signed copy of your Will, which can make things easier for your family. Be sure to share the attorney's contact info, but you already know that because you paid close attention to our "Organizing Contacts" section. (See page 52 for a refresher.)

WHAT HAPPENS IF . . .
YOU DON'T NAME AN EXECUTOR?

If you don't create a Will, or if you create a Will but don't feel like naming an executor (perhaps you were in a sour mood that day?), someone in your family will need to petition the court to become the administrator of the estate. This takes time, is expensive (of course), and might require that they put up a bond against the estate, similar to making sure someone doesn't skip bail. And why would you want to put anyone through that?

There's a ton of other stuff that needs to be done after a death, some of which could be time sensitive, that can't even be started until an executor or administrator is in place. It could be as simple as shutting down a credit card or gaining access to an apartment to clean it out, which requires legal documentation. And let's just say no one wants to find themselves fighting with a mobile phone company who doesn't believe your dad is dead.

---

responsible for any real or perceived malfeasance. You want them to be thorough not only for your family's sake, but for their own as well.

Understands finances and ideally business: Being an executor isn't easy, and if they're not fully up to the task, they need to be willing to follow through on the next point or else they may have a nervous breakdown.

Willing to get help if they're in over their head: Even some of the smartest and most fiscally responsible people we've known have hired an estate attorney to carry the load. Asking for help isn't a sign of weakness or failure.

Usually, it's necessary because the person didn't have enough time to devote to the task and realized the cost of an attorney was worth it.

Patience: The process may take a long time. We're talking months or even years if complications arise.

The person with this magic mix of qualities may not be a family member but rather a competent, honest, and intelligent friend or close colleague. Also, some states have laws about whom you can name as an executor, which makes it a good idea to consult an estate attorney when making your decision.

If you don't feel like you have anyone in your life to entrust with this role, you may appoint a professional, such as an estate attorney or an accountant. The typical fee when naming a pro is often a portion of the estate. Sometimes attorneys even offer affordable estate planning packages in the hope that they'll be hired to eventually settle the estate. If this is the case, let your family know you trust this person but to still keep a lookout during the proceedings to avoid being taken advantage of, like excessive billing hours or a lack of transparency.

How to Get a Will Done: Use an Attorney or DIY?

Once you've made all the decisions laid out in this section so far, it's time to make it official. If you're looking to get something done this very second, there are lots of online legal services that can help you create an official Will. If you're the type who needs things to be 100 percent to your liking, hire an estate attorney or use an online service that offers actual legal advice from attorneys.

Ideally, you'll want an estate attorney's assistance to avoid any trouble down the road if someone contests your Will in court. However, we want you to have something in place, so don't use finding the right attorney as an excuse for putting off getting it done.

Quick and Basic: Online and software-based Wills have become quite common, allowing you to create one that covers all the bases (assets, beneficiaries, guardians, and an executor). Quicken WillMaker Plus is around $90 and also offers a whole host of other legal docs, including a POA, Living Trust, and more. Then there's LegalZoom, Rocket Lawyer, LawDepot, and many others. Just Google "create a Will" and you'll find plenty of options.

We could go on forever listing examples, and all these services offer pretty much the same thing: a user-friendly experience (for the most part) that walks you through the process, a nominal fee (some are free, others are well under $100), and an official document that only needs to be signed by you and two witnesses after you print it.

For the More Involved: As we mentioned earlier, if you have complex financial arrangements,

such as intricate real estate holdings, overseas assets, elaborate investments, or Trusts, then you're going to need some help. This means working with an attorney or an online service that offers advice from

Plan of Attack

YOUR LEGAL DOCS: POA AND WILL

DECISION TIME

DECIDE WHO'LL BE YOUR POA

- Five minutes if the choice is obvious and they accept.

- Two to three hours if you need to choose among family or friends, and a bit longer if you decide to hire a professional (estate attorney, financial advisor).

DECIDE WHAT GOES IN YOUR WILL AND WHO GETS WHAT

- Less than an hour if you have a simple estate and want it divided evenly among your heirs.

- Two to four hours if you have a complicated estate and need to allocate money and assets among heirs differently.

PICK AN EXECUTOR
(Plus an Alternate Executor)

- Five minutes if the choice is obvious and they accept.

- Two to four hours if none of your choices are up to the task and you have to look into hiring a professional.

PICK A GUARDIAN (and an Alternate) FOR KIDS OR AN ADULT WITH SPECIAL NEEDS

- Five minutes if you and your spouse/other legal parent immediately agree on the person and alternate guardian (this almost never happens).

- It could take weeks or months if you're at an impasse, so we're giving you a hard deadline: five days. Here's how it works: You have to keep confronting this topic until you arrive at a decision. If you can't decide after five days, you need to attend free mediation and work it out.

TIME AND COST TO GET YOUR POA AND WILL

ONLINE

- Time it Takes: Less than an hour

- Extra Benefits: Some sites offer full estate planning packages that include an Advance Directive, Revocable Living Trust, and Transfer on Death Deed for a bundled fee.

real lawyers. The best way to find an attorney isn't much different from finding a good doctor, electrician, or dog walker. Get recommendations from friends, family, or other attorneys.

- Average Cost for Just a Will: $0-$50

- Average Cost for Just a POA: $20-$50

- Average Cost for a Bundle (No Trust): $150-$300

- If You Include a Trust: Add $250-$1,000 (or more)

WITH AN ATTORNEY

- Time to Find an Attorney: Five days

- Time Spent with Attorney Creating Documents: Two hours

- Extra Benefits: If you're hiring an attorney, you might as well go all the way and throw in an Advance Directive, Living Trust, and Transfer on Death Deed.

- Average Cost: $300-$500 for the basic documents. Add $1,500-$3,000 if you include a Trust. (This varies, depending on how many documents you create and whether you're doing it alone or with a spouse or partner.)

Once you have some options, meet with them to find out if you get along and approve of their working style and skills. And, of course, don't forget the price tag. According to legal website Nolo.com, costs can range from $300 for a simple lawyer-drafted Will to $1,200 for something more involved. If you opt for an hourly rate, it should range from $150 to $200—keep your eye on the clock so it doesn't cost way more than it should. Following our suggestions and making these decisions in advance should speed up the process and save you money.

Where Should You Keep Your Will?

We're not yet living in a world where digital Wills are pervasive and legal, but perhaps they will be one day. For the time being, here are your best options:

Safe at Home: Put it in your personal safe, a locked filing cabinet, or anyplace you feel comfortable having it. If you store it in a location that requires a combination, password, or key for entry, you have to share that information (in your password keeper, of course) or it won't be of much assistance when it's needed.

With an Attorney: Many estate attorneys, personal attorneys, and some financial advisors will be able to store your Will securely in their office. If you choose to store it with your attorney, tell your family so they're not tearing up the house looking for it.

With Your Executor: Since executors are in charge of making sure your Will gets executed, it makes sense to see if they'd be willing to safely store it for you. Then let your family or beneficiaries know the executor has it, once again to avoid confusion and manic searching.

Safe Deposit Box? Nope! We didn't speak very highly of these earlier (see page 28), but in case we didn't make ourselves clear: Do *not* store your Will in a safe deposit box, mainly because it presents a circular access problem. Frequently a family needs the Will to get legal access to the safe deposit box. So if the Will is *in* the safe deposit box, well, you see the problem. (You do, don't you?) Unless the box is jointly managed—and your survivors are authorized to access it—the bank will require a court order, which just amplifies the misery.

How It Works:
You Die with a Will

Here's a way to visualize what's set in motion after a death. Think of a Will as a three-act play you were forced to attend because your coworker was in it (just be thankful it's not improv, because those shows are hit-or-miss at best):

Act 1: The executor presents the Will to probate court.

Act 2: The probate proceedings can take anywhere from three months to three years, depending on state laws and the complexity of the estate. In short, get comfy. The executor can't distribute property, sell assets, or pay off debts until the court grants approval.

Act 3: The court validates the Will. Victory! Now the executor can get to work and start paying off debts and handing out assets to the beneficiaries.

How It Works:
You Die Without a Will

Let's play this out from a different angle—if you didn't create a Will. The quick version: The court gives your closest surviving relatives everything, including assets and custody over minor children. Your estate will still have to go through the probate process, and "intestacy laws" (*intestate* is the fancy word that describes a person who dies without a Will and whose assets outweigh their debts so there's something to distribute) kick in to determine who gets what.

We're not trying to be dramatic when we say this can be a disaster that lasts years and creates a Grand Canyon–sized rift in your family. You might think your family will be able to work things out peacefully, but when grief starts to subside, greed is often waiting to fill the void.

Having a Will versus not having a Will can make the difference between a couple of months and a couple of years to gain access to financial accounts needed to pay off debts or keep up with a mortgage, not to mention all the legal fees. So, please, do a Will.

Pour-Over Wills: Splitting the Difference

A Pour-Over Will funnels any assets in your name into an already-created Trust when you die.

This essentially means that any assets you hadn't moved to your Trust before your death are automatically moved (or "poured") into the Trust after your death. Once in the Trust, those assets will be subject to the terms and stipulations of the Trust.

Why create one? It's like having a safety net for any assets you may have forgotten about or intentionally left out of a Trust that you would like moved into one after death. This can help your heirs avoid probate, or at least make the probate process

DOES A WILL HAVE TO BE NOTARIZED?

Nope, a Will is still valid if you don't get it notarized. In some states you may have to get a self-proving affidavit—this is where the witnesses swear under oath that they witnessed you signing the Will—and that needs to be notarized.

go faster. Though probate laws vary from state to state, for the most part the assets that "pour" into the Trust will avoid probate if they total less than $100,000. However, you should check with a trust and estate attorney in your state to learn about your state's laws.

To create a Pour-Over Will, a Revocable Living Trust must already have been properly established. Apologies for getting ahead of ourselves by talking Trusts before explaining them. (For more on Trusts, see page 86.)

What If You Don't Want a Will?

We're not here to judge. If you don't think you need one, the least you can do is give your family and loved ones a heads-up. Otherwise they could spend months, even years, searching for a document that doesn't exist. Plus, it gives them plenty of time to start sharpening knives for the inevitable battle over everything you had.

And though we said we wouldn't judge, let's get real: Unless you want your family to fight, you should have a Will. Even if you despise everyone in your life, that's all the more reason to have an official document letting them know how you feel.

WHEN YOU'RE ALIVE *OR* DEAD: Trusts

A Trust allows you to put a barrier between you and your assets. It can be to protect them from taxes, lawsuits, nosy people, and other things you want to avoid. Trusts can get hyper-complicated, but that tends to happen when they're designed to protect and ultimately disperse a wide range of valuable holdings. They can also be tailored for smaller purposes.

FIVE REASONS TO GET A TRUST

1. **To avoid probate court.** Again, probate is the legal process by which a Will is validated. It's

long and slow and painful. If all your major assets are in a Trust, they can pass to your heirs and beneficiaries without having to go through the courts.

2. **To maintain control of assets in the event of incompetence.** If you become unable to manage your assets because your health or mental fitness declines, the rules set forth in the Trust are generally protected more so than in a typical bank or investment account.

3. **To put space between you and your assets.** You can create the type of Trust that takes ownership of your assets, which may allow you to qualify for Medicaid and serve as a shield from creditors and personal lawsuits.

4. **To pay Life Insurance premiums.** Many people (including Adam) have a Life Insurance Trust to keep insurance separate from

THE FOUR MAIN COMPONENTS OF A TRUST

- **GRANTOR:** The person who creates the Trust (also known as the *donor*, *settlor*, or *trustor*).

- **PRINCIPAL:** The property or assets themselves, including money, that are held in the Trust and managed by the trustee(s).

- **TRUSTEE:** The person, people, or entity (such as a bank) who agrees to hold the principal and is responsible for managing it, filing taxes, and distributing it according to the rules of the Trust (the grantor may also be the trustee). When the person who created the Trust dies, a successor trustee is tasked with following the rules of the Trust to manage or distribute whatever was in it.

- **BENEFICIARY:** The person or people who ultimately receive the property or assets in the Trust.

their estate because it gets taxed much differently.

5 To maintain control over assets after they've been passed to another. When a significant amount of assets is involved (cash, property, valuables), Trusts can be established to maintain control of how those assets are used after death. For example, a Trust's sole purpose could be paying college tuition for a grandchild. In this scenario, the money in the Trust can be used only to pay that tuition and can't be used on behalf of anyone other than the grandchild.

Before you consider creating a Trust, you need to identify the goal you want it to fulfill. The five things we just mentioned are a good place to start, and from there it's all about working with an estate attorney or financial advisor to make those goals a reality.

What About Estate Taxes?

This is one of the major reasons people *think* they need a Trust, so let's clear this up: Avoiding estate taxes is *not* the reason most people need a Trust. It's a compelling topic of conversation, like imagining what you'd do if you won the lottery, but you still have to pay taxes on money held in a Trust. They're just not "estate taxes" because a Trust isn't part of an estate (the act of putting things in a Trust separates it from the estate—that's why most people create them). As of 2020, to even qualify for estate taxes you need to have more than $11.5 million. And then you're taxed only on the money above that threshold. (So if you had $12 million, only $500,000 would be taxed at the federal level. State laws—and their tax rates—vary.) Again, compelling for idle conversation, but not realistic for most people. If this applies to you, speak with a financial advisor or estate attorney—because, you know, you can afford it.

Living Trusts vs. Testamentary Trusts

Although all Trusts must be set up by you during your lifetime, not all of them immediately go into effect. Many Trusts go into effect *after* a person dies, leading people to believe they can be set up on behalf of a person after their death. And although an heir can set up a Trust with the assets left to him or her, it wouldn't be on behalf of the deceased—it would be their own Trust. The two basic types of Trusts are a Living Trust, which goes into effect now, and a Testamentary Trust, which goes into effect when you're gone. Here are a few more differences between the two.

A Living Trust: It becomes effective the moment it's created. This is the one you hear about the most (with the exception of "Trust Funds")

and is usually established to avoid probate court (see page 84). In short, this means that when you die, the assets in the Trust are no longer considered your property and can skip the courts and pass seamlessly to the beneficiaries. Be aware, though, that only the assets in the Trust can avoid probate. If something is not included in the Trust, then it has to go through probate before it can be distributed.

Another good part of Living Trusts is the level of privacy they create around the assets—and the way they are distributed. Only the trustees know the terms, which is why when a rich or famous person dies with a Trust, the media can only speculate about what they may have had. If they didn't have a Trust and their estate has to go through probate court, it becomes a public record and we get all the juicy details. However, Living Trusts are more expensive than Testamentary Trusts for various reasons, including paperwork and retitling assets.

A Testamentary Trust:
A Testamentary Trust is created as part of a Will and becomes effective only after death. It's used primarily to control how or when a beneficiary receives assets. It could be that your child doesn't receive a payout until they turn a certain

HOW TO CHOOSE TRUSTEES

Just like naming an executor (see page 79), you want someone honest and financially competent, whose beliefs are aligned with the goals you had in mind when creating the Trust. Although some Trusts may require trustees with extensive experience in investing or accounting, others may benefit from trustees who have close personal relationships with the beneficiaries or the grantor.

If there's no one in your life who is up to the task, you can appoint someone close to you to act as a trustee but specify that they hire professionals to advise them, which is common for executors as well.

age—eighteen, twenty-one, or fifty-five if you really want to make them sweat—or complete a certain task like graduating college. You make the rules. After all your assets pass through probate, they hang out in the Trust until those rules are satisfied.

A Testamentary Trust, which is usually affordable since it can be bundled with a Will, can be difficult to change—because it's bundled with a Will. Any changes to the Trust also require you to revise your Will, which might be a hassle if you plan to make lots of changes. Also, you don't get privacy with a Testamentary Trust. If that's your reason for creating a Trust, you might want to focus on the living version.

Trust Flavors: Revocable or Irrevocable

All Trusts need to be either Revocable or Irrevocable. But don't get tripped up by these big words, even though the pronunciations can be tricky. *Revocable* (RE-va-kah-bull) means you can change it; *Irrevocable* (IR-rev-ah-kah-bull) means you can't.

Revocable Trusts: You retain ownership and control over everything in the Trust and can change it whenever you want. If you need to name different trustees or beneficiaries, have at it.

Why Choose This? Most people opt for Revocable Trusts to avoid probate. When you die, the Trust becomes Irrevocable and whatever's in it can be distributed according to the rules of the Trust and not the rules of the probate court. You can move assets in and out of the Trust whenever you want without too much hassle, but these assets are taxable because they're still considered yours even though they're technically in a Trust. It also won't help if you have a liability judgment against you or any creditors on your tail. For that you need asset protection, which is one of the benefits of Irrevocable Trusts.

Irrevocable Trusts: You give ownership and control of the property in the Trust to others (trustees) and therefore no longer own or control the property, making you unable to change it without going through major hoops. It's like getting a regrettable tattoo removed. It can be done, but how much pain do you really want to endure?

Why Choose This? Irrevocable Trusts are generally established to avoid or reduce taxes. Since the assets are no longer considered your property, you're not responsible for paying taxes on them. (To be clear: Taxes still need to be filed for the Trust, but any taxes owed come out of the Trust and not your personal accounts.) It might not be easy for a person to essentially give up ownership and control of their most prized or valuable assets, so people need to choose wisely and carefully.

Putting assets into an Irrevocable Trust requires a formal transfer of property, meaning the property must be retitled in the Trust's name. If it's a house, your name on the deed is replaced with the name of the Trust—which means the person who created the Trust no longer has the right to sell, give away, invest, or manage the assets. You also can't change the beneficiaries or revoke the Trust.

So far, we haven't really made this type of Trust sound—what's the word we're looking for?—good. What's the point of having money or property if it's not yours anymore? The main benefits are that these assets are protected from lawsuits, creditors, and taxes that you'd have to pay if they were still yours. They tend to work better if only one family member is set to receive a particular asset, because it means less squabbling among relatives. There's also the ability of the giver to then qualify for government benefits, such as Medicaid, without having to spend the money they planned on leaving to their heirs. Finally, this type of Trust comes with privacy, which means only the trustees will know what's in it and how it will be distributed.

This Can Get Complicated

If the primary goal of the Trust is to avoid excessive taxes and qualify for benefits you wouldn't get if you had too much money, you'll likely want to set up an Irrevocable Trust. If the goal is to maintain control of assets in the event of incompetence, you'll likely want to go with the Revocable option.

The rules of the particular Trust you're establishing will likely dictate the style of Trust you choose. This is why we can't stress the following enough: Hire a professional! Especially if you're looking to do something complicated. An attorney can help you decide what to do, set it up, manage retitling property if necessary, and navigate state and federal laws that can make it even more perplexing. Also, if you don't follow the rules properly and mess something up (even by accident), it can void all the effort that went into creating the thing in the first place.

A Matter of Trustees

Let's get away from the Trust for a moment and focus on the trustee, who's responsible for keeping accurate records of all transactions; preparing, filing, and paying income tax returns for the Trust; and adhering to any and all applicable state and federal laws regarding how the Trust is administered.

This sounds like a lot to do, because it is. So think hard about who you know who can (and will) do all this work. It can be you (for a Revocable Trust), your family members or (really smart) friends, fee-based professionals (such as accountants or attorneys), a bank or Trust company, or any combination of these people.

Then there are successor trustees, who need to be named if you have only one trustee. If something happens to that person,

the successor will step into the primary role. If you're the only trustee, then you have to name a successor, since you won't be able to rise from the dead to manage anything anymore.

Why Do All This Work? Beneficiaries!

You're not going through this hassle because you love paperwork and have spare time to kill. You're doing this so your beneficiaries—kids, other family members, an organization or charity—eventually receive this property. It's easy to lose perspective, so visualize the person or people you would be helping by jumping through all these hoops.

How to Get It Done: Trusts

A Trust is essentially setting up a business entity, which requires its own bank account and likely its own tax return every year (forever). Although there are many online legal services that can help you create a Trust, we believe it's wiser to work with an attorney or advisor to avoid complications. There are also online services that offer personalized legal advice from an attorney, which can be a more affordable option.

The cost can vary based on the type and complexity (like a Will), and the method of establishment. Online legal services can charge

CREATING A TRUST

DECISIONS YOU HAVE TO MAKE: Start with your reason for creating a Trust; choose trustees (if other than yourself); choose beneficiaries (and alternate beneficiaries); and determine how it's funded and how much effort needs to go into annual maintenance.

TIME IT TAKES TO MAKE THESE DECISIONS: Two hours if you're extremely confident and clear with your choices; three to five hours if you need to do more research.

TIME IT TAKES TO DO IT ONLINE: Around an hour because it's like taking a very long survey and some of the questions might be perplexing unless you're well versed in Trusts. (If you are, you probably already have one and just need to share the details.)

COST: $250–$1,000

TIME IT TAKES TO DO IT WITH AN ATTORNEY/FINANCIAL PROFESSIONAL: One to two hours if you come prepared.

COST: $1,500–$3,000. (It varies, depending on the complexity of the Trust and if it is done jointly with your spouse or partner.) There may be other costs, such as retitling property, opening new accounts, and filing annual tax returns.

LEGAL DOC RECAP: Online platforms offer decent and affordable Wills and POAs for simple estates. Trusts can be complicated, which is why we suggest meeting with a professional, to assure it's done correctly—or to determine if you even need one, which a reputable financial advisor or estate attorney should tell you right off the bat.

THE COMPROMISE: It's always better to have something in place than to have nothing in place. Don't avoid doing these documents because you haven't found the perfect attorney. Start by trying an online platform and think of it as a just-in-case Will and POA. You can always bring those documents to an attorney for review later. If later never comes, at least you'll be offering your family and heirs some level of protection today.

anywhere from $30 to $300, and consulting with a lawyer can generally range anywhere from $1,000 to $3,000 (or more). Plus, you need to include other possible fees (like an annual tax return), and they can add up if you expect the Trust to be in effect for the duration of your life. You may also meet with a pro and find out that you don't even need one or would be fine with bundling a Testamentary Trust with your Will.

Although the cost of consulting with an attorney may seem high, their job is to ensure that the Trust you're setting up is valid and legally sound, which can potentially save you or your heirs money. But, like a Will, if you're looking to set up something extremely simple, you can try your hand at doing it online first. Think of it as a practice swing. If you find yourself getting in too deep, stop! Otherwise you'll *need* to hire a professional to undo all the damage. (This is a bit like going to a bad dentist and then having to pay double to get whatever they did to your teeth corrected.)

LETTER OF LAST INSTRUCTIONS

Legal documents tend to be black and white (literally and figuratively), which is why including a Letter of Instructions (or Letter of Last Instructions) is a thoughtful gesture. This letter serves no legal function, but it can give the people you left behind insight into the decisions you made, why you made them, and ways to go about handling final arrangements.

A traditional Letter of Instructions tries to cover everything in a person's life, but that's not always realistic. Detailing your entire life in a few pages is too much to ask of anyone, which is why we want you to create a laser-focused Letter of Instructions pertaining only to your Will, Trusts, and other practical or logistical areas (for example, phone access, passwords, location of documents), where you think your family may be confused or wanting to know more.

Or perhaps you're the type who doesn't like to explain yourself or your decisions. That's cool, because you don't have to. But if you have three kids and cut one out of the Will, you might want to explain why. If you set up a Trust that doles funds out to an adult child over time because they can't be trusted with vast sums of money, make it clear. If you name an unlikely guardian— like a close friend and not a family member—you can help the snubbed party try to understand your reasons for doing so.

We mentioned that this letter isn't legal, but if things get contentious— heirs fighting over assets, a less-than-ideal relative trying to get custody of your kids—it could be used to sway

Plan of Attack

LETTER OF LAST INSTRUCTIONS

TIME: One hour. This is a culmination of all your legal decisions and is something you should be thinking about in the back of your mind throughout the entire process. Take the time to create a quick rough draft with all the things you want to include. The example we included gives you a good idea of the structure and what you might want to say. Return to the document a few times over the course of two weeks until you're satisfied that it gets your message across clearly and warmly. (Or coldly, if you plan to give someone bad news: "You. Get. Nothing! And here's why. . . .")

the court in favor of your decision. Or it could be completely ignored. Courts pretty much do what they want—we can only hope for the best.

You don't include the letter as part of your Will, POA, Trust, or Advance Directive (see page 120); you just need to be sure it's found by the people who will need it. Storing it alongside these documents can ensure safe delivery. Also, if you're worried someone in the family might destroy the only copy and throw the family into chaos, make extras. (It's unlikely, but we've watched a lot of soap operas.)

To help illustrate what a letter may look like, a close friend of ours shared the one she wrote for her kids. We changed the names, but feel free to use it as a template when writing your own.

■ ■ ■

To My Executor and Trustee:

Please consider this letter an extension of my Will and an effort to help my children and family members understand my wishes.

First and foremost, it is my wish that my children read this letter in the company of my executor or trustee.

Please be sure Milo and Dani understand that I wish their inheritance to be spent to further their private school education, college education, sleep-away camp or summer enrichment programs, or extracurricular activities, in addition to any purposes that the trustees deem appropriate. While Milo and Dani are minors, I also hope that they continue to see Dr. Winnie as their primary pediatric physician. As adults, I hope they will use this money, if not for the above items, then on a home. (Don't forget to negotiate!)

I want to be sure Milo and Dani know the funds allotted should be used for their benefit and no one else's.

I truly hope they will stay in close contact with their grandmother, aunts, uncles, and cousins. Make sure they celebrate holidays together. If I am not here, I hope that they both are still with my family to celebrate holidays.

Most important, to my children: I love you with every molecule of my heart. I wake up every day believing in you, knowing that you'd grow up to be amazing. I'll always be with you—in your heart, in your soul, watching out for you, protecting you, and cheering for you.

Wherever I am, I'm thinking of you and smiling.

Love,
Mom

MONEY YOU OWE
DEBT, CREDIT & INSURANCE

■ ■ ■

Back when phones had only one ringtone, bills were a stack of paper on a table. You'd go through each one, fill out what was required, write a check (remember those?), put a stamp on the envelope, and do your best to remember to drop it in the mail.

Technology revolutionized this process, mostly for the better. Now you might not even receive paper statements. When a bill is due, you might get an email alert, but it doesn't matter, because you likely have it on autopay. This makes bill paying less of a hassle, but it also removes the physical transparency.

If you handle the majority of the bills for your household, it's difficult for anyone else to understand the behind-the-scenes process. They'd need access to the email account associated with the bill, the payment method (is the account linked to a credit card or a checking account?), and the login credentials to make or change

HOW THIS HELPS AFTER YOU'RE GONE
(Deconstructing your debts)

- Similar to the breakdown of your assets, which we discussed in the "Money You Have" section (see page 28), this provides a clear picture of your finances . . . only from the other side.

- When settling your estate, taxes and debts need to be paid off before heirs get their share.

- Credit cards and other forms of payment need to be managed to avoid unnecessary expenses or possible fraud against your estate.

- Any insurance payouts owed can be collected, since this money is often a financial lifeline.

a payment. The good news is we've already explained how to compile and share your passwords in Level 1 (see page 8), so that's no longer a worry.

Simply being able to access an account doesn't help organize all the money flowing out of your life. To paint the full picture, we're going to help you organize all your bills using two basic categories: expected and unexpected.

For lazy folks looking to circumvent this process, we have a shortcut, but it'll force your family to do the heavy lifting, and it involves math and credit card statements. Before deciding, however, hear us out on the options.

CREDIT FOR ORGANIZING

Let's start with the most basic (and ongoing) form of debt before digging into the specifics: credit cards. If you're the type of person who charges everything, the statements tell the tale.

Some of the charges are easy to track because they show up every month, like utilities, groceries, cell phone, or subscription services like Netflix. Some are obvious and would make sense to anyone peeking in, such as clothing, pet supplies, or restaurants. Others are the ones you don't even recognize at first glance: "Who charged something at MEGA-OU812? Did my card get stolen?!" Once you calm down and do a search, you realize: "Oh, it was that juice I got at the mall."

How to Start

If you don't want to organize and explain all your expenses, the least you can do is share your credit card information. But know in advance that it can be a hassle for anyone who might need to commandeer your finances either temporarily or permanently. The following is a starting guide to recording and tracking your plastic rectangles.

What cards do you have? Visa, American Express, MasterCard, Discover, a card from a specific bank or store (Target, Walmart)? If this isn't easy to answer, then you probably have too many cards.

How do you pay for it each month? Is it on autopay from a particular bank account? Do you manually pay it online when it's due? Do you still send a check in the mail?

Share some helpful specifics: What are the last four digits, security code, and expiration date of your cards so you know they're up to date?

What rewards are there for each card, and how do you access them? The main benefit of credit cards—besides not carrying around all the cash you need for everything all the time—is to get something back for using them. Do you get miles, cash back, or maybe shopping reward points that can be used on Amazon or at Disney World?

Can the login details be found with the rest of your passwords? Is it coupled with a bank account (example: a Chase Visa)?

Do you still receive paper statements? Where do you keep them?

Most cards offer a year-end summary, which tries its best to categorize the charges in a pdf. Print these out and put them in a folder with other financial info. If you're not into paper, keep the pdf in a folder on a shared drive in the cloud (examples: Dropbox, Google) with other important financial documents, like your tax returns.

This is also where one of those budgeting or financial tracking tools we mentioned in Level 1 (see page 24) come in handy. These record all your transactions and can help someone else make sense of your finances free of paper cuts. Plus, unlike year-end statements, these programs make it easy to edit transactions and keep them properly categorized. For example, a coworker told us his neighborhood grocery store is always categorized as "printing." If he didn't correct it, someone would be very curious about why he's been spending more than $300 a month on printing for the past six years.

Although credit card statements tell the full story from a high-level and labor-intensive point of view, let's take a look at where your money actually goes (or went).

The Great Debate: Paper vs. Paperless

Almost everything we do that was once paper is now digital. Even a ninety-five-year-old grandma who's never touched a computer has a digital profile. Although you can still request paper statements and send checks in the mail, companies want to eliminate paper, postage, and other costs that feel increasingly unnecessary. It also helps the environment, but it's probably more about the money. This is why many companies offer incentives if you opt for electronic delivery, such as $5 back or a minor discounted rate.

But not everyone is on board, especially those who trust things they can physically hold in their hands. An online survey by

Consumer Action reported that, depending upon the type of bill, close to half and up to three-quarters of respondents "choose paper over electronic notifications for insurance, utilities, medical, mortgages, credit cards, and property taxes."

Paper is real. Paper doesn't become inaccessible for a period of time because it's undergoing maintenance. If you have a dispute with a company, you can produce a piece of paper and make your case in black and white. But paper is only the physical proof. When it comes to action, like paying a bill or contacting customer support, we tend to do it digitally because it's faster and more efficient. But there's undeniable security in having something to hold in your hand. Most of the legal documents we described in the first part of this Level need to be on paper for them to be official. Sometimes, despite the paperless tide riding high, it's a jump ball.

The Solution: Find a happy medium. Going paperless doesn't have to be all or nothing. Having things on

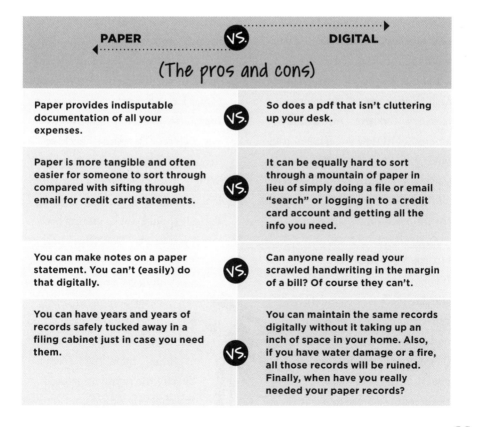

PAPER vs. **DIGITAL**

(The pros and cons)

PAPER		DIGITAL
Paper provides indisputable documentation of all your expenses.	vs.	So does a pdf that isn't cluttering up your desk.
Paper is more tangible and often easier for someone to sort through compared with sifting through email for credit card statements.	vs.	It can be equally hard to sort through a mountain of paper in lieu of simply doing a file or email "search" or logging in to a credit card account and getting all the info you need.
You can make notes on a paper statement. You can't (easily) do that digitally.	vs.	Can anyone really read your scrawled handwriting in the margin of a bill? Of course they can't.
You can have years and years of records safely tucked away in a filing cabinet just in case you need them.	vs.	You can maintain the same records digitally without it taking up an inch of space in your home. Also, if you have water damage or a fire, all those records will be ruined. Finally, when have you really needed your paper records?

paper can be comforting, but keep in mind how often you check and pay for everything online. If you can't quit paper, make your monthly bills digital, print out a year-end summary for each of your cards, and keep it with a copy of your tax return. We also implore you to keep all your statements in an orderly fashion, so you don't drive your family crazy if they need to make sense of them all.

Finally, consider using one of the financial account aggregation tools mentioned in Level 1 (see page 24). They can solve the record-keeping problems many of us have faced for a long time. Once they become part of your routine, you'll wonder why you've been making it so hard on yourself for so long.

BILLS: THE EXPECTED

The only surprise regarding these monthly, quarterly, or annual bills is how many you have and how much they cost. The majority might be consolidated on credit cards, but maybe a few are paid in cash or draw from your debit or checking accounts. Once again, the amount of money you have to pay doesn't matter, at least for planning purposes. You just need to identify all the following expenses along with the information we suggest.

Home Related

If you own your home, the natural starting place is your mortgage. What's your mortgage company's name, the account number (if applicable), the location of your mortgage paperwork, the account you use to pay it,

and the mortgage term. If you have a mortgage agent or specific contact at the bank, make sure that name goes in your contacts.

If your home is paid off (lucky you!), you still have property taxes to pay twice a year (or once in some cases). If you rent, indicate how you pay each month: online, check, or drop it off with a building manager? Where do you keep your lease, when is it up, and how much of a security deposit should you be getting back when you vacate? Don't forget to include the landlord or management company's info among your contacts.

If you're in an assisted-living facility or nursing home, treat it like a rental. Specify the payment method and share the admission contract or other relevant paperwork, as well as a main contact for any issues that arise.

If you own other real estate, what type of property do you have? Is it a rental used for business, is it a time-share, or is it actual land you plan to do something with eventually? If you're renting, treat it like a rented apartment. If you're paying it off, treat it like a mortgage.

Utilities et al.

Now that you know how to organize all the details about your home (see page 30) and have made it clear how you pay for your home, how do you keep it operational? The reason these bills tend to fall through the cracks is not that they're secret, it's that they're mundane. How you keep the lights on isn't a thrilling story to share around the dinner table. Here's a handy list to make sure you're not forgetting anything:

- ❏ Electricity/gas
- ❏ Water
- ❏ Heating oil/propane
- ❏ Internet, cable, home phone (landline or bundled services)
- ❏ Security monitoring system or company
- ❏ Cleaning/landscaping
- ❏ Garbage removal

You need to explain how you pay for these services, particularly if they're complicated or unorthodox. Do you have any set to autopay? Do you pay some in cash, like to that kid in the neighborhood who cuts your lawn? For the accounts you pay online, make sure you share the passwords in your password keeper or whatever other document you're using to collect them.

Vehicle Related

If you're wondering why it's important to share payment details about your vehicles, we've got two words for you: repo men (or women). If you finance your car, where's the original title, what's the name of the finance company, how do you pay for it each month, and when is the projected date of the last payment? If your vehicle is leased, you probably get the gist by now, but just to be clear: Whom do you pay and how do you pay them, where do you keep the paperwork, and when does the lease end?

There are other expenses related to a sweet, or at least reliable, ride. Do you have a gas station credit card, a toll pass account, a roadside assistance program, and/or extras like in-car satellite radio or wireless data? Do you live in a city and put your car in a lot? If so, where's the lot and how do you pay for it?

(Almost) Everything Else

Beyond your home and your wheels, there are myriad expenses that typically need to be added to your list. And these don't include the unexpected ones, which we'll tell you how to "expect," sort of. In the meantime, start, as always, with your phone. Then proceed to the less-important things like taxes and tuition for your kids (we joke—it would've been funnier if we hadn't been distracted by our phones).

Cell Phone: We give mobile phones a special call-out because for some unholy reason, canceling a service plan, whether you're alive or dead, has become one of the biggest hassles on earth. The best you can do is share the login information for your current plan in your password-keeping method of choice (hello, passwords again!), and explain the contract details and how you pay. Also, pray for a reasonable and sympathetic service rep over the phone, though you'll likely have to visit a store to terminate service (without being charged fees) or to transfer the account to another name (if it's a family plan).

Subscriptions: It seems like every company has instituted a monthly or annual subscription model, which is easy to keep track of on credit card statements. Simply write down (ideally in a digital document, since it's much easier to manage) a clear picture of what you have, whether it's an entertainment or streaming service (Netflix, Hulu, HBO, Spotify), a recurring food delivery (FreshDirect, prepared meals-in-a-box, Chewy.com pet food and supplies), shopping (Amazon Prime, Costco), digital storage (Dropbox,

THE PSYCHOLOGY OF THE EXPECTED

If you were to picture all your bills, you'd notice that the vast majority of them are completely expected. Even vacations are expected unless your life (and budget) allows you to jet off at a moment's notice. We don't want to get into the psychology of how debt messes with our emotions, but it can be hard to face the fact that more of our money seems to be going out than coming in. It can be even harder to let your family know this too.

Clear all that from your head and don't get wrapped up in the dollars. In the same way we don't care about how much money you have, don't worry about how much money you owe. All we ask is for you to stay focused on keeping it practical, thorough, and honest.

iCloud), magazines and newspapers, or any other service that shows up regularly at your door or digitally through a device.

When you create a list of all your subscriptions, you might be shocked at how many you have, how much you spend on them, and how few you use often enough to justify the expense. This is where the financial aggregation tools we mentioned (see page 24) come in handy, because some are specifically designed to monitor all your subscriptions and offer ways to easily cancel the ones you don't want anymore.

Memberships: These aren't much different from subscriptions, with the exception that you usually get an ID card to prove you're a member. They're also a bigger hassle to cancel, specifically when they involve gym memberships, which are notorious for locking people into contracts and making it difficult to cancel without having to physically go to the location and incur cancellation fees (or worse, be put into collections). The same may apply to golf or tennis clubs, as well as fitness or dance classes that require an up-front payment without any refunds. For many of these, your executor will have to go to the location or send a certified letter providing proof of death to recoup any money owed and cancel the membership. But there are helpful ones, too, like AAA, AARP, or social and charitable organizations that shouldn't be left off your list.

Loans & Big Debts: We know these can be a huge burden to bear and a constant source of anxiety in your life, but they still need to be confronted. Aside from your home and car, do you have any other loans or debts looming over your life? Is it a line of credit, a personal loan (including ones from family or friends), or a dreaded student loan? Although you might not have many nice things to say about the financial institution that issued the loan, you should share details about whom you pay, how you pay it, related documents (like the original loan agreements and invoices), account numbers, and when you expect it to be paid off if you stay on track.

Taxes: Aside from state and federal income taxes, and a biannual property tax bill, are there any others lurking in the dark waiting to ruin your day? It's best to have an inkling of whether you're getting a nice refund come mid-April or begrudgingly writing a check.

Gifts & Tips: It's great to have a big, loving family, but it can get expensive around the holidays and when birthdays seem to be every other week. Same goes for weddings, bar/bat mitzvahs, confirmations, *quinceañeras*, anniversaries, and other joyous events that require gifts or cash. These dates are right there on your calendar, so you can't say they're much of a surprise.

Along these same lines, do you give tips or gifts to vendors and service people around the holidays? If so, make a list with amounts. It could be postal carriers, garbage collectors, cleaning staff, security guards/doormen, the super for your building, parking lot attendants, or a host of other people. Tipping can be extremely confusing for those who aren't involved, forcing them to give too much, too little, or nothing at all.

Tuition: Student loans tend to hog all the attention, but there's a whole thing that happens before (and during) the debts: school. Whether it's preschool, private school, college, technical school, graduate school, or anything else, what and for whom do you pay for education? This may involve financial aid, scholarships, tutoring, and special-needs programs as well.

Alimony & Child Support: If you're responsible for paying an ex, what's the payment schedule and duration? Are there any stipulations if something happens to you? Perhaps it's factored into a Life Insurance policy, Will, or Trust—your ex must remain as a beneficiary or receive a portion of your estate until you're no longer required to pay.

BILLS: THE UNEXPECTED

Inevitably in life, there are bills that seemingly come from nowhere, repeatedly. Sometimes you drop your phone into the toilet. And root canals don't send out save-the-dates three months in advance.

Although unexpected bills are harder to quantify and predict, there's nothing stopping you from estimating what they may be and *how* you would go about paying them. Look through old credit card statements, find big transactions, and ask yourself, *What are the odds of this happening again?* Even if the answer is *possibly*, include it on your list, perhaps with advice on what you'd do better for them next time.

Medical expenses tend to be the most backbreaking (pun intended). According to a survey conducted by West Health Institute in conjunction with NORC at the University of Chicago, "About 40 percent of Americans report skipping a recommended medical test or treatment and 44 percent say they didn't go to a doctor when they were sick or injured . . . because of cost."

This is also why nonprofit news service Kaiser Health News reported in 2019 that "of the $5 billion [GoFundMe] says it has raised, about a third has been for medical expenses from more than 250,000 medical campaigns conducted annually." We don't want you to spend too much time worrying about this next question (or you'll be a nervous wreck), but if a medical emergency were to strike your family, would you be able to come up with the money without going bankrupt or having to rely on the kindness of others?

When it involves anticipating possible emergency home expenses, you should make notes of possible issues when creating your Home Operating System (see page 45).

Check to see if the water heater is on its last legs, if the gutters are hanging off the house, or if the washing machine is one spin cycle away from laundry heaven. Same goes for vehicle expenses, which can also be a financial killer. If you're generally aware of things that might break, you can at least brace yourself for when the things actually break.

We're keeping the unexpected expenses short on purpose because it could be a book unto itself. You can drive yourself crazy manufacturing worst-case scenarios about every situation in your life, but that's no way to live.

Tax Returns: A Buried Treasure of Information

Think about all the information on a tax return. There's a veritable trove of data that can point your family in the right direction if they need a clearer picture of your finances. Here's a list of vital details lurking on those drab government forms we're forced to file each year:

❑ Social Security number

❑ Income from jobs

❑ Investment income

❑ Business income

❑ Deductions and credits

❑ Financial accounts (or at least the ones that accrue interest)

- ❏ Property taxes
- ❏ Interest and dividends
- ❏ Prior tax payments
- ❏ Taxable alimony
- ❏ IRA/pension details
- ❏ Rental property income/expense; profit/loss statement
- ❏ Social Security benefits
- ❏ Miscellaneous income like gambling winnings, scholarships, and medical savings accounts

We're well aware that releasing one's tax returns has become quite the political hot potato, but you're not releasing yours to the *Washington Post*. You're making them easy to find for the more-than-capable executor who will need to unravel your estate one day.

If your taxes are prepared by a financial advisor or accountant, their info is front and center in your contacts (see page 52). If you do your own taxes using software or an online service like TurboTax, share the login information along with the rest of your accounts.

Regardless of how you get your taxes done, let someone know where you keep your past returns. If something happens to you, these are an ideal financial blueprint. If you're the type who doesn't bother filing taxes, you might want to start. Like, immediately.

Plan of Attack

MONEY YOU OWE

TIME: Four hours to identify and list all the bills, loans, debts, taxes, and other things that cost you money. We suggest doing a rough estimate on paper, then using a financial aggregation app (see page 24 if you aren't using one already) so nothing is left to chance.

COST: This depends on how much you want to rely on the following resources:

▶**App: The majority of the ones we recommend in the "Money You Have" section are free, but they might hit you up with suggested offers (which is how they make money). If you opt for a paid one, it should be less than $100 a year.**

▶**Software: If you have a program on your computer like Quicken, it's less than $50 a year.**

▶**Human: This depends on whether you choose a fee-based or commission-based advisor, which is also covered in the "Money You Have" section (see page 28). Again, ask them when you meet with them.**

Running a credit report can also uncover assets or debts you didn't know existed.

SO. MUCH. INSURANCE.

Insurance is all about getting back what you lost or providing for those who lose you. Until either of those things happen, it's generally considered an expense to cover much larger expenses.

Insurance You Likely Have

We'll keep these brief since they've probably been a part of your life for a long time.

Health: Rather than get into the weeds of health insurance and coverages, focus only on the aspects you need to keep your primary coverage organized. Who is the provider (is it public or private?), how is it paid (through work, government assistance, on your own?), what is the deductible (if you even know), and how do you log in to the portal (shared with the rest of your passwords, of course)?

After you take care of your main source of coverage, do you have any other plans such as dental, vision, or supplemental? Share the same info about those too.

Finally, if you take any medication, how does your prescription plan work? Is it bundled with your insurance or is it a different plan? Don't worry about the types of meds you're

taking, because we cover that later (see page 116).

Car/Vehicle: This is the one type of insurance that's required in almost every state, unless you don't own a car. Then keep walking/riding/subway-ing, buddy. For those of you who vroom around, what insurance provider do you use, how do you pay the premiums, and how do you file a claim if you get in an accident? Do you use one of the handy apps (passwords!) or do you have to make a call?

Additional auto coverage you may want to consider getting if you haven't already is called Uninsured Motorist Coverage, which pays out if you get hit by a driver who doesn't have insurance.

Home/Property/Renters: Use the same train of thought as you did for auto insurance. Whom do you use, how do you pay, is there a digital component (passwords!), how do you file a claim, and do you have any additional coverage like umbrella or liability (and other possibilities listed on page 110)?

Insurance You Might Need

Think of this next part as a soothing bedtime story in which your family gets a huge payday . . . if you die. Relaxing, right?

Life Insurance: Here's how Life Insurance works. You buy a policy and pay the monthly or annual fees (a.k.a. premiums) on time. If you die, the insurance company pays your family, or whomever you named as the beneficiaries, the amount of money specified in the policy. Like the lottery, there's a choice to receive the money all at once (lump sum) or in installments (annuity). Unlike the lottery, this is an investment that can actually pay off.

There are two main types of Life Insurance, called Term and Whole Life.

Term Insurance covers you for a set amount of time. If you have a twenty-year plan, keep up-to-date on payments, and cease to be living within those twenty years— YAHTZEE!—your beneficiaries get the money. The premium can vary dramatically, depending on age, health, and family history, but the standard cost for a $500,000 policy is around $50–$70 a month for twenty years. If you're still around after those twenty years, the plan expires, and you have to get a new policy if you still need it and can afford it (but on the bright side, you're still alive!).

Whole Life Insurance (also called Permanent or Universal Life Insurance) never expires. You either pay it all at once, which is expensive, or in installments over a set period of time (like twenty years), which is also expensive but it lasts forever. How expensive varies, since the polices are customized to the person being covered. However, industry averages suggest upward of ten times a Term Life Insurance policy. That means a $500,000 policy can start at $400 a month under the most optimal conditions. Unlike Term Life Insurance, you still have the option of accessing the money while you're alive, either by investing it in the stock market or taking some out as a cash loan.

Insurance You Should Consider

The following type of insurance might be a tough reality to face, but it can be a lifesaver when you need it most. However, if you wait too long to buy it, you will miss out on all the benefits.

Long-Term Care Insurance: Brace yourself for some harrowing statistics: According to the Administration for Community

Living, 69 percent of people turning sixty-five will need some type of long-term care services at some point in their lives. The average duration a person requires care is three years, which makes it an extremely expensive part of life.

This is why it's smart to look into Long-Term Care Insurance (LTC), which can help pay for the care and services you'll need if you suffer from disabling medical, physical, or cognitive conditions. It can cover many different forms of care, including in-home health care, nursing homes, adult day care, long-term care facilities, and Alzheimer's care facilities, among others.

DOES HEALTH INSURANCE COVER LONG-TERM CARE?

Although some health insurance policies may cover some of the costs of long-term care, most, including Medicare and Medicaid, will not pay for a full range of LTC services. A certain amount of "skilled nursing" (short-term care in a nursing home) is usually covered, but this doesn't include home care or assisted-living facilities. If you need long-term skilled nursing care, an LTC policy can get it for you.

THE COST OF LTC: Did we happen to mention it's pricey? We won't offer any hard numbers because it varies greatly, but a standard policy with better-than-average coverage can run you a few thousand a year. However, it's not as expensive as paying for the care required out of pocket, which can quickly deplete any savings. It's most affordable if purchased before age sixty, because the insured's age plays a role in determining the premium. In addition, a long-term care policy has no "surrender" value, which means if you never require long-term care, the money that you put into the policy is gone. But that's a good thing since you beat the odds!

ALTERNATIVES TO LTC INSURANCE: If there's no way to afford an LTC policy, and you don't want to deplete all your savings meant for your kids and other beneficiaries, you can set up an Irrevocable Trust (see page 89), put all your assets in it so they're no longer yours, and receive government coverage to get the care you need (mainly Medicaid). It might not be the white glove treatment you desire, but it'll be better than going broke and receiving the same medical benefits anyway.

Insurance You Should Know About

These types of policies are often situational and based specifically around your life. Owning tornado insurance if you live in the Great Plains makes sense, for example. Not so much if you live in Louisiana, where flood or hurricane insurance (or getting hit in the eye with beads during Mardi Gras) is much more relevant.

Let's lightning-round this. If you're not familiar with some of the insurance types listed below, you'll get a general understanding and perhaps want to look into them more. If you already have it, then you need to organize the details like all your other types of insurance.

Liability (or Umbrella): It provides protection from lawsuits often involving personal injury or property damage and can be bundled with other types of insurance like property, renters, or auto.

Critical Illness: This covers the costs that health insurance doesn't if you experience a heart attack, stroke, cancer diagnosis, or other often catastrophic medical emergency or diagnosis.

Identity Theft: This helps recoup costs associated with having your identity stolen.

Funeral: We go much deeper into this in Level 3 (see page 204), but as a sneak preview, this is when you make sure your family can pay for your send-off, and in some cases you even prepay to lock in the prices.

Catastrophe (Earthquake/Flood/ Hurricane/Terrorism): If you don't live in a high-risk area, you might be covered by Hazard Insurance (for example, you live in Florida and experience an earthquake). If you live in a high-risk area—say, San Francisco—and experience an earthquake there, this kind of insurance can come into play.

Longevity: Also known as a Longevity Annuity, this is like getting a regular paycheck when you turn eighty (or older), so you're guaranteed income for the rest of your life.

Kidnap and Ransom: This is for people who regularly work or go to school in high-risk areas where kidnapping is a possibility; insurers deploy specialists to get the insured back and pay for expenses. Unfortunately, the ransom must be paid by the person or company/institution who took out the policy.

Tuition Refund: If a student must drop out of school because of serious physical or psychological problems, this can help recoup tuition and other related expenses you might not be able to get back if you simply asked the school (which is worth a shot too).

Travel: Travel insurance is an extra you can tack on to a trip, so you can get reimbursed because of last-minute cancellations, delays, or lost bags.

Disability Insurance: Similar to long-term care, no one wants to think they could become disabled. According to a recent study, half of American adults don't have enough savings to cover three months of living expenses and wouldn't be able to immediately pay an unexpected $400 bill.

If you're interested in any of these policies, do some Google searches, read the fine print, and ask every possible question you can think of before making a purchase. You may think you're covered for something, but on page 342, subsection 95, Part B you find out you aren't. Then you'll get really upset, yell at a helpless customer service rep out of frustration, and feel bad for the rest of the day.

YET. MORE. INSURANCE.

It'd be easy to write "Everyone should have Life Insurance!" See, we just did. But for some it's not financially possible. Others may be denied because of age or health issues. For everyone else, first determine if you really need it, what "riders" are appropriate for you, and when it's time to meet with an agent.

Who Really Needs Life Insurance?

If you have kids or other dependents, or care for an adult with special needs, you need insurance to make sure they're taken care of in the event you cannot do it yourself. To put this in even simpler terms, if you're the main source of financial support for your household, you need insurance.

If you don't think you need insurance, consider this: You might be young, or think you have no use for a policy, but the older you get, the more expensive and unattainable Life Insurance becomes. You may not have a family or any dependents now, but you could one day. Even if there's no one in your life you want to give it to, and you have the means, you could name a charity or institution as a beneficiary and help others as a last gesture of kindness.

HOW TO KEEP YOUR POLICY ALIVE

It's vital to keep your Life Insurance policy in good standing. Don't ignore any invoices or notices you get in the mail or via email; set reminders on your calendar so you remember to pay the premiums on the agreed-upon payment schedule. There's a chance a policy could be voided because of nonpayment within a grace period or a violation of the conditions like filing a false claim. If your family thinks you have a valid policy and you let it lapse, either by accident or on purpose, it can be a huge problem if they ever need it. You should also review whom you've chosen as beneficiaries after major life events—births, deaths, marriage, divorce, and so on—in case you want to make changes.

How Much Insurance Do You Need?

If you don't know how much insurance is right for you, be realistic and ask yourself the following questions:

If your family had no money coming in, how long could they continue to live the way they're living now? If you have expenses that could outlive you, such as a mortgage or college tuition, how long could your family make those payments? You may have some coverage as a workplace benefit, but is it enough? It usually isn't, and if you change or lose your job, that coverage disappears.

Take a moment to think about everything we've mentioned in this book so far to get a general idea of how much you spend. The money you have, your debt situation, house payments, car payments, utilities and bills, and other expenses all factor into the larger equation. By considering how much money your family will need to live, you can begin to determine how much insurance you should buy.

Who Benefits from Your Insurance?

To understand who will reap the rewards of your insurance, here are a few examples of the types of beneficiaries you can name in a policy:

- ❏ A person or a group of people (family members and loved ones)
- ❏ A Trust you've established
- ❏ A charity or nonprofit organization
- ❏ Creditors
- ❏ A company you own
- ❏ A funeral home
- ❏ Your estate

Some states and policies may have beneficiary restrictions, which is why you need to go through a licensed agent. You also need to name contingent beneficiaries in case something happens to your primary ones.

Insurance Riders: Like Side Orders

Insurance policies are a bit like the base model of a car—they offer a set level of coverage with conditions, restrictions, and requirements. To make changes to that basic coverage, you can add riders, which are additional provisions that customize a standard policy—like adding power windows, a bigger engine, and heated seats. They're not necessary, but they make things a lot comfier. Here are four common types of riders:

Accelerated Death Benefit: Also known as Terminal Illness Insurance, this provides financial assistance if you've received a terminal diagnosis and usually have less than a year to live.

Accidental Death & Dismemberment (Double Indemnity): This provides your beneficiaries with an additional payout, often double the amount they'd normally receive, if your death occurs as a result of an accident. (It's also the name of a classic movie from 1944 you should totally watch.) The dismemberment part is just as it sounds: payment if you lose a body part or a bodily function (mobility, sight, hearing, and so on).

Family Income Benefit Rider: This is if you'd like the benefits to be paid out in installments over time, often equal to the policy holder's monthly income, rather than all at once. This helps guard against spendthrifts who could burn through the whole benefit in the time it takes you to watch the movie *Double Indemnity*.

Long-Term Care Rider: This is for people who want long-term care coverage but don't have the means to buy a separate Long-Term Care Insurance policy, which we explained a few pages ago.

You Need an Agent!

The concept of Life Insurance isn't necessarily complex, but the reality of getting a policy can be complicated and time consuming. Enter the licensed agent. Their job is to help you understand how much insurance you need in terms you can easily understand.

When you meet with an agent, he or she should present you with options that meet your criteria. The agent should then clearly explain the details, advantages, and drawbacks of each option. They should provide understandable answers to all your questions, and you should never feel pressured into making a purchase. Here's how to judge your potential agent in three steps:

1 **Is the agent properly licensed?**
They must have a current up-to-
date license issued by the state
in which they sell insurance. Just
ask them. If you're still unsure,
which is a red flag in itself, check
with your state's insurance
department.

2 **Are they experienced?** Not in
worldly affairs, but in working
with people in your situation.
In some cases, the agent may be
able to provide you with client
references.

3 **Does the agent have lots of initials
after their name?** Many insurance
agents complete additional
training and courses to obtain
advance credentials. Some popular
credentials include Chartered Life
Underwriter (CLU), Chartered
Financial Consultant (ChFC),
Certified Financial Planner (CFP),
and Financial Services Specialist
(FSS). These credentials often
signify a commitment to the
profession and ethical business
practices.

Once you've decided on an agent
and purchased a policy, which can
take between one and three months
(depending on medical exams and
level of coverage), they should be

available to review the details of the
policy every few years.

What to Share About Your Policies

Insurance can be one of the trickiest
and most complex (but necessary)
parts of planning. For all the policies
you have, and those you may buy,
be sure to include all the pertinent
information for each policy in the
appropriate place:

❏ The name of the insurance
provider (this goes in contacts)

❏ Where you keep the policy,
which includes online portals
(passwords!)

❏ Account/policy number

❏ Name of primary and contingent
beneficiaries or dependents
(if applicable)

❏ Type of policy, such as Term
or Whole Life

❏ Start and end date (if it's Term)

❏ Tips on filing a claim
(example: "Use their app—
it's a snap" or "Take a photo
of the invoice and email it to
their claims department")

It's easy to neglect these details,
but when you have an accident, need
to file a claim, or have to dispute an
exorbitant charge that almost triggers
a panic attack, easy access becomes the
most important thing in your world.

■ ■ ■

Plan of Attack

INSURANCE

STANDARD OR REQUIRED INSURANCE: Your health, auto, and property insurance details should be included among your bills (since they're an ongoing expense), and each should take no longer than ten to fifteen minutes to organize.

TIME IT TAKES TO GET LIFE INSURANCE: One to three months. We wish we could say this is as easy as getting car or property insurance, but it's not. You can take assessments online, but once it gets serious, you have to commit to the process. This includes deciding what type of insurance would best benefit your family (Term or Whole Life), how much you need, what provider is most appealing to you, and how much you can afford. Next steps are speaking with an agent, getting medical tests to determine the death benefit, doing the paperwork, and paying the premiums.

COST: This varies based on age, health, and amount of coverage. If you're under 40 and in good health, a Term policy could be around $30 a month for $250,000. If you're 40-60, it could be double that for the same coverage; if you're over 65 and in poor health, it's probably not an option—you might be interested in Final Expense Insurance (see page 206).

TIME IT TAKES TO GET LONG-TERM CARE INSURANCE: Two to four hours to research LTC Insurance companies, fill out an assessment, and speak with an agent. If you move forward with the process, it could take a few months to finalize.

COST: Like Life Insurance, there are many factors at play, but it could range from $1,000 a year on the low end to more than $3,000, and the rates can change throughout the duration of your policy.

LTC NOTE: If you think you'll be able to qualify for Medicaid because of your financial situation, then you might not need LTC, since the government will be picking up the tab. This is also why you might want to look into creating an Irrevocable Trust to keep your assets safe for your heirs.

OTHER INSURANCE TO RESEARCH: Go through the list on page 110 and ask yourself whether any of the insurance types listed apply to your life. If they don't, move on. If any do, spend fifteen minutes doing a quick search to see if it makes financial sense. Perhaps you'll find it might be offered by a company already insuring your car or property. Or maybe the cost will be too high compared with the benefits. Either way, now you're aware of it for the future.

YOUR MEDICAL CHECKUP

■ ■ ■

We'll do our best to keep this medical section as quick and painless as, well, *not* going to the doctor. You already did most of your medical heavy lifting in Level 1 when you learned about organizing your doctor and specialists (see page 51). Now it's time to focus on your actual health in a way that's helpful and not too overwhelming for your family to understand.

YOUR PERSONAL MEDICAL JOURNAL

Talking about medical problems is rarely fun. People tend to downplay the bad stuff because they don't want anyone to worry. How many times have you heard a variation of the phrases "I'll get to the doctor when I have time" or "I'm doing everything they're telling me to do" only to find out later neither is true? Medical problems combine many of our biggest fears: the possibility of a dire diagnosis, having to make extreme lifestyle changes to get our health back on track, and facing our own mortality.

Ideally, a person dealing with all these traumatic issues at once would be open and honest with the people they love. In reality, they often keep their health conditions a secret until it's too late. On three different occasions, one of our coworkers found out about surgeries his parents had after the fact. (They said they didn't want to worry him or his siblings, but it had the opposite effect.) If you're facing an illness, it's important to ask for help, no matter how hard that is. If you're tasked with helping someone else face an uphill battle, try your best to be as supportive and delicate as possible. These might be the last few years, months, or days you have with someone you love.

But since we're here to help you get *your* life organized, forget about everyone else for a moment. The best way to keep track of your own pressing or personal medical issues—and provide a definitive record for those who might need it—is with a Personal Medical Journal.

Unlike medical records, which are cold, clinical, and filled with lots of jargon, this is a more casual and realistic way to keep others in your life apprised of your health. Like the way we helped you understand how to create a Home Operating System (see page 45), it's quite simple. But instead of walking around the rooms of your home and making notes, you'll be taking a tour of your body.

Start by listing existing or current conditions. Anything that you manage on a regular basis, or that involves treatments, should rise to the top. Any low-maintenance chronic condition that simply flares up from time to time sinks to the bottom. Think of each issue as an item you're writing on an index card and then pinning to a 3D rendering of your body. An example of the template can be found on the next page.

Even if you don't adhere to our exact format, try to include as much detail as possible and don't forget about any related medical documents or records (if they can be accessed via an online portal, include the login info with your passwords) and equipment that would need to be returned to avoid a huge bill from the insurance company (including the type of device, make/model, and equipment provider).

Voilà! You just helped someone easily understand one of your important health conditions. You can do this for everything like kidney problems (dialysis), high cholesterol (medication/diet), heart conditions (pacemaker and stents), autoimmune diseases (arthritis, multiple sclerosis, lupus), hearing loss (hearing aids), or anything else that ails you.

Start from your head and work your way to your toes and categorize the conditions based on level of urgency. If you think they're all of equal importance, do it alphabetically. Your journal can be a digital document or handwritten, though we suggest digital so it's easier to update and share. The method doesn't matter.

PERSONAL MEDICAL JOURNAL

SAMPLE

CONDITION

Type I Diabetes

APPOINTMENTS & TREATMENT

I have an insulin pump that automatically administers the correct dosage and needs to be refilled every three days; I have a standing appointment with my endocrinologist every four months (Dr. Rooney); I monitor my blood twice a day using my glucose meters (I keep one in the kitchen and one in the car).

MEDICATION

My insulin is auto-delivered twice a month through Capsule (I keep the login information with my passwords); I also have a recurring alert on my phone, so I don't run out.

HOW I MANAGE IT

As much as I don't enjoy it, it's been a part of my routine for so long that I've learned to cope. I pack snacks so I'm not tempted to stray from my diet (you know how much I love double chocolate cookies . . .), I keep lotion on me at all times for when my skin gets irritated, and if I'm experiencing any symptoms like extreme fatigue, blurred vision, or peeing much more than normal, I check my levels and might even email my doctor to be safe.

Next up are chronic problems that aren't life threatening but still something you have to manage. This might include allergies (unless they're life threatening, in which case they should go with the preceding important conditions), migraines, irritable bowel syndrome, past injuries that affect your walking or range of motion, eyesight issues (glasses prescription, cataracts), and anything else that would be helpful for your family or doctors to know. Use the same template and go from head to toes again (or toes to head if you want to mix it up).

Finally, it's time to organize something that can be an actual lifesaver for those you love: your family medical history.

Do women in your family have a history of breast cancer? Do the men have a history of prostate cancer? Do you know of any heart or respiratory problems, blood disorders, muscle or spine conditions that may be hereditary? It's common for parents to tell their kids about these problems, but they can easily be misunderstood or forgotten. Perhaps something that affected your grandparents and skipped a generation could be completely preventable and treatable if you catch it early.

We glossed over your official medical records, but you should share those as well by filling out a HIPAA authorization form—ask your doctor for one or just Google it and download—which allows someone you trust to view them. The Health Insurance Portability and Accountability Act of 1996 was created to make your medical records easier to access while also protecting your privacy. Like everything involving health care, it's mind-numbingly complicated, but it's helpful for adult children caring for their parents and parents whose kids are going to college.

Plan of Attack

CONSTRUCT YOUR PERSONAL MEDICAL JOURNAL

GATHERING RECORDS

TIME: Two to three hours if you use the method and template we've provided (see the facing page) to document all of your current ailments and general medical history. Add an extra two hours to complete a family history, since you may have to research this information. We suggest using a digital document to keep track of everything, but a handwritten journal works too (just keep it up to date, please).

ADVANCE HEALTH CARE DIRECTIVES

When you can't make health decisions for yourself, this is the North Star that guides your loved ones and doctors in the right direction. It might sound like an 1980s action movie—*Advance Directive*, starring Sylvester Stallone and Bruce Willis!—but it's really the universal term for how you'd like to be treated in the event of a medical emergency or at the end of your life. It's made up of two parts:

Naming a Health Care Proxy: This person advocates for your care when you can't. We call it a Proxy, but it can go by different names such as Health Care Power of Attorney or Medical Power of Attorney (not to be confused with the financial/legal Power of Attorney), Health Care Agent, Representative, or Surrogate.

Filling Out a Living Will: This spells out the types of medical treatments you *do* or do *not* want during a major medical emergency or toward the end of your life.

The bulk of the effort you'll spend when filling out these documents will be devoted to decision making. These decisions are not really all that pleasant to think about, but they're much easier to make now than when you're in a hospital connected to tubes.

Why You Need an Advance Directive

In the event of a medical emergency, things move really fast, and regrettable decisions can be made. An Advance Directive helps eliminate some of those regrets before they happen. Emotions always run high during stressful situations, but if you prepared this document outlining your wishes during a more peaceful time, it can cut through the emotional haze and provide a clear direction. Finally, if you don't make these decisions, you're forcing someone else to bear the burden and live with it for the rest of their life.

How to Choose a Health Care Proxy

If you become incapacitated and can't speak for yourself, you'll want someone you trust to speak on your behalf. This person needs to know what types of treatments you want, will stand tall in the face of adversity (namely, pushy doctors and pesky family members), and will make sure you get the care you want. Enter your Health Care Proxy. But before you settle on someone, it's important to understand what they'll be able to do.

For starters, they can make choices about your medical care and pain management. This includes the ability to request or decline life support treatments, medication, or surgical procedures. Your Health Care Proxy can also decide *where* you can seek medical treatment, including moving you to different facilities. They can view and approve the release of your medical records and apply for benefits on your behalf, including Medicare or Medicaid. Finally, they can take legal action on your behalf to ensure that your medical decisions are honored.

Now that you understand the power of a Proxy, here are the characteristics you'll likely want in whomever you choose. They should be a person you trust implicitly and one who understands your values. They should be someone who has a clear understanding of how you want to be treated in a medical emergency. And your Proxy should be willing to follow your decisions, even if they don't agree with them or are put under pressure from family or medical professionals.

Finally, your Proxy needs to have endurance. Their responsibilities could drag on for weeks, months, or even years. Your choice might be a member of the family, a lifelong friend, or an associate you feel will put emotion aside and stick to what you want. You want someone who will remember that these are *your* decisions, not *theirs*, and will always act accordingly, even if things get tough.

TIP: You should also choose an alternate or secondary Proxy in case your first choice is unavailable during an emergency.

Tell the Proxy They're the Proxy!

When you choose someone, it shouldn't come as a surprise to them.

There was an episode of *Grey's Anatomy* where one of the doctors was clinging to life after being electrocuted, leaving the rest of the staff with two options: let him die or do a risky procedure that might kill him. When the nonelectrocuted doctors consulted the electrocuted doctor's Health Care Directive, they learned, to their shock(!), that he had named Meredith Grey as his Proxy. (For those who don't watch, she's the star . . . hence her last name being the clever play on words in the show's title.) When Dr. Grey found out, she was stunned.

"But he can't make me next of kin without talking to me first," Grey says.

Oh, but he *can*, Dr. Grey. And he *did*. We forget how the episode ended. Maybe he lived, maybe he did not. Maybe two attractive doctors started making out and the credits rolled. The point is, it's possible for you to be a person's Proxy and not know about it until you're the final word on whether they live or die. This is fine for a prime-time drama, but a terrible thing in real life.

The first rule of naming a Proxy is that you need to tell them well in advance that they are your Proxy. The second rule is that you should have an open and honest conversation with them so they know how you'd like to be treated and the types of care you'd like to receive. It could be that this person isn't the right fit. What if they're unwilling to pull the plug even though that's what you want? What if they're all too willing to pull the plug when you want to be kept alive no matter what? Better to get this all sorted out well ahead of time.

Although it might be difficult to share these decisions with your family, it's important to do so to avoid confusion. It's possible that some family members won't understand the choices you've made and may even try to talk you out of them. Stand your ground and let them know this is about the medical care *you* desire. Tell them these aren't easy decisions to make, you want their love and support, and you will offer them the same consideration for whatever they choose for themselves.

LIVING WILLS

Think of a Living Will as an emergency medical treatment checklist for the important players in your life. Your doctors will use it as a guide to manage your care, and your Health Care Proxy will use it to make sure what you want is getting done.

What a Living Will Is (and Is Not)

If you're worried that a Living Will gives medical professionals permission to kill you, you're being way too dramatic. (Perhaps you should try out for a part on *Grey's Anatomy*?) Living Wills are primarily about life-support treatments, specifically if you're suffering from a terminal or progressive illness or a major accident where you're unlikely to recover. A Living Will is used only if you are deemed incapacitated and mentally incompetent by at least one doctor. Even then, it can be overruled if it jeopardizes your care.

Evaluating Life-Support Treatments

All life-support treatments have pros and cons—something we may have learned when COVID-19 made ventilators front-page news. For each treatment, consider the following questions, which you should go over with your doctor if you have concerns.

(continued on page 126)

WHAT HAPPENS IF . . . YOU DON'T HAVE A LIVING WILL

Those of a certain age in the 1990s and early 2000s probably recall the name Terri Schiavo. When Schiavo was twenty-six, she had a full cardiac arrest. After she spent eight years on life support, doctors determined she was in a persistent vegetative state, and her husband got a court order to remove her feeding tube.

Her birth family believed she was still conscious and fought to have the feeding tube reinserted. For the next seven years Schiavo's husband and family fought in court. The battle even reached the highest level of government when President George W. Bush signed legislation to keep Schiavo alive. Eventually, the original decision to remove the feeding tube was upheld, and Schiavo died in 2005.

Regardless of which side you believe was right, if Schiavo had created a Living Will, it could have eliminated a lot of heartbreak for all involved. It would have prevented her husband from getting pitted against her family, and the final decision would've been hers alone.

The only upside to this highly upsetting and divisive moment in history was how it made Advance Directives front-page news, waking millions to the importance of creating one, regardless of age. If you don't have a Living Will, the default course of medical treatment is almost always to do everything possible to keep you alive at all costs. Or to force your family into making the call to suspend treatment and live with that decision for the rest of their lives.

To save the people you love this agony, all you have to do is make your choice clear in a Living Will. The only bad decision in this case is none at all.

LIFE SUPPORT

The following are the most common types of life-support treatments, how they work, and their possible side effects. Please bear with us. We're fully aware that this part isn't much fun.

	VENTILATORS	FEEDING TUBES	CARDIOPULMONARY RESUSCITATION (CPR)
How They Work	A ventilator (a.k.a. respirator or breathing machine) provides air to your lungs through a tube if you're unable to breathe on your own. This tube can be inserted through the mouth, the nose, or an opening made in the throat.	Also known as tube feeding, this provides nutrition and fluids through a tube inserted into the nose, stomach, or intestines.	If your heartbeat or breathing has stopped, CPR can restart both. Techniques range from blowing air into the mouth (mouth-to-mouth resuscitation) and pushing on the chest (chest compressions) to electric shocks delivered to the heart (defibrillation) to breathing tubes inserted into the windpipe (intubation).
Side Effects	Apart from being uncomfortable and impairing your ability to speak, a ventilator, according to the National Heart, Lung and Blood Institute, may lead to infections (the most common being pneumonia), lung damage, and damaged vocal cords.	The possible negative side effects include aspiration (inhaling the liquid food into the lungs), organ puncture, and infection, according to the National Center for Biotechnology Information (NCBI).	The American Heart Association reports that conventional CPR can cause fracturing of the ribs and/or the breastbone (sternum) in at least one-third of cases. However, they also report that "the chance of surviving an out-of-hospital cardiac arrest is near zero for a victim who does not immediately receive high-quality chest compressions . . . followed by additional therapy within minutes."

What It Does to (and for) You

BLOOD TRANSFUSIONS	DIALYSIS	ANTIBIOTICS
If you have lost a significant amount of blood, it may be replenished with an intravenous supply from a donor.	If you have experienced kidney failure, measures may be taken to mechanically filter your blood as the kidneys would. Dialysis usually entails removing blood from the body, filtering the blood, and returning it.	If you've developed a bacterial infection, antibiotics may be used to kill it.
According to the Centers for Disease Control and Prevention (CDC), "Negative side effects of blood transfusion therapy are uncommon but can include blood transfusion reactions, infections, the development of red blood cell antibodies, and iron overload in different organs of the body."	Depending on the type of dialysis you receive, possible side effects include infection, muscle cramps, itching, and low blood pressure, according to the Mayo Clinic. Sessions can be up to three times a week (or more), and take up to four hours or longer per session.	The most widely reported side effect is antibiotic resistance. According to the CDC, although the benefit of antibiotics has been enormous, "these drugs have been used so widely and for so long that the infectious organisms the antibiotics are designed to kill have adapted to them, making the drugs less effective. People infected with antimicrobial-resistant organisms are more likely to have longer, more expensive hospital stays, and may be more likely to die as a result of the infection."

(continued from page 123)

- ❑ What purpose does the treatment serve?
- ❑ What are the side effects?
- ❑ What type of medical equipment will be used, and how will it affect my body?
- ❑ Does this treatment usually improve my overall health, or does it simply extend my life?

Additional medical forms that aid people closer to the end, specifically a DNR and POLST, are covered later (see page 192).

Where to Store Your Advance Directive

An Advance Directive isn't one of those documents that requires privacy or discretion. You shouldn't keep it locked in a safe or hidden away in your secret fortress of solitude. For it to be of any use, it has to be available when it's needed. And you never know when it'll be needed, so here are some suggestions:

> **TIP:** Play it extra safe and also store a digital copy in a shared folder or an online platform, be it a health care portal or a site like Everplans. Although it's always preferable to have the physical copy, this digital version can still be handy in a pinch.

1. Keep it with other important household documents (emergency contact list, Wi-Fi password, Home Operating System, Personal Medical Journal).

2. If you've been experiencing health problems, keep it on your fridge or someplace in plain sight; you should also keep a copy in your car, since many unexpected medical emergencies are the result of an accident.

3. Give a copy to your Health Care Proxy.

4. Give a copy to your doctor.

Visit Your Advance Directive Every So Often

Once you have an Advance Directive, review it periodically to think about whom you named as your Proxy and to verify you're still on board with all the decisions you previously made in your Living Will. Things change over the course of your life—people move (and pass) away, and you may have a change of heart about certain medical treatments—so always keep everything as current as possible.

SECOND LIFE: Donating Your Organs

You don't need to wear spandex, see through walls, or have a billion-dollar suit of armor to be a superhero. All you need to do is become an organ donor.

Many people view organ donation as a final altruistic gesture to help others, and almost all religions support it. Every state has its own donor registry; if you've registered through your local Department of Motor Vehicles, you may get a sticker or some other sign on your driver's license identifying you as a donor. As long as you do it in some form, you'll be in your state's donor registry.

It also appears as an option on most Advance Directive forms, offering another shot if you never did it through the DMV or a state registry. You may want to tell your family, your Health Care Proxy, and your doctor you're a registered organ donor so they can support your decision to donate.

How the Donation Process Works

Here's some background so you can sound well versed on the topic if it comes up at a cocktail party. And what cocktail party is complete without a discussion about giving away your organs?

Organ donation in the United States is regulated by the nonprofit Organ Procurement and Transplantation Network, which is administered by the United Network for Organ Sharing under contract to the US Department of Health and Human Services.

If you have a fatal accident or illness and are admitted to the hospital, your family or your Proxy will tell the hospital team treating you that you're a registered organ donor, which can help them prepare.

(continued on page 130)

WHAT CAN BE DONATED?

Think of this as a menu of lifesaving (or life-improving) goodness.

ORGANS: Kidneys, heart, lungs, liver, pancreas, intestines

TISSUE & OTHER VITAL BITS: Corneas, skin, heart valves, bone and cartilage, veins, tendons and ligaments

SIDE MISSION:
WHEN LIFE GETS GOLDEN

How far in advance do you plan vacations? A few months, usually, right? You book the flights and hotels, arrange for time off from work, get the kids out of school, and start looking forward to it from the moment you make the final arrangements. We view eldercare in this same anticipatory light because it's never too early to think about how and where you want to live when you're older.

Granted, the circumstances may not be very vacation-like. You could be having trouble getting around and taking care of regular daily activities (like cooking, cleaning, and driving) or become ill. But you don't have to wait for something to happen to start getting a handle on your options.

THINGS TO CONSIDER RIGHT NOW

Take the following things into account when preparing yourself mentally for decisions you, or your family, will need to make:

HEALTH: Will you need doctors and nurses on staff to help with any medical problems? Even if you're not ill, perhaps you want easy access to medical professionals, just in case.

FINANCES: Do you have the means to live where you want, for as long as you want? Did you even read what we wrote about how expensive Long-Term Care Insurance can be on page 108? (It's OK if you didn't. You can always go back. It's not going anywhere.)

LOCATION OF FAMILY MEMBERS: Do you want to be near family and friends, or will they travel to you?

DEGREE OF INDEPENDENCE: Do you like doing things on your own, or are you OK with someone else pitching in and helping out with your daily routine?

It's hard to predict all of these things in advance. No one likes to picture themselves as anything other than able-bodied and healthy. But knowing what to expect and preparing yourself and your loved ones for different possibilities is an achievement in itself.

THREE TYPES OF ELDERCARE HOUSING

IN-HOME CARE: This option is for those who want to continue living at home (and who doesn't?) but may need some help with daily activities like cooking, cleaning, and hygiene.

This level of care may require some modifications to your home to reduce the chance of accidents and make caregiving easier—like installing ramps for a wheelchair, widening doorways, installing a stair lift, and adding railings in the bathrooms and shower.

Cost: This can vary greatly, depending on your current living situation and the level of modifications needed for your home. Although this is probably the preferred option for many, it also has the most variables, especially as your health declines.

ASSISTED LIVING: This option is best if you can manage your own care but need occasional help with daily activities, such as cooking, cleaning, and other routines that might become difficult to do on your own.

Although this type of care moves you out of your home, you can still have a healthy degree of independence—like living in a small apartment—with the added benefit of having doctors and nurses on staff at all times.

Cost: Assisted-living facilities generally require a down payment and monthly fees that range from $1,000 to $5,000. The costs vary based on location, size and style of the room, and services and amenities offered. Medicare won't cover the cost, though some facilities accept Medicaid, as well as Long-Term Care Insurance (again, see page 108) and

HMO/managed care plans, but you'll have to pay the bulk of the cost out of pocket.

NURSING HOME: This is for those who need a high level of medical care—there are doctors or nurses on the premises at all times—in addition to help with daily activities.

Cost: Since nursing homes provide the highest level of care, they're also the most expensive, averaging around $6,000 per month. To lessen the financial burden, Medicare covers short-term stays (usually about 100 days) and Medicaid might cover the costs (you have to qualify, and not all homes accept it). If you don't have the financial means, you'll need a large savings account or generous family member willing to foot the bill.

IN THE AUTUMN OF YOUR LIFE: It's understandable to want to ignore the fact that all humans eventually need some type of care. It's also not an easy conversation to have with your family, especially if every time you try it ends with a vague "We'll figure it out when the time comes." You may think one of your kids will take you in and set up a cozy room, but what if they can't?

The key is to face this head-on, know your options, and work toward getting a financial plan in place. Preparing today can help you stop worrying about tomorrow.

(continued from page 127)

No, You Won't Be Killed for Your Organs

If you're worried that doctors will let you die so they can put your parts into another human, that won't happen.

The hospital needs absolute confirmation that you're brain dead before moving ahead with the donation process. To determine brain death, a neurologist will perform a series of tests (often more than once) to see if there's any brain activity. Brain death is not a coma. It is, in fact, death. If there's no brain activity, the death will be confirmed by a neurologist and the body will be kept on life support to maintain the organs until they are removed.

At no point will your care be compromised. This isn't a Lifetime movie where a doctor wants to harvest your kidneys to save his dying son. This is real life where medical professionals keep you alive at all costs. Once that's no longer an option, donation becomes a chance to save others.

There's Never Enough to Go Around

We've come across countless donation stories where a family turned the worst day of their lives into a positive force in the world. Whether it was the eleven-year-old boy in China who succumbed to brain cancer and donated his kidneys and liver or the sixteen-year-old football player whose sudden death ended up saving his own grandfather with his kidney, these stories of tragedy have become symbols of love and hope.

According to OrganDonor.gov, there were more than 113,000 men, women, and children on the national transplant waiting list in 2019, and twenty people die each day waiting for a transplant. If you still have reservations, please reconsider because it's the best gift you can give.

Plan of Attack

CREATE YOUR ADVANCE DIRECTIVE

MAKING BIG DECISIONS

TIME: Around a minute to download your state's form (incasethebook.com/advance -directive-forms); an hour to understand the decisions you need to make if you're already sure of what you want. And if you're unsure and want to speak with a doctor, bring the form along to your next appointment.

COST: Free if you do it yourself; a fee if you do it with an attorney as part of an estate planning bundle.

LET'S GET DIGITAL

∎ ∎ ∎

What happens to all your digital accounts, services, and property after you die? Way back at the beginning of Level 1, we stressed the importance of sharing passwords and codes (see page 2). We've even peppered many of the sections with *(passwords!)* to emphasize how prevalent they've become in our lives. Now we're ready to cover the accounts and services those passwords unlock, and what you want done with them today or after you're gone. The official name for this is a Digital Estate Plan. (Note how the words *estate plan* can be off-putting but become infinitely cooler once you put the word *digital* in front of them.)

WHY YOU NEED A DIGITAL ESTATE PLAN

With the lines increasingly blurred between our on- and off-line lives, it's more important than ever to have a plan for your digital holdings. With one in place, all your digital accounts and services can be deleted, managed, or transferred to someone else after you're gone. You can also ensure that all paid or recurring services are closed and not draining money from your bank account or racking up credit card debt. Finally, a plan will provide guidance and direction about what you want done with

your digital assets and overall online presence.

In the same way that you need to organize your physical possessions, if you don't get a handle on your digital life, you're leaving a huge mess for your family when you sign off from this world.

How to Classify Digital Assets and Accounts

Although there are likely many different components to your digital world, we've narrowed it down to two overarching types.

Hardware: Computers, smartphones, external hard drives, tablets, digital music players, e-readers, digital cameras, wearables, and other digital devices

Online accounts & services: Email and communications, social media, shopping, entertainment, online storage, and accounts associated with your day-to-day life

Yes, we managed to squeeze all this stuff into two neat, compact points. But we're fully aware that, in practice, it's a large, virtually invisible universe to process. For this section, we're drilling down on digital accounts that often play by their own set of rules, which is why you might want to keep this next part a secret.

Digital Estate Laws & How to Bend Them

Things are about to get a little legislative, so hang tough, because it's worth it. Almost all fifty states have passed laws that give a person's family (or executor) the right to access and manage *some* of their digital assets after they die. Much of this is to the credit of a nonprofit called the Uniform Law Commission. They created the Revised Uniform Fiduciary Access to Digital Assets Act (2015), which is aimed at allowing executors, trustees, or the person appointed by the court (*conservator* or *fiduciary*) access to a deceased person's digital assets. Although it's not yet the law of the land, and there are still stipulations and complexities involved, it shows there's been forward momentum and progress regarding the issue.

To give you some perspective: When we first started Everplans in 2012, fewer than a dozen states had these laws. Now, almost all of them do.

Even with these laws in place, many of the accounts we use on a daily basis are governed by the "terms of service" or "privacy policy" of that particular service (such as Gmail, Facebook, or Amazon), which still want to determine what should be done with an account

HOW THIS HELPS AFTER YOU'RE GONE
(Mapping your digital existence)

■ The maze that is your digital life, which also includes physical backups, can be navigated by someone other than yourself.

■ Your family will know what to keep, transfer, cancel, memorialize, and delete.

■ They can avoid some of the frustrating steps these services have in place when all you want done is to have an account shut down.

■ The person you name as Digital Executor can use this information to help settle your estate.

after a subscriber's death. Although massive services like Facebook offer something called a Legacy Contact, and Google has an Inactive Account Manager, this supposes that you take the time to get your digital affairs in order ahead of time. Since people don't often do this, and legislation may not fully (or quickly) solve the problem, you might need to take things into your own crafty hands. This means sharing passwords and instructions with someone else. Digital services don't like it when people do this, but there are things they do that we don't like either.

To be fair, many companies have these rules in place to provide security or privacy. If multiple people can access the same account, it's more likely to be compromised. That's all well and good, but giving up this much control over your information can be hard for many to

accept, which is why you may have to paint outside the lines on occasion to get what you want. For example, think about all the digital purchases you've made up until this point of your life—books, music, games, movies, and TV shows—that simply evaporate once you're gone.

Before the digital age, entertainment was physical. You bought albums, books, DVDs, or any other type of media, and those things were yours. You could keep them forever, give them to a friend, donate them, or burn them. If they got ruined or destroyed—like a tape you played so much it broke—you had to buy a new one, which was also yours to do with as you pleased.

It doesn't work that way anymore. If you've ever made a digital purchase, you're basically renting that thing for the duration of your life. When you die, you can't pass it down the same way you would an actual book or album. It's more convenient to be able to carry a library's worth of books on your tablet, but the sense of ownership has become muddled.

Sharing (Passwords) Is Caring

So, what can you do if you're worried about losing your digital assets one day? Many people share the details of the accounts that contain purchased media with an heir who can take ownership of that account. All they have to do is log in and change the email address, and it's theirs. It might get a little messy having more than one account, but it's better than letting media worth hundreds or thousands of dollars disappear or need to be repurchased.

Some of our most cherished possessions are books handed down from our grandparents and parents. If every cookbook of the future is digital, and the companies that provide those books get them back when you die, how is that fair to your kids?

Perhaps this won't matter as much to future generations as it does to us, since the delivery of media has changed drastically over the years. Or maybe it's up to us to keep the concept of permanent media alive.

Take Netflix, for example. You pay around $10–$15 a month to access thousands of movies and

TV shows and have no expectation of ownership. Each month new programming is added, and movies and shows are deleted because Netflix no longer has the rights to them. Most of the time you never even notice when something's removed—unless it's a movie you always like to watch when you're sad, or the one show that got your kids to settle down for an hour or two. You might feel disappointed for a moment, but then you find something else to watch (because there's *always* something else to watch!).

It's hard to tell at this point if companies like Amazon and Apple will pivot toward tighter or looser control over media ownership. At least for now, the only surefire way to acquire books, movies, and music that you can share and bequeath is to buy the real deal or create a Digital Estate Plan that accounts for all these things.

In some instances, the device itself can be preserved and frozen in time. For example, some people might turn off the Wi-Fi for Grandma's Kindle so it never accidentally syncs to the Amazon servers, ensuring that you don't lose the dozens of books she downloaded (and put a sticker on the device "Grandma's Library—Never Sync!"). It seems low-tech, but so is printing

GET A PASSWORD MANAGER, THE REMIX

Far be it from us to tell you what to do, or to repeat what we already stressed in Level 1 (see page 2), but in this instance we're willing to go all in on password managers. Currently, everything digital requires some sort of password or code. Although the world is starting to transition toward fingerprint ID and facial recognition, the backup entry is always a password or code. To remind you, once again, why it's important:

- You need to remember only one password.

- You can easily share some or all of your passwords with someone you trust.

- You can auto-generate strong passwords for greater security.

If you're *still* unwilling to hop aboard the password manager express, you'll need to provide instructions alongside each of your accounts in whatever password storage method you choose. It's easy to include in a digital document or note-taking app, but if it's a handwritten list, you'll need to find space on the page for it. If you don't keep track of your passwords anywhere, then we're calling your family right now and staging an intervention.

DON'T FORGET YOUR GADGETS: Include access codes to all your devices (computers, smartphones, tablets), since your family may need to use them to access your accounts or services, especially if they exist only as a mobile app.

words on sheets made from dead trees and gluing them together. Whatever you choose to do, just have something in place, unless digital purchases don't matter to you as much as they do to many collectors.

Classifying Each Account

Not all digital accounts and services are created equal. You should be able to classify each of your accounts as you start to peel away each layer:

1 **Personal:** Emails, texts, photos, document storage

2 **Value (with a credit card attached):** iTunes, Amazon, eBay, domain names

3 **Social:** Facebook, Twitter, Instagram, LinkedIn

4 **Transferable:** Streaming services, food delivery, travel

As a reminder, we're not including off-line services that might be in your name and benefit others in your household, such as utilities, banking, house and car payments, and health insurance.

These, as we already mentioned, need to be associated with the service they provide, since the process to transfer or close them is more nuanced. (And by *nuanced* we mean "pain in the butt," which is covered in the "Money You Owe" section.)

How each of these are managed will vary, depending on the nature of the account or service. You may want some assets to be archived and saved, others to be deleted, erased, or ignored, and others transferred to family members, friends, or colleagues. Ideally, you should specify what needs to be done for each digital account or asset. If that's too much to ask, you should focus only on the ones that matter and let the rest disappear, never to be logged in to again. But first, you need to get a full picture of what you have.

YOUR DIGITAL ACCOUNT MATRIX

It's backbreaking work to clean out another person's packed house. It's mind-breaking work for your family to manage your digital estate if they don't know what you have and what you want done with it all.

The most efficient way to begin organizing your digital accounts and services is to focus on the ones that provide the most value to you right now. Even though you may have dozens (or even more than a hundred) accounts, this short list will provide the most value to the people who have to deal with them when you're gone. The rest will fall into place, or by the wayside, as nature intended.

We've done our best to list as many digital accounts as possible to put you on the right track, but they're always changing. If we had written this section in the early 2000s, MySpace would have been at the top of the list and we'd look like idiots. For this reason, please cut us some slack if we highlight something that doesn't have relevance by the time you read it.

Here are the main things you need to consider for each account you have:

Level of importance: If you were to delete it today, how would it affect your life? One way to clean things up is to kill the useless accounts as you're getting a plan in place.

Single sign-on: Do you use the credentials for this account to log in to other accounts, such as using your Google account to log in to eBay?

Payment method: Is there a credit card, a bank account routing number, or another form of cash attached to a given account? If you canceled the card or closed the bank account, would it interrupt or delete the service?

Ultimate fate: Should it be deleted or transferred, or do you just not care?

This covers all the bases on general organization, but like we said earlier, not all accounts are created equal, and some require special treatment. Let's start with those.

The Big Five

The majority of your accounts can be organized into neat categories, like communication, shopping, and entertainment. Then there are the "mothership" accounts that stand above all the rest because they provide multiple services and play by their own set of rules. Here they are:

GOOGLE

Remember when you first heard the word *Google* and how ridiculous it sounded? Now it's almost dizzying how interwoven it is into our digital lives.

Gmail: If you're one of the 1.5 billion people who use Gmail as your primary email, you understand its importance. Aside from general communication, this is how you might get your billing statements and confirm your accounts. If someone needed to reset a password to gain access to an account, this is likely where it would go down. If you're a private person who doesn't want their email to be read, you can use their Inactive Account Manager option (see page 138).

Other Google Services: Google Drive, Chrome, Contacts, Calendar, Maps, YouTube, Android, Home, Nest, Chromecast, and Photos. As you can see, Gmail is only the tip of the iceberg. You can identify the rest of the services associated with your account when you log in and view this page: myaccount.google.com. Or maybe you could think about it like this:

❏ Do you have documents and spreadsheets uploaded to Drive?

❏ Are your passwords saved in Chrome?

❏ Are you concerned about your browser history because you never bothered using Incognito, which allows you to view whatever you want without saving it?

❏ Is your calendar loaded with appointments and contacts?

❏ Do you subscribe to YouTube services (music, TV), and is it connected to a Chromecast so you can watch it from the comfort of your couch?

❏ Do you have a Google Home device that provides Amazon Echo-like functionality and home automation?

❏ Do you back up all your images and videos using Google Photos?

❏ Do you use an Android-based phone that ties all these services together in a mobile environment?

❏ Do you sign into other sites or apps using your Google account?

❏ Do you also use it for work?

❏ Are you scared yet?

Depending on the depth of your digital relationship with Google, you can see why granting someone access to your account and telling them what you want done with it after you're gone could be the most important aspect of your Digital Estate Plan. Google is so pervasive, it even has a way to somewhat painlessly allow a person you trust to manage your account after you're gone.

Inactive Account Manager: Google's post-death solution is based on your level of inactivity, which means people use Google so frequently (checking Gmail on a phone, doing a search, or watching a YouTube video while logged in) that not using it for a period of time is considered odd behavior. You can set your inactivity time from three months to a year and a half. If you don't access any of their services within that time frame, Google sets off a series of events that will either delete your entire account or share it with someone you named as a "trusted contact."

To set up Inactive Account Manager, Google "inactive account manager" or use this link: myaccount.google.com/inactive. From there, it walks you through the steps.

Tread Lightly Before You Delete: You have to be very careful not to jump the gun and delete a Google account unless you're sure you won't need it.

The same rule applies to all primary email accounts that serve as a major source of information. It'd be like torching a filing cabinet filled with every contact and correspondence you have just because you wanted it gone. What's the rush? You can always delete it later. Better to keep it active and secure until you're sure it's no longer required.

FACEBOOK

There are other, more important services than Facebook, but with 2.6 billion users (many of them real people, not fake profiles), it carries a lot of weight. It's also become a major source of single sign-on, which is when you use Facebook to log in to other sites, so you don't have to create a new set of credentials.

Facebook has also become the hub for millions of people's online identity, a kind of modern phone book without the need for a phone. You can pretty much get in touch with anyone at any time, as long as they regularly check Facebook. It's possible that Facebook and its other popular messaging platform, WhatsApp, could be just as important as a primary email account.

Memorialization & Naming a Legacy Contact: Memorializing a Facebook account after death has become a

standard practice. Anything the deceased posted is still visible, and, depending on their account settings, a "Remembering" badge is added to the profile and friends can still add memories and comments on their wall. If a Legacy Contact was appointed, that person can update the main photo, respond to friend requests (but can't add new friends), and include a pinned post at the top of the profile (for example, a final message). They can't access any direct messages, which are kept private. To have full access, a person would need the login information (passwords!).

Instructions to Delete: If you want to remain virtually visible to the world, take the memorialization and Legacy Contact path. If you want your account deleted the way Facebook suggests, name a Legacy Contact and select the option that you want your account deleted. If you want to do it unofficially, give the person in charge of your digital estate your login info and have them delete it the same way you would if you were still alive. This person would need access to your email and phone if two-step verification is required to complete the process.

Warning: Time Is Not on Your Side. Although Facebook has been working to make the process better, there's a chance that anyone can submit a memorialization request and make it a huge pain to get it unmemorialized. It's sometimes done by a person who may not have even been close to the deceased. They just want to play TMZ and break the news about a death without perhaps considering what the family or close friends may be going through. If this happens to you, your family will be at the mercy of Facebook, so beware.

AMAZON

What started as a place to buy books in 1994 has become a superstore behemoth with more than 100 million Prime members. Although the majority of people use it to shop, Amazon has found a way into almost every aspect of our lives, including streaming (Prime Video), music (Amazon Music), digital books (Kindle), photo storage (free with Prime), groceries (Amazon Fresh and Whole Foods), and hardware that's either connected to your TV (Fire), guarding your home (Ring), or listening to you right now and awaiting instructions to tell you the time, weather, or a joke (Echo). It also has an entire world you might not know about called Amazon Web Services, which provides cloud computing to a decent-sized chunk of the internet (Everplans included).

Although much of it operates within its own ecosystem—you

might not use your Amazon account to log in to other accounts, for example—Amazon is a massive universe that allows you to share your account and benefits with two adults, four teens, and four children via Amazon Household. If the main account holder dies, it can get tricky, which is why each (trusted and responsible) member of the household should have access to the main account.

Purchased Content: Like most of the digital media purchases we mentioned earlier, these are a one-time agreement between Amazon and the person who bought it. When you delete an account, all that goes away. If you've been building a substantial library of digital books over the years—Kindle was released in 2007—you can't put them in a box and hand it to your grandkids to enjoy. This is why you might want to keep the account alive, either by having someone take it over or by

removing any payment options (a credit card is required only for Prime) and keeping it dormant to access those purchases.

If you want to let a Prime subscription lapse, it's not the end of the world, but you should check a few things beforehand. Will any auto-deliveries be interrupted? Do you need to download any backed-up photos? There are also video watchlists and music playlists, but anything subscription based can be re-created on another person's Prime account.

Sellers: There are 5 million marketplace sellers on Amazon, which range from individuals operating like they would on eBay to small businesses using it for distribution. We had a Side Mission (see page 74) about running a small business, but here's a little insight into any moneymaking (or losing) ventures: They have to be included as part of your estate. We talked about how an executor must gather up all the assets. Money (including points or gift card balances) in a seller's account is considered an asset.

Instructions to Delete or Transfer: Before you delete an Amazon account, be aware of all the implications. It might be easier to simply take it over if you want to keep using it. That way you don't have to set up the same exact thing again. You'll need to

change the email to your own, which means you should have access to the previous email in case it requires verification. (Passwords to the rescue again!) Any canceled credit cards will need to be updated to prevent a disruption in service.

APPLE

As one of the most valuable companies on the planet, Apple has created its own world of products that work together from platform to platform. If you've got an iPhone, MacBook, iPad, Apple Watch, or Apple TV and use any of Apple's services (iCloud, Safari browser, Apple Music, photos, games, video . . .), then you'll want to follow a route similar to the one you did with Amazon.

The Keys to the Apple Kingdom: The Apple ID is digital gold and grants access to all of these services. Anyone who might be taking control of your iKingdom needs the username and password, as well as the associated email account (to update or reset the password) and the access code to the iPhone (if two-step verification is enabled—something you will have already taken care of because you're so on top of all this).

Instructions to Delete or Transfer: Once again, don't do this on a whim, because once it's closed, or inaccessible, it's almost impossible to get it back. For a company that was built to make computing easy, deleting an account is confusing and arduous. For this reason, you may want to tell the person to change the email on the account to their own—or one they set up on the side—just to keep them from spending hours or days trying to figure it all out. What you should do is outline all the things that need to be managed, such as photos, texts, contacts, passwords, and everything else associated with that Apple ID. If you've made a lot of purchases, mainly because iTunes was the first legit marketplace for downloadable music, you might want to do the same thing we did with the Kindle: Freeze it in time and keep using it without connecting it to the internet.

We're fully aware that some of these solutions seem crazy in an era with such amazing technology. The problem: These companies, along with the majority of the human race, don't want to think about death. However, as more and more people who use these products start to leave us, they're going to have to come up with better solutions, like offering an easy way to merge or transfer these accounts into your own. If they included a feature like that, it would render this entire section of the book completely unnecessary, but that's a sacrifice we're willing to make. (We're so noble sometimes.)

MICROSOFT

Microsoft might not be happy following Apple, but they're still doing just fine, mainly because more than 1.5 billion people use the Windows platform. They have Outlook.com (formerly hotmail.com), Office, Skype, Xbox, LinkedIn (betcha didn't know Microsoft owned that), and other services that fall into many of the same categories we already covered.

The Keys to the Micro Kingdom:
The Microsoft ID (formerly known as Passport) consolidates every Microsoft service, much like all the other major "special treatment" providers we've mentioned. A person with this will have full access to all the Microsoft services you have.

Instructions to Delete or Transfer:
We think you know the drill by now. The few differentiators with Microsoft are Office, Xbox, and LinkedIn. If you pay for a LinkedIn Premium account, you'll want it canceled. If you pay for an Office 365 subscription or Xbox Live account, you'll have to make arrangements for those too. Otherwise, you can either have someone take them over by changing the email and payment options or let them all disappear into the abyss.

Don't Go Overboard!
You don't have to be an overachieving completist. When you take an

inventory of all your accounts (detailed in the next six pages), make a quick decision using these criteria:

If I delete this right now, what are the consequences? If the answer is "My entire digital world would collapse" or "It has a lot of my personal information that I'd like deleted," then you know it requires effort. If the answer is "Nothing at all," then you can let it slip away like a thief in the night.

Does anyone else need it? You might not care about an account,

but someone in your family might need it. This also opens a door—or portal, if we wanted to sound extra futuristic—to having a digital estate conversation with your family so you can all be on the same (web)page.

Finally, feel free to include some personality in the instructions. A little levity can help keep the person tasked with the job from getting depressed while shutting down and deleting your digital universe. (For more digital matrix info, go online here: incasethe book.com/digital-account-matrix.)

Plan of Attack

MAKE A DIGITAL ESTATE PLAN

DOING THE DIGITAL DANCE

TIME: You can tear through this much more quickly once you organize all your passwords from Level 1. To speed things up even more, recognize early in the process which accounts really matter and which simply need to be shut down or transferred (see "The Big Close-Out" chart that follows).

- If you're keeping track of accounts using a password manager, add your instructions in the Notes field.

- If you opt for a digital or hard copy document, include the

word *Instructions* under the login info and then add them.

- If your password list is handwritten, you may need to start a new document, since there might not be room on the page (or sticky note).

Limit yourself to thirty minutes for each account that really matters. The ones that don't have much significance but still require instructions should take less than five minutes per account. For the ones that really don't matter, keep it under thirty seconds (Delete or Ignore will suffice).

THE BIG CLOSE-OUT

Now that we've gotten those monsters out of the way, let's dig into the categories. We're presenting them in a stylish chart to give you a sense of what type of account fits into each category, a quick take, and examples of instructions you should leave behind. If any of these types of accounts applies to your digital life, make a mental note of what you want done with it. If it doesn't, that's one less thing to worry about.

	EMAIL	SOCIAL MEDIA
Likely Culprits	The biggies we already covered (see page 137). The others are work, personal, AOL, and Yahoo.	Twitter, LinkedIn, Instagram, TikTok, Snapchat, Reddit, Pinterest
Quick Take	If you use one of the big providers we already covered, then you're ahead of the game. If you use another service, treat it the way you would Gmail or Outlook.	Without Facebook (which also owns Instagram), this section seems kind of naked. The one standout is Twitter, which requires a plan along with Facebook if you use it to log in to other accounts. The other social media sites depend on your level of usage. If you couldn't care less about Pinterest, let it go. As for Reddit? We're putting you here because we love you and have nowhere else to put you. (Please don't be mean to us.)
Example of Instructions	"Don't delete this until you no longer need it. Monitor it for bills, statements, and people who are trying to get in touch with me. Almost every account I have is tied to this email, and you can use it to gain access, reset passwords, and change the email for that service to one of yours if you want to keep it going. I'd appreciate you not snooping too much on things that are personal, but since I'm gone, I'll have to rely on your honor. HUGS!"	"I used Twitter sparingly, so feel free to delete it. Same for LinkedIn. I know it might seem important to keep me alive online, but apart from Facebook it really doesn't matter to me."

SHOPPING

eBay, big-box stores (Walmart, Target, Bed Bath & Beyond, etc.), Etsy, coupon sites (Groupon, Rakuten, Shopify, etc.)

This is only about buying, not selling. We know big-box stores might not seem like official digital accounts, but if you use them like Amazon and have auto-deliveries that need to be transferred, they're close enough. Your level of usage of digital-only services (eBay, Etsy, Poshmark) should determine their fate, but it's best to have them deleted unless there's a reason to keep them around. If you have rewards due from coupon sites, explain how you use them so they don't go to waste.

"Delete eBay since I won't be making many purchases anymore. (That's a joke!) Seriously, I have credit card and banking info there that you don't want compromised. I still have discounts at Walmart and Bed Bath & Beyond—you might want to use them before they expire, and then you can delete. I have cash-back rewards from Rakuten, which you can cash in for a gift card that will be sent to my primary email. Or you can request that a check be sent by mail or to my bank account, which should be included in my estate."

PAYMENTS & MONEY MANAGEMENT

PayPal, Venmo, money management services we covered in "Money You Have" on page 28 (Mint, YNAB, Trim, etc.), Kickstarter, GoFundMe

If it's a payment account that still holds money, it needs to be rolled up into your estate. If you use the account only to make payments, delete it once you're sure it's not being used for anything on autopay. The money management sites, which are extremely handy for keeping track of your finances while you're alive, are just as helpful for your executor when you're gone. They can be used as a real-time checklist and monitoring system to see that the assets are being moved into new accounts and there aren't any new charges posting. Once all activity ceases and they're empty, they can be deleted.

Crowdfunding accounts can inform your family about your charitable interests but should be deleted unless you leave behind instructions to donate to a cause through one of these platforms. If a member of your family sets up an account to raise funds to pay for your funeral, it should have nothing to do with your personal account.

"I want all of my payment information and sources shut down to prevent unnecessary expenses and fraud. This includes PayPal and Venmo. I used Clarity Money to keep track of all my bank account and credit card transactions, and you can do the same until everything is closed down."

THE BIG CLOSE-OUT

	CLOUD STORAGE	**STREAMING:** Music, Movies, TV, Gaming
Likely Culprits	Dropbox, Box	Netflix, Hulu, Spotify, Pandora, HBO Max, Disney+, Roku, PlayStation Now, Steam, FandangoNow, and so many more
Quick Take	Before Apple, Google, and Amazon got into the storage game, these were much more relevant. Dropbox still has millions of users (for now), and those files need to go somewhere.	Many of these services are regularly shared among family and friends. They even let you set up separate profiles within each account. You may already share the login credentials, which makes it easy for another person to take over the account or cancel it if they don't use it regularly. The only time you might want to offer more guidance is if you made any purchases on entertainment platforms like FandangoNow, PlayStation/Xbox, Sling, or one of the giants we already mentioned (Apple, Amazon, Google). Music is mainly about preserving playlists and favorites. If this is important, you'll want to relay these musical suggestions in Level 3 (see page 180). Gaming was a breeze when it was only disks—now it's much more complex. Most consoles require a login to access games, even if you own them, and online profiles are usually tied to one person. This makes them relatively useless to pass on to other people unless it's a game where you've built up a lot of credit and someone else can step in to take control.
Example of Instructions	"I was a very active Dropbox user for many years before transitioning to Google Drive. You can disconnect the account on my computer, and everything in those folders will remain intact. Add those to the rest of my digital files, which should be sorted and stored in one place." (Note: We cover how to do this on page 150.)	"As the next official holder of the family Netflix account, it's now up to one of you to take up the mantle. Change the email to one of yours, change the payment method since my card won't be active forever, and read a book every once in a while." 

SOFTWARE LICENSES	FOOD DELIVERY, MISC. SERVICES	TRAVEL
Adobe, McAfee, Quicken	FreshDirect, Grubhub, Yelp, Postmates, Craigslist, TaskRabbit	Airbnb, discount travel sites (Booking.com, Expedia, Hotels.com, Priceline)
Licenses can be expensive, but the model has changed over the years from one long serial number that gives you access to a program forever (like Microsoft Word and Apple's Final Cut Pro) to an annual subscription-based fee (like Microsoft Office 365 and Adobe Creative Cloud). Is it worth it for your family to keep paying for a service they won't use?	Accounts that are shared among the family for food deliveries or groceries require someone else to become the main food master and provide updated payment details to keep recurring deliveries on track. For handyman-like services you found on Craigslist or another app, include your method of using the service; if you found someone who's great at fixing things, they should go in your contacts with a clear description of what they provide and how much they charge.	Airbnb accounts for travel (not providers) are tied to one person, so it might not make sense to transfer one. Those who use discount travel sites can have someone take them over by changing the email and profile name if there are worthy rewards available.
"I bought a Microsoft Office license years ago that's on a few of my computers and should never expire. The serial number is included with my passwords. Any subscription-based software isn't worth the expense and hassle because you can't transfer them to another machine. Keep using them until they lapse on my machine, then it's up to you if you want to pay for them on your own."	"Make any changes to FreshDirect or Amazon Fresh by logging in with my credentials and switching them over to yours so you still get the regular deliveries. Also, I've had luck using Craigslist when I've had trouble with bigger projects that didn't require a contractor (like when we redid the kitchen floor). Just be careful not to let a serial killer into the house."	"Once you cancel my credit cards, all those travel sites shouldn't matter anymore, but you can delete them just to be safe (the discounts were good, but the rewards never really amounted to much)."

THE BIG CLOSE-OUT

	TRANSPORTATION	TICKETING	BUSINESS & NETWORKING
Likely Culprits	Airlines, car rental companies, Uber, Lyft	Ticketmaster, StubHub, Fandango	CareerBuilder, Monster, Indeed, Meetup
Quick Take	Airlines and car rental accounts, although not fully digital, can't be transferred since they're almost always tied to one person. There's a difference between logging in to someone's account and showing up at an airport pretending to be them. This doesn't mean you should delete them, because there could be lots of miles or free rental days available. These might be associated with a credit card (see page 97), but if they aren't, then contact the company to see about getting them transferred. Ride sharing apps follow a similar pattern.	If you purchased tickets to a big event far in advance—some concerts and shows sell them upward of a year before a tour—your family would need access to the associated account to attend the event, get a refund, or sell them. Otherwise, it's mainly about making sure rewards or refunds don't go to waste. (If you're a season ticket holder for any sport or event, you'll want to explain exactly what to do if you want those tickets kept in the family.)	One of the benefits of being dead is that you no longer need a job, making these accounts easily deletable without requiring explanation (unless it's LinkedIn, which we bundled with Microsoft). Meetup can potentially help your family learn about people or groups that were of interest to you.
Example of Instructions	"Before you cancel any of my airline or rental accounts, contact them, explain the situation, and find out how you can transfer available miles or free days into your account. If I have any discounts or credit with Uber, use them up and then delete."	"I bought almost all my tickets on StubHub. Log in and check that there aren't any future games or shows you can resell or attend. Going to the movies twice a week built up a lot of points— use them, and think happy thoughts of me."	"I used to host a mentorship Meetup with my old colleague Peter three times a year to help young entrepreneurs hone their business model. It'd be nice if they could keep this going, because it helped a lot of people."

HEALTH & FITNESS	VIDEO CONFERENCING & MESSAGING	CONTENT SUBSCRIPTIONS
Home fitness equipment and subscriptions like Peloton and NordicTrack, and wearables like Fitbit (now owned by Google), Weight Watchers (WW), MapMyRun, or Runkeeper	WeChat, WhatsApp (owned by Facebook), Slack, Skype and Teams (owned by Microsoft), Snapchat	Newspapers and magazines (*New York Times*, *Wall Street Journal*, *Vogue*, etc.) and news aggregators like Flipboard or Pocket
No one can take over your body, but they can take over the devices you used to track your body or keep it in shape.	What do you want done with all the texts and messages you've ever sent? We're asking you because we have no idea. We'd want ours deleted because they're no one else's business. Video services like Zoom, UberConference, and others don't matter since they can't be used in the afterlife (as far as we know).	Content walls don't care who's reading; they just want someone to pay.

"Delete all my monitoring data since it's clearly of no use anymore. Give my Fitbit to whoever wants it (they can reset it and make their own account). If I have any credits on my diet plans, try to get a refund or simply cancel them before they send more gross stuff I hated eating. Same goes for using the NordicTrack that became a clothes rack."	"I'm giving you access to my phone, but I'd appreciate it if you didn't read my texts, because I wouldn't want you to do that when I was alive. Delete these accounts by either logging in to them and following the instructions for deletion or reset my phone to delete everything once you no longer need it to access my other digital details."	"When we shifted from newspapers to digital, I always remained a patron of my favorite outlets. All these subscriptions should be canceled. I encourage you to support any pay outlets you prefer, if only to keep them in business."

Physical Files:
Backups & Hard Drives

Today, the cloud dominates file storage, but it wasn't always that way. Here are the types of storage devices you'll find either belonging to someone over forty or in a museum: floppy disks, Zip and Jaz drives, CD-ROMs, and DVDs. If you had an external hard drive, it meant you were a big spender, because they were pricey. As they became more affordable (thanks, Black Friday deals), they were a necessity to protect your data. It became normal to have a drawer full of these metal boxes loaded with data from every computer you ever had.

It's hard enough to sort through physical possessions. Add in terabytes of unsorted data, much of which could be duplicates, and it's a herculean task to behold. Sure, there could be gems hidden on those backups, the same way you might find a priceless heirloom in a box in the attic, but searching through every file could take a lifetime. You and your family have better things to do.

Then there's the question of why you need a backup hard drive in the first place. To restore a current computer if it has a meltdown, right? That means backups for older computers aren't of any use beyond nostalgia

and peace of mind. The operating systems and programs probably won't even work anymore.

Then there are the memories: mainly documents, photos and videos, and emails (if you can still access them). If you care about these things, you'll be interested in our photo-sorting method in Level 3 (see page 165). If you want a quick solution, here's one idea: Gather up all the external drives you have and light them on fire, then run away. (And yes, we're joking. *Please do not do this!*)

OK, here's the real process: Begin by gathering up all the external drives you have in one box. This includes thumb drives too. Go through them, one by one, and start sorting. Anything you want to keep—mainly photos, videos, and documents—should be moved into a folder on your desktop titled "Stuff from External Drives" or some naming convention so you know what it is. Once you complete a drive, reformat it so there's no going back. Repeat until all the drives are empty. Use one of the drives to back up your current computer, because it's important to do it for computers still in use. Now instead of having twenty external drives, there's only one and it's filled with items worth keeping.

Not very scientific, but there's really no other way. If you're the sentimental type, you will waste hours stuck in memory holes. You'll probably want to keep everything or find it too daunting and want to give up. If that's the case, then don't even bother looking and just reformat the drive.

"You want me to delete everything?!" you just thought, incredulous. *"Are you people monsters?"*

Perhaps, but here's reality: If you haven't needed these drives for years, why do you need them now? We completely understand the hoarding mentality (just ask our coauthor Adam, the man saves *everything*), but what would your family do if they were tasked with making sense of decades of hard drives? You haven't touched them in years, so why should they? It's up to you to mine the drives for what's important. If you don't want to do it, then let them go.

One last point about external hard drives, and it may get a little adult. Back when the internet first started, the naughty materials people currently access online would be downloaded. Perhaps some of these drives are loaded with stuff you don't want your family to see. We read a thread on Reddit about what was found on dead people's computers, and it was overwhelmingly porn related. We tastefully tackle this topic near the end of the book (see page 221), but now that we teased it here, does that give you enough motivation to start sorting and deleting? Thought so!

Naming a Digital Executor

Once you've identified what you want done with all the accounts that matter, you need someone who'll make the instructions you leave behind a reality. Enter the Digital Executor—the person you designate to help manage and settle your digital estate. It sounds a lot more official than it is, especially since it's not legally binding in most states. But you didn't get this far in life by following the rules, did you? Also, most Wills include this option, so you won't have to do much extra work to get it done.

Do This: Appoint this person in your Will or make it clear to your executor that they're also responsible for your digital accounts and assets.

Don't Do This: Include passwords or what you want done with your digital accounts in your Will. As we've already mentioned, a Will becomes a public document and you *don't* want this private information floating around for identity thieves to steal.

So Do This: All the instructions you leave behind should be in a separate

Plan of Attack

place, whether in the Description (or Notes) field of your password manager alongside the account or in a document where you keep all your passwords. As you add new accounts, or rethink the importance of accounts you already have, updating your records should become part of your regular password storage process.

Logging Off

If the concept of sharing your digital information with another person makes you uncomfortable, then you're being completely sane and normal. And here's the thing: You don't have to provide access to these accounts right now, but you do need to organize everything in one place to save your loved ones a ton of headaches down the road.

The whole point of a Digital Estate Plan is to allow someone you trust to close down your accounts, repurpose devices, and transfer services without going completely crazy. There's a reason why some of the most popular pages on the Everplans website involve closing digital accounts after someone dies (and we have instructions for more than 200 of them!). We've also received countless emails from people begging us to help them close an account when someone they loved passed away without leaving any details behind. As sad as it makes us feel, there's nothing we can do at that point. They're at the mercy of Twitter or Facebook or the hundreds of other possible services that don't make it easy for a person who's grieving.

You don't need to personally experience this sort of frustration and pain to spring into action. Take the time to get everything in order and you'll be lifting a huge virtual weight off whoever you leave behind. Plus, we won't receive as many depressing emails about closing accounts anymore. This is what people refer to as a classic win-win.

■ ■ ■

Break Time

Talk the Talk

Until now, most of the advice we've offered has been about gathering up your own information and organizing it for someone to decipher later. Here we'll tell you how to coax that information out of someone else, typically a reluctant family member. Because it's hard to have difficult conversations about touchy subjects with your loved ones without yelling, breaking household items, and storming out of the room. Usually.

Talking with family can be littered with emotional, and sometimes suspicious, land mines. When topics include money, medical issues, or death, it can be even more terrifying.

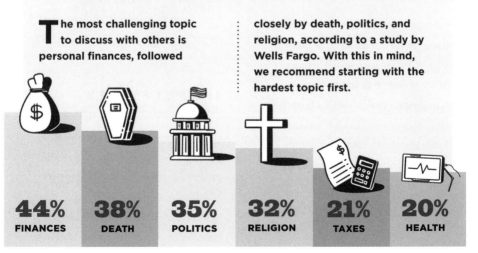

HOW CHALLENGING ARE TOPICS TO DISCUSS?

The most challenging topic to discuss with others is personal finances, followed closely by death, politics, and religion, according to a study by Wells Fargo. With this in mind, we recommend starting with the hardest topic first.

44%	**38%**	**35%**	**32%**	**21%**	**20%**
FINANCES	DEATH	POLITICS	RELIGION	TAXES	HEALTH

Consider for a second that people would rather talk about no longer being on earth than money. The Wells Fargo study also revealed that although people aren't comfortable talking about money, it's one of the biggest stresses in their lives, often causing sleepless nights. You'd think turning to family would assuage these fears, but silence often prevails. Let's imagine how one of those awkward conversations can go:

❏ A general overview of their financial situation

❏ Do they have a Will and Power of Attorney?

❏ Where do they keep their important documents?

❏ Is there an up-to-date Life Insurance policy?

❏ What should be done in a medical emergency?

❏ What are their general funeral wishes?

> **You:** Dad, do you have Life Insurance?

> **Dad:** Why, would you want to kill me for the money? [laughs]

> **You:** [nervous laughter] Um, no, Dad, just wondering . . .

> **Dad:** Don't worry about it . . . Now pass the salt, Cheery McGee.

Perhaps you could sit with your family and ask these questions straight up. Good for you. Feel free to skip this section and go spend more time with your perfect family. But many families don't have this open line of communication, so they need to employ different tactics to get what they need without things getting heated.

We're here to prevent family discussions about serious issues from turning into a bad sitcom. To start, we're going to prep you with some stealth tactics to gather what you need. This isn't about lying; these are ways to broach sensitive topics without setting anyone off.

Here are the things you'll want to find out:

THE MONEY TALK

How many times have you been given the wrong change at a store or restaurant and just accepted it? Maybe the line was too long or the cashier didn't seem particularly friendly or you thought a few cents wasn't worth the hassle. Or maybe you have no qualms about making sure you get back *exactly* what you're owed regardless of how you're perceived by the unpleasant cashier or the long line behind you.

When speaking with your family about money, it can go either way, since most people tend to get touchy when discussing their finances. According to Yahoo! Finance, the best way to approach this issue going forward is to simply make money a normal topic of conversation.

YET MONEY IS HARDER TO TALK ABOUT THAN DEATH

When it comes to talking about money, Wells Fargo also found that "71% of adults surveyed learned the importance of saving from their own parents. Despite this, only a third (36%) of today's parents discuss the importance of saving money with their children on a frequent basis, with 64% indicating they talk about savings with their kids less than weekly or never."

Let's stay focused on the problem and solution: How do *you* comfortably discuss money with *your* family?

Whenever a person prefaces a conversation with "We need to talk . . . ," odds are it won't be a pleasant experience for at least one of you. Most money conversations seem to be couched in ulterior motives, especially if the only time your family talks about money is during a crisis or when a person needs some. However, if money can become an unconditional part of your ongoing conversations (it's peppered throughout all the other stuff you talk about), it won't be so awkward.

You don't have to break out bank books and give specific amounts, but regularly discussing financial tips or experiences with kids, siblings, and parents will make it less taboo. If the first time your family talks about money is when an estate needs to be divided after a death, you're playing with fire. Start small—savings, investments, monthly budgets, advice you got from your parents or trusted advisors—and work up to bigger conversations once everyone's on board.

GENERATION GAP

A person who worked their whole life to amass savings has a completely different perspective from someone in their early twenties just getting started. Although you might never see eye to eye with someone twenty or forty years your junior or senior (especially when it comes to music), you have to try to understand their point of view.

Ideally, when it comes time to talk, you should have a clear idea of what you want to accomplish. If you're one of the wise family elders, you can dictate the tone and make everyone comfortable enough to ask any questions they may have, even if it's a fifteen-year-old grandkid bewildered by the concept of a mortgage (or a thirty-five-year-old adult bewildered by the concept of a mortgage).

Finally, don't be coy. Unless someone is demanding specific figures you're unwilling to offer, try to answer as openly as possible. For example, if your Will says that all your assets will be divided equally among your adult children, tell them that. The entire point of normalizing money discussions with your family is to limit surprises, not heighten the suspense and turn it into a free-for-all after you're gone.

STEALTH TALK:
How to Gather Info from Loved Ones

There's an old interviewing trick that gets people to disclose information without even realizing they're doing it: Turn a question into a challenge. For example, if you wanted to find out someone's views on spanking a child, you could simply ask and get a tepid, nonengaged response. But if you say, "I think spanking is the worst possible way to discipline a child," then you're challenging the other person to give a response. What they say, and how they say it, gives you all the information you need, and in this case, it could help you decide if that person would make a good guardian if you have underage kids.

After interviewing hundreds of people, we've learned that people love to be interviewed. Even if they act like they hate it, deep down it makes them feel validated that someone is taking the time to listen to what they have to say. It gives them a chance to talk about themselves, explain their successes, warn about their failures, and share their views and life lessons. It's typical for celebs and athletes to be interviewed, but how often does anyone lavish that kind of attention on your family and friends?

If you want to find out what types of documents your parents have completed, set the stage and then sit back and listen. And remember: This shouldn't be about

determining net worth, the value of a Life Insurance policy, how much inheritance each person in the family will receive, or obtaining a complete inventory of assets. This is about finding out whether documents exist and where they can be found, if necessary, and what other plans have been made or should be made.

LEGAL DOCS

Goal: *You want to find out if your subject has created a Will.*

Plan of Attack: If *you've* already created a Will—something we strongly encourage—bring it up in a playful manner. Say something like, "I've finally done my Will, which makes me an official adult." Then use your triumph as an excuse to ask your interview subject if they've done one yet. If they have, tell them you're looking for suggestions for where you should store it. This will reveal the location. Bingo!

If you haven't created a Will, mention that you've been interested in doing it but don't know where to start because it all seems so complicated. This almost always gets the subject to reveal if and how they've created theirs (people love being advice and referral heroes).

If you find out that the subject doesn't want a Will, find out why.

It could be that they don't see the value in having one and think that if the family can't amicably come to an agreement over the remaining assets after they're gone, they deserve to fight. Regardless of why, at least you know that when that person dies, you won't have to waste time searching for a document that doesn't exist.

If You Get Shut Down: There's a possibility your family might think you're fishing for financial information. If anyone says something like, "Are you worried about being cut out of the Will?" or "Why are you all of a sudden so interested in this?," use some finesse . . . and perhaps this easy-to-remember anecdote to get the ball rolling.

Anecdote: What's in the Box? Mention the story of a family that couldn't locate a Will, so they had to spend months in court figuring out the estate. A year later when they finally got around to sorting through their father's basement, guess what they found at the bottom of a box of old bank statements and receipts? Yep, the Will. By then it was too late, because the estate had already been settled. If their father had kept it in a folder or with an attorney, or had

simply told someone, he could have saved everyone from lengthy court proceedings, expensive lawyers, and tons of avoidable stress.

The goal here is to hammer home the point: If you can't find their Will after they're gone, then it's as if they never drew it up.

Last-Resort Tactic: Change the topic and live to fight another day. You've planted the seed and can now approach them at a later date to get the information.

LIFE INSURANCE

Goal: *You want to know if your subject has an active Life Insurance policy and the name of the company that provided it.*

Plan of Attack: Like you did with the Will, you're trying to ascertain if a policy exists. If there's no policy, or the policy lapsed, it's best to know so you won't waste time searching for money that isn't there. From there, you want to find out the company name and the location of the documents. Here are two ways to approach this topic:

If You Have Life Insurance:

Say you recently paid your premium, and mention the company you're working with and the level of service you receive. This will get your subject to chime in with the name of the company they've chosen. Then tell them where you keep the policy in case something happens. You might keep it in your desk, but you've been thinking about buying a fireproof safe. Or maybe you don't even have a paper copy and it's all digital. By asking, "What's the smartest way to keep it secure?," you're opening up the floor for useful suggestions and valuable intel about where they keep theirs. Pretty sneaky, right?

If You Don't Have Life Insurance:

Say you have limited coverage through your job and express an interest in getting Life Insurance with more ironclad benefits but don't know where to start. You might find out that your grandpa had a twenty-year Term policy that he let lapse after the kids were grown. Or your father bought a Whole Life policy at a great price when he was young. From there, keep your inquisitive streak alive by asking what company they liked working with and where they kept (or keep) the documents.

Finding out if someone has Life Insurance isn't exactly in the danger zone of conversation starters. Just don't pry about the value of the policy.

Anecdote: Surprise—Your Late Husband Had Life Insurance. A woman we spoke with had no idea her late husband had Life Insurance until a cousin approached her at the funeral and mentioned he had sold him a policy twenty years earlier and it was still in effect. What's even more interesting: The husband had made his estate plan, including his Will, accessible and easy to find, but never mentioned that he had an active policy. The money was a welcome and helpful surprise, but she'll always wonder: Why did he keep it a secret?

If You Get Shut Down: If you're getting resistance, or the person appears uncomfortable, change the subject. For all you know, they used to have a policy but had to let it lapse because of financial problems.

Last-Resort Tactic: We don't really see failure as an option here. If a family member has a policy, it's not really a sensitive subject. If a family

member says they don't have one, your work here is done.

MEDICAL DECISIONS

Goal: *You want to know your subject's medical wishes and find out if they've created an Advance Directive (or would be willing to do so with your help).*

Plan of Attack: You don't want to make this discussion about current or suspected health conditions, because that's how arguments happen. Even though you may have valid concerns about a family member's lifestyle choices, judging their habits (eating, smoking, drinking, laziness) will get you nowhere.

Instead, focus on responsibility and paperwork. Remind them that you'd have no idea what to do if an emergency happened. Tell them you've created your Advance Directive, and ask if they've created theirs. If they haven't, you can help them, since you now know what to

do. Let them know you're up at night worrying that you might make the wrong decision about their care and have to live with it for the rest of your life.

Anecdote: Ever Hear of the Daughter from California?
In *The Conversation: A Revolutionary Plan for End-of-Life Care*, there's a concept called the Daughter from California Syndrome, which is when a relative who has shown very little interest in a person's gradual decline in health arrives on the scene near the end and immediately asserts their dominance over the situation. They'll disregard treatment options, argue with medical professionals, and try to make other family members feel guilty about not doing everything possible to keep the ailing person alive. This behavior is usually born out of guilt and denial, but it's generally viewed as a nuisance to the medical staff, who have worked with closer family members to construct a thoughtful plan for the patient. So, is there a "daughter" or "son" like this in your family? Who is it? (Beware: It could be you.)

If You Get Shut Down: If you're not making any progress, refer to the story about Terri Schiavo we mentioned earlier (see page 123).

Last-Resort Tactic: Complete your own Advance Directive and show it to your subject. Perhaps you named them, or someone present when you bring up this topic, as your Health Care Proxy, meaning that you have some backup. You can also print out the form from their state and help them fill it out (see page 130).

FUNERAL WISHES

Goal: *You want to find out if your subject wants to be buried, cremated, donated to science, shot into space, or whatever else is possible and legal. Also, you need to know if they've already purchased a burial plot, and ideally, if they've prepaid for any funeral arrangements.*

Plan of Attack: You need to be cool about this. The absolute wrong approach to this topic: "Mom, how do you get this bacon so crispy . . . Speaking of crispy, what are your thoughts about cremation?"

Some people plan their funeral in advance, but most leave the planning up to the family. Either way is fine as long as the family is aware, especially if your subject already owns a plot (you don't want to accidentally buy another). Arguing over the final disposition of the body, and the type of funeral ceremony, can create one of those family rifts we've been trying to avoid this entire time. Don't screw it up now!

This is where age and experience often have a decisive advantage. Generally, the longer you live, the more loss you experience, and you start viewing this as a practical discussion rather than something depressing and unspeakable.

If your family has experienced a loss in the past year, or your subject mentions a funeral they recently attended, you can seize the opportunity to let them know what *you* want. It might sound strange, but try to keep it light to get them talking, and always speak about it in the distant future.

Ideally, your subject will break in and say something like, "Just put me in the ground and move on" or "I want the biggest ceremony this town's ever seen." You still need to be mindful, because death is one of the last topics people want to discuss (aside from money), so don't be graphic or morbid.

Anecdote: Funeral Strippers Are a Thing. Most people want a big turnout at their funeral, but some cultures have taken it to the extreme. Did you know that in parts of China and Taiwan, where a well-attended funeral can be a sign of good fortune for the deceased as they venture into the afterlife, they had to crack down on strippers being hired to woo larger crowds? Speaking of which, if you don't tell me what *you* want, then I might be forced to make your final farewell a bawdy burlesque show. (Note: If the subject is actually receptive to this suggestion, you may have painted yourself into a corner.)

If You Get Shut Down: Be honest and say that you're curious. If you know the subject regularly visits the grave of a loved one, find out what type of flowers they bring. Ask if there are family plots or if making arrangements in advance is a smart thing to do. Talk about how expensive funerals have become (between $7,000 and $10,000) and see if that's an issue. Anything that gets your subject to reveal what's on their mind and what they might want is a win.

Last-Resort Tactic: Don't press too hard, but definitely revisit this topic when it might be more appropriate. No loving family member wants their death to be a burden, and some might not care about a funeral at all. If that's the case, then at least you know it'll be up to you and other survivors to make the call.

LEVEL 3

THE FINISHING TOUCHES

Memorabilia, Letters, Funeral Planning, and Obituaries

HERE'S WHAT YOU'LL HAVE
WHEN YOU'RE FINISHED WITH THIS LEVEL:

- An organizational plan for all your meaningful photos, recipes, and family heirlooms.

- A record of your personal history, interests, beliefs, and life lessons so everyone remembers you the way you want to be remembered.

- A model for writing letters to your family and friends they will cherish for the rest of their lives.

- A complete understanding of everything you need to know about planning a funeral.

- Your own obituary (if you're up for it).

We spent this entire book getting all the serious moving (and stationary) pieces of your life under control. In Level 3, you get the chance to sit back, unwind, and let the people you love know the real you.

Let's begin with *Titanic*. Not the tragic event that killed more than 1,500 people in 1912, but the 1997 blockbuster movie that captivated the entire world. How did this movie, which had an ending everyone already knew, become one of the most successful films of all time? It made you care.

Early in the movie they explain exactly how the massive ship sank, going so far as to show a computer simulation. We're sure some people in the audience were like, "Welp, no mystery here, maybe I can catch the rest of *Good Will Hunting* on the other screen."

Then Grandma Rose starts telling her story. It becomes so engrossing that by the time the iceberg hits hours later (it's a *long* movie), you're completely invested. You already know how the boat broke apart and even how many people perished. But now it isn't cold hard numbers and computer graphics, it's actual people with personal stories. Add in some melodic Celine Dion, and what

was once a tragedy on its way to becoming a historical footnote is now relevant and meaningful for generations to come. Like for our colleague who's in her twenties and has been absolutely obsessed with the movie for most of her life.

The sum of your life isn't simply numbers, tasks, legal documents, and possessions. On paper, most of us are pretty much the same, give or take a few zeros. The real meaning of your life is what you experienced, how you affected other people, how they affected you, and the lessons you want to live on after you're gone.

Whether you're a young Jack dying in the freezing ocean because there wasn't enough room on that board for two (seriously, there wasn't—*MythBusters* proved it) or you're Rose throwing a priceless diamond into the ocean (it was never hers to begin with), then dying peacefully surrounded by (photos of) loved ones, what's your story?

Here's how to tell it.

MEMORIES
THE KIND YOU SEE, TASTE, AND HOLD

■ ■ ■

Think of the emotions you feel when looking at a photograph and remembering exactly what was happening when it was taken. When you hold a cherished item one of your parents passed along to you. Or when you taste a familiar meal that immediately transports you back to your grandma's kitchen when you were a kid. These are the feelings you want to capture and, ideally, transfer to the next generation.

PHOTO FINISH

We all have too many photos. It's time to get them under control so they're not lost in the cloud. Or the attic. Handing down photos from one generation to the next used to be a simple act of passing along a few framed photos, some leather-bound albums, and packed shoeboxes.

And, given all the effort that used to go into taking those photos, they held a certain power and value. You had to buy film, conserve the number of exposures so you didn't run out, get that roll of film developed (when you had time), hope the person who developed them at the Fotomat* didn't judge you too harshly, toss out half of them because they were blank or completely out of focus (digital viewfinders weren't a thing), and then put them in an album (if you got around to it).

Now, you can immediately take a photo of anything and share it everywhere. It could be an adorable

*If you don't know what a Fotomat is, imagine a shack in the middle of a parking lot that operated as a drive-thru, with an awesome 1970s vibe.

shot of your child frolicking in a field, a receipt for an expense report, or a funny-looking french fry. According to InfoTrends, 1.2 *trillion* digital photos were taken worldwide in 2017. Some are posted on social media or shared among family and friends, but most are left unsorted and unnamed on phones and computers, backed up on hard drives, or stored in the cloud. To help bring order to this digital disarray, consider these questions:

❏ What do you want to happen to them?

❏ Would your family know how to access them if something happened to you?

❏ Do you want your kids or grandkids sorting through an unmanageable number of digital photos to find the best ones?

❏ Should some of these photos disappear forever?

These digital assets are important because they've become our new memories. And we have too many of them. Here's how to trim the fat and honor the photos that deserve it.

Hard & Fast Rules

The first rule is to never have a single point of failure. For example, if you never back up your phone and it falls out a car window, those irreplaceable digital photos can be gone forever. Second rule: Don't get married to a particular photo storage platform. If the company running that platform changes rules or the way photos are stored and viewed, your photo archive could be in jeopardy.

Cloudy Backups: This is where the majority of your digital photos live, at least the ones you've taken since personal cloud storage became a thing (most likely when Dropbox launched in 2008). Since then, Google Drive, iCloud, and OneDrive have taken care of Android, iOS, and Microsoft users, and Amazon Photos has added unlimited storage as a Prime perk. Your cloud sorting and storage method should be a combination of security and quality.

When it comes to security, you want to guarantee they never get deleted, stolen, made inaccessible, or rendered unviewable. The storage giants may change the rules at some point in the future by making it difficult to export a copy of your photos in an open, nonproprietary format. We've seen this happen with

HOW THIS HELPS AFTER YOU'RE GONE
(Organizing keepsakes)

- Your family won't need to sort through tens of thousands of photos to find the best ones.

- People will actually know who's in the photos and when they were taken.

- Favorite family recipes can still be enjoyed exactly as you remember them.

- Heirlooms will end up in the right hands and won't end up in donation bins or the trash.

music and video formats. Today's standard format is tomorrow's joke. Yes, we're laughing at you, floppy disks.

Since the beginning of photography up until the early 2000s, photos were primarily on paper. In the past two decades, it's all changed and keeps on evolving. We have photo files on backups from the mid-'90s that are incredibly difficult to view. Who knows what it'll be like thirty years from now?

To assess quality, you'll want to select only the best and most meaningful images. Looking through a shoebox of a few hundred photos that span decades is fun. Looking through the few hundred photos from your last vacation can be a chore. Add in the 25,000+ photos from the rest of your camera roll and it's just too much. If you took 400 photos on your last vacation, pick ten to thirty of the best and archive the rest.

Physical Backups: A computer often serves as the mothership for photos, giving you a fast way to edit, rename, and delete large batches of them (sorry, smartphones). It needs to be regularly backed up, which brings to mind a stack of external hard and thumb drives. We covered them in Level 2 (Digital Estate Plan, see page 150), and now it's time to deal with the photos taking up all that virtual space.

Backups are the new film negatives, which were those orange-y strips of plastic that came in an envelope with your developed film that allowed you to get more prints. Backups are lifesavers when your computer melts down, your phone is destroyed, or your data is deleted from the cloud. For those in favor of this classic digital storage method for photos, the best you can do is label each drive like you would the cover of a photo album, since they all look alike ("FAMILY, 2012").

Hardware won't completely future-proof your images for two reasons, the most obvious being that they break. The second issue is obsolescence, but more often they break before they become obsolete. This doesn't stop them from being a cheap and reliable option, as long as you realize that one day they may become a collection of rectangular paperweights.

Digital Deluge: Organizing Your Files

The onslaught of digital photos is one of the newer challenges we face, one that can be approached from a few angles. If, for example, you take all your photos on an iPhone, consider the following options:

1. Pay for extra iCloud storage (currently, 99 cents a month for 50GB) and make sure it's backing up the original full-sized images, so you never have to think about it.

2. Get a second cloud service like Dropbox or Google Photos to automatically dump a copy of all new photos or videos into a folder.

3. Periodically sort through photos and remove all the accidental pictures of your feet, unnecessary duplicates, and screenshots of what you needed to pick up at the store.

4. Create one organized and manageable photo archive on your main home computer.

5. Every six months or so—set recurring reminders on your calendar—copy all the new photos to an external hard drive. We recommend an SSD drive, since they don't have as many moving parts inside that break . . . although they can still break.

6. If you're really paranoid, make a second copy of the drive to keep at a secondary location, like a parent's house (or a safe deposit box if you choose to go against everything we've said about them throughout this entire book).

Cloud Pricing

You can take a chance and trust in Google, Apple, Microsoft, or Amazon Photos, all of which have decent (and almost creepily accurate) search functionality, even though what's free (or 99 cents a month) today could be expensive tomorrow. There are also security and privacy concerns when you give an algorithm full control over your personal memories.

FAMILY 2012

- **AMAZON PHOTOS:** Unlimited full-resolution storage with Prime membership, $20 per year for 100GB

- **DROPBOX:** 2GB free, $120 per year for 2TB

- **GOOGLE PHOTOS:** 15GB free for all Google services, $24 per year for 100GB

- **ICLOUD:** 5GB free, $12 per year for 50GB

- **MICROSOFT ONEDRIVE:** 5GB free, $24 per year for 100GB

Disclaimer: Prices and storage limits may have changed by the time you read this.

Restrain Yourself

Sometimes having limits can be a good thing. Five gigabytes of storage equals about 1,000 photos. If you want to avoid paying a storage fee for the rest of your life, you can thin the herd to only the best whenever you hit the limit. Not easy, but 1,000 photos are still more than most of our grandparents ever took in their entire lifetime.

From professional photographers we learned there's no perfect solution, but many workable options exist. Each has their own favorite programs (like Adobe Lightroom or even Google Photos) and workflow that suits them, but their situation is much more intensive. They may have only a few days (or hours) to sort and edit hundreds or thousands of photos into a tight collection for a client, be it a wedding or a media outlet. You're not under that kind of pressure, so keep it basic and stay consistent.

It could be as simple as taking a few hours around the holidays and scrolling through that year's photos, choosing only the best fifty or one hundred, and then using those to create an annual collection. If you're really ambitious, you could become the photo point person for the family and include the best snaps taken by your spouse and children in one family collection. Although this may be too much work for you to manage, the least you can do is train them on a reasonable workflow, so you all know exactly where and how each person's photos are stored and organized. On the next page, we explain how to incrementally tackle your mountain of photos so the best are on display or easily accessible, and the worthwhile extras can disappear into an archive never to be looked at again.

> TIP: You can use an online service to get really nice prints to display around the house. Some popular ones are Snapfish, Shutterfly, Amazon Print, and Walmart Photo. (Yep, Walmart.)

How to Get Framed: Physical & Antique Photos

Even though we live in a world of digital photos, every family still has some good old-fashioned prints.

Although we'd like to introduce a fancy way to help you organize classic physical photos, sometimes the simplest way is the best. Start with sorting them into three piles:

1. **Album-Worthy:** These photos are worth preserving.

2. **Box-Worthy:** These photos are worth keeping but not worth honoring in an album (these are mostly similar to or duplicates of better photos you have).

3. **Don't Care:** These can be shredded or tossed into a shoebox with "Don't Care" written on the side so your family knows they weren't important to you.

After the sort is complete, add some color (even if your photos are black and white) by including the following details on the back of each photo, either by hand or with a sticky note: the name(s) of people in the photo; the date and location if you can recall them (a rough estimate is fine); and any brief, relevant historical data (example: "Aunt Stephanie's farm, Missouri").

This shouldn't feel like a chore. It should be a pleasant journey through the past, which you can do in increments while you're bingeing a show, watching a game, or lounging around on a rainy afternoon. Basically, instead of messing with your phone, sort and catalog your photos.

You should still keep your phone close, because it's a great way to preserve these photos. Take a photo of your photo, or have it digitally scanned if you want super-high quality. And be sure to include pertinent information in the file title ("Grandma-Zeina-Ohio-1945.jpg"). You can even send it around to family or friends. Suddenly, a photo that's been hidden in a drawer for decades can instantly brighten their day.

Also, don't neglect the photo albums that have already been filled, or half filled, over the years. Or any antique photos you may have on the walls of your home or in storage. A close colleague of ours told us a story about finding a stack of classic black-and-white photos of people who appeared to be his ancestors when cleaning out his late parent's home. Since he never had the chance to ask

Plan of Attack

PHYSICAL MEMORIES

SORTING & ORGANIZING PRINTED PHOTOS

TIME: Two hours to gather them all up—this includes albums, antique framed photos, packed boxes, and those you still keep in the folder from when they were developed. When they're all in one place, take an hour to sort them into the piles we outlined earlier (Album-Worthy, Box-Worthy, Don't Care). The final step of identifying the photos should be broken into four one-hour shifts over the course of a month to avoid fatigue. This also includes photos hanging on your walls that might be a mystery to everyone but you. Add some extra time for the photos that require research from family or friends (because there's always an aunt or cousin who knows everything).

COST: $50–$75 for new photo albums, sticky notes, pens

SORTING & ORGANIZING DIGITAL PHOTOS

TIME: One hour to list out every place you have digital photos on your computers, mobile devices, and external backups (including thumb drives) and in the cloud. Depending on how many you have, start consolidating them into one centralized collection, which should be done in four one- to two-hour shifts over the course of a month. Back up the main collection on a hard drive and decide on a primary and secondary cloud service. If you're already using multiple cloud services, clean them out so you don't have different collections floating around.

MAINTENANCE: At least once a year, spend two hours sorting the photos you've taken since your last backup, prune your collection to the best, and add them to the main collection. Set a reminder so you don't forget!

COST: External drives: around $80 for 500GB SSD. Thumb drive: less than $10 for 32GB, around $30 for 128GB. For cloud pricing, see page 168 and decide what works best for you.

---

about them, he told us how sad he was to realize he would never know who these people were.

To prevent this outcome, these priceless images need relevant information on their backs too.

Providing even the most minor details will keep them alive for generations, and you can get all warm inside thinking of your grandkids holding the same photo many years from now and knowing exactly who's in the picture.

DELICIOUS HISTORY

Think of recipes as passwords to tastiness. Start by asking yourself the following: How do you keep track of recipes now? Are you an index card traditionalist? Do you have a stained and battle-worn notebook? Have you gone digital and created a document or do you rely on a recipe app? Regardless of the method, your goal is to preserve them so future generations don't lose their appetite. Literally.

Let's get the basics out of the way, especially for those who love to cook but don't have a recipe system in place that others would be able to understand. Think back to Levels 1 and 2, specifically the parts about

RECIPES AS MEMORIES

Cooking family recipes transports you back in time with smells, tastes, and memories. Abby's late beloved babysitter Lidia used to make the most incredible empanadas and shared the recipe before she died. Every time Abby misses her, she makes those empanadas and they bring back the warmest memories. Plus, she gets to share the deliciousness with her kids, which makes it a new memory for them.

organizing your passwords, the Home Operating System, and your Personal Medical Journal. All of those involved committing things you have in your head, or scattered all over the place, to one easy-to-understand system. How are recipes any different, apart from being an absolute joy to share and eat? The basic template for recipes is as simple as it gets:

- ❏ Name of recipe
- ❏ List of ingredients
- ❏ Preparation/cooking instructions
- ❏ Additional instructions and tips
- ❏ Optional: Sprinkle in family stories and history related to the recipe.

You can toy with the format, but this is the information that needs to be included. We're even going to take it one step further and include two of our very own favorite recipes to show you how it should look.

Abby's Mandel Bread (word for word as she has it)

INGREDIENTS

½ cup peanut oil

1 cup sugar

3 eggs

1 tablespoon vanilla extract

3 cups flour

1 teaspoon baking powder

½ teaspoon salt

1 cup chopped walnuts
(optional)

½ cup coconut (optional)

Strawberry jam
(or a jam of your preference)

Cinnamon, sugar, chocolate chips
(optional)

❶ In mixing bowl, mix ½ cup oil (I use peanut oil), 1 cup sugar, 3 eggs, and 1 tablespoon vanilla extract.

❷ Add 3 cups flour, 1 teaspoon baking powder, ½ teaspoon salt, 1 cup chopped walnuts, and, if you want, ½ cup coconut. I prefer walnuts but no coconut.

❸ Mix well and put in fridge for 30 minutes to 3 hours. Line a baking sheet with foil. Divide the dough into three equal parts.

❹ With two parts of the dough, make logs on the baking sheet. Using a spoon or your thumb, make an indentation down the length of each and fill with strawberry jam. I use a lot of jam (and sometimes include chocolate chips). Pinch the sides of the dough together to try to enclose the jam.

❺ Flatten out the third part of the dough, create two long pieces,

and cover as much of the jam that's still sticking out on each log (use water on your fingertips since it can get sticky). I sprinkle them with cinnamon and sugar (optional).

❻ Bake at 350°F for 40 minutes. Let cool. Cut the logs into slices and lay them on their side on a baking sheet, sprinkle with cinnamon and sugar and bake for 20 minutes, then turn them over and sprinkle with more cinnamon and sugar.

❼ Shut off the oven and leave them in until they get to the crispness you like.

ADDITIONAL INFO/TIPS

I like strawberry jam, but you can use whatever jam you prefer. I like them crispy, so leave them in for at least 5 minutes after turning off the heat—sometimes up to an hour. This recipe was adapted from my grandmother's and my mom's recipe, and from Melanie Nussdorf. The peanut oil was a mistake that my mom made one time, but it was so good that now it's the only way I make them.

Adam's Chili (Pulled directly from Adam's spreadsheet)

INGREDIENTS

8 strips thin-sliced bacon

3 large yellow onions

8 garlic cloves

Salt and pepper

2 lb. ground sirloin

4 teaspoons paprika

2 lb. cubed steak
(or other thin sandwich steak)

28 oz. can diced tomatoes

12 oz. can tomato paste

1 chopped poblano
(or other medium-hot) pepper

½ chopped serrano
(or other hot-hot) pepper

6 teaspoons ancho chili powder

6 teaspoons chipotle chili powder

¾ teaspoon red cayenne pepper

4 teaspoons oregano

4 teaspoons cumin

2 bottles of beer (12 oz. each)

2 Hershey chocolate bars
(1.5 oz. each)

30 oz. can small red beans
(or pinto beans)

1 Cook the bacon in a pan until crispy. Reserve the grease in the pan. Set aside the bacon on paper towels for later.

2 Sauté chopped onions and garlic in bacon grease until translucent and a little soft. Season with salt and pepper. Place in the pot.

3 Brown ground sirloin in leftover grease from onions/garlic. Season with 2 teaspoons of paprika. Remove while medium rare. Place in pot.

4 Brown cubed steak in 1 tablespoon of leftover grease from sirloin (you will probably need to drain most). Season with the remaining 2 teaspoons of paprika. Remove while rare. Slice into small bits. Place in pot.

5 Add diced tomatoes with tomato paste, chopped peppers, chili powders, cayenne pepper, oregano, cumin, and 1 bottle of beer to the pot.

6 Bring to a slow boil and then simmer for at least 2 hours.

7 Add chocolate, bacon, and the other bottle of beer and simmer for 30 minutes.

8 Add beans and simmer for 15 minutes.

9 Serve with sour cream, shredded cheese, cornbread, rice, raw onions—whatever.

WARNING!

Be careful with the serrano and cayenne pepper—if you wipe your eyes after handling, you'll be really sorry.

- **You can substitute any thin, sandwich-y kind of steak for cubed steak if you can't find it.**

- **You may want to add only half of the cayenne powder initially, then taste the chili after a couple of hours—it gets spicier the longer it cooks.**

- **You might not need to add all the beer. If the chili looks wet enough, just drink the beer instead.**

We'd love for you to make Abby's bread and Adam's chili and tell us what you think. We also want you to send your family favorites to **us@incasethebook.com** so we can try them out. And we will!

Greetings, Cards

There's nothing like a classic tin box full of index cards on a kitchen counter. The cards themselves can be considered heirlooms, but what if everyone in the family wants them? One former Everplans team member and her sister did her family the greatest kindness by organizing, transcribing, and scanning all their grandmother's index cards into a book, *Ruth Whitman: A Life in Recipes*, making sure to preserve as much of the original handwriting as possible. She gave everyone in the family a copy, and the reaction was incredible, ranging from "You captured our past so beautifully" to "You stirred up so many family traditions and memories!"

If making a book is too intense a project, you can take photos of the cards and share them in a digital "Family Recipe" folder so others can access them. Although we love the history of handwritten recipes, there's always a worry that they could go missing or be accidentally ruined (spills happen). Same goes for recipes you may have cut out of a magazine, printed from a site, or ripped from the pages of a book.

Delectable Digital Delights

If you want to take your family heirloom recipes to new digital heights, settle on a system that makes it easy to add and update recipes, access them at a moment's notice—especially if you need to gather ingredients at the store or you're at a family member's house over the holidays—and share them with others so they can enjoy them too.

If you want an app to do the heavy lifting, check out Paprika, BigOven, and Cookpad (among the slew of recipe apps available). Although these can be handy, you should still heed the advice we offered about digital photos. Technology's forever changing, and there's always a risk when putting all your eggs in one virtual basket. A software program you love today

RECIPES

CULINARY CULLING

TIME: One-day time limit to round up all your recipes into a centralized place. To keep it from becoming an encyclopedia, take three one-hour shifts and focus only on personal recipes, ones handed down from parents and grandparents, and family favorites until you have the best of the best.

DIGITAL: If you're creating a digital cookbook in a Word document or Google Docs, start plugging away using the format we suggest (or one you're comfortable using) until your pile is empty. Add new recipes at regular intervals or as they begin to stack up.

PHYSICAL: A bunch of online services allow you to self-publish your own family cookbook. Do a search to find a reasonably priced option that walks you through the process regarding format and design. This is a great option for a family heirloom cookbook, but not the best solution for one you'll be using, updating, and sharing on a regular basis.

APP: Almost all recipe apps have ways to import so you don't have to type them all in, but you may have to do some editing so they're easier to decipher.

COST: A physical book varies, depending on the service you choose, ranging from $30 all the way into the hundreds. You can do it on the cheap if you create your own, but it'll take longer. Most apps are a one-time cost to download (around $5–$30) or free with in-app subscription options.

could be obsolete tomorrow, forcing you to redo all your hard work.

When it comes to preserving something as important as family recipes, we suggest you choose a method that makes them always accessible regardless of what the future may hold. When Adam stores or creates a recipe, he's all about business. He puts all the relevant text (ingredients/instructions) into a Google Doc or spreadsheet in his Drive recipes folder. This allows him to "quickly cut out all the unnecessary storytelling that every food blog seems to have in the middle of a recipe." Since Google offers really good search capabilities, he doesn't need them to be in an app or database.

Abby uses a similar method so her recipes are always at the ready (she saves all recipes in Gmail in a Recipe subfolder). She currently sticks to the basics when organizing her recipes, but always tells her kids the stories behind each scrumptious creation. Both of these methods allow for practicality, sentimentality, or both.

Even if you want to print out all your recipes and keep them in a binder, at least your family will know they can always make new copies, so no one ever goes hungry.

PERSONAL ANTIQUING

You already understand the type of valuable or meaningful assets that should go in your Will or be clearly assigned to an heir. There are others, perhaps less financially valuable but nevertheless meaningful, that might get overlooked or end up in the wrong hands if you don't tell the story behind them. It could be a set of cutlery you bought on your honeymoon in Italy, or a classic table clock that was passed down from your grandparents to your parents. If it has a story behind it that would resonate with anyone in your family, tell it!

Stories of people finding notes left attached to personal items give us the happy chills. It's a beautiful way to express love and say goodbye, but it doesn't have to be a surprise. Cleaning out a late parent's home while grief-stricken could lead to discarding items that have a story to tell. The same goes for a family member swooping in and taking everything, especially if they think those items have value. A person who

works closely with Everplans told us how an in-law looted all the classic furniture from a deceased parent's house before anyone had a chance to claim anything. Although this was many years ago, and she's not even sure she wanted any of it, it's still a minor point of contention among the family.

All it takes to guarantee this doesn't happen is a prominently placed note somewhere in your home, or included in a Letter of Last Instructions, saying something like this: "There are personal notes attached to many items in the house. Be sure to check the back and bottom of each before you discard anything you might not want."

There is no template for what to include on these notes. You can offer the personal history of the item ("Bart, this letter opener was on my desk from my first day on the job until my last. Love, Dad"), a brief cute thought ("Dina, your father bought me this vase on our tenth anniversary, and it always craved fresh flowers"), or simple ("Yoko, I wanted you to have this"). It doesn't have to be much, but it's best to include the name of the person who should get it to prevent disagreements about where it should go. If Sarah wants the Thanksgiving serving bowl, but there's a note with Casey's name, it's pretty clear to everyone in the family who should get it.

HEIRLOOMS

TIME: Three 1-hour shifts over the course of a month to make a list (or spreadsheet) of all the heirlooms you would want others to have (include names next to the items). This list serves a dual purpose because it can be used by your family as an inventory and let them know who's getting what. Once the list is final, grab some Post-Its, or index cards and tape, and start tagging the back or underside of each thing with personal notes.

■ ■ ■

TELLING THE STORY OF YOUR LIFE

◼ ◼ ◼

N ow that we've gotten the physical stuff out of the way, it's time to tell people who you really are. Think of all the personal lessons, tips, and knowledge you'd like to leave behind, whether it's information about your family history, things you've loved about life, or lessons you want to pass on to future generations. Technically, this is called an Ethical Will, but we don't like that name because it sounds like a typical Will with high moral principles. It needs to be livelier than that. Picture yourself on an exciting game show where there are no wrong answers.

We're about to start a lightning round of questions. However you choose to capture these thoughts—handwritten journal, Word document, notes app—it's vital that someone knows where you keep your answers so they can be shared with others.

ROUND 1: Your Personal History

These are easy for you but might stump your kids because they never asked. This stuff might seem obvious, but think about it this way: How many of these questions do you wish you could have asked someone who's no longer alive?

For example, do you know where your grandparents were born? How about the song your parents chose for the first dance at their wedding? Or where they went on their honeymoon?

- ❏ Where were you born?
- ❏ What traits did you inherit from your parents?
- ❏ What was your family like when you were growing up?
- ❏ What pets did you have throughout your life?
- ❏ What was the first car you drove or owned?
- ❏ For military veterans, what do you want to share about your service?

IF MARRIED:

- ❏ How did you meet your spouse?
- ❏ How did the proposal go down?
- ❏ What were the most memorable moments from your wedding?
- ❏ Any family-friendly details to share about the honeymoon?

IF DIVORCED:

- ❏ Briefly explain why you got divorced (or go into detail if you feel compelled to do so).
- ❏ What lessons did divorce teach you?

ROUND 2: Your Favorite Things

You shouldn't have to think too long about the things you like most. You're not trying to impress your peers; you're just letting the world know what inspired, impressed, entertained, enlightened, or made you happy. The categories below are just a guide. Feel free to add (or subtract) as many as you like. If you make this a digital document, you can include links and other forms of media to make it even more lively. Name your favorite . . .

- ❏ Place in the world
- ❏ Vacation spot
- ❏ Song or album
- ❏ Book
- ❏ Movie
- ❏ TV show
- ❏ Video game
- ❏ Board game
- ❏ Sports team
- ❏ Musician
- ❏ Actor/actress
- ❏ Athlete
- ❏ Writer
- ❏ Artist
- ❏ Hobby
- ❏ Meal
- ❏ Dessert
- ❏ Beverage
- ❏ Quote or saying

ROUND 3: Your Experiences

Imagine you're being interviewed by a well-regarded reporter on a popular news show about how you spent your life. Let each answer flow naturally, and trust the first thing that pops into your head. You don't have to force a reply for ones that don't apply to your life, and each needn't be a cathartic breakthrough. It just needs to be from the heart.

- ❏ What are your fondest memories?
- ❏ Which events had the greatest effect on your life?
- ❏ What are you most proud of?
- ❏ What are you most grateful for?
- ❏ What were the happiest moments of your life?
- ❏ What are your favorite family holiday traditions?
- ❏ What was the best gift you ever received as a child?
- ❏ Who were the people who most influenced you?
- ❏ What's your biggest regret?
- ❏ What is the hardest decision you ever made?
- ❏ What was the most difficult time in your life?
- ❏ When things got tough, where did you find comfort?
- ❏ How do you define happiness and success?

- ❏ What significant historical events did you live through, and how'd you feel when they happened?
- ❏ From whom would you like to ask forgiveness?
- ❏ Whom would you like to forgive?

This started general and then got heavy toward the end, but it's a good progression to consider. It may help remind you of all those innocuous moments in life that ended up having a lasting effect. And who knows, maybe whoever reads it might see how a job in high school or a brief encounter with a person you knew for only a short period of time, for better or worse, changed the course of your life.

HOW THIS HELPS AFTER YOU'RE GONE
(Documenting You)

- ■ The people closest to you will know your history, favorite things, life experiences, beliefs, and hopes for the future.

- ■ The details of your family tree will be accessible to anyone who wants to know about your heritage.

GENEALOGY & FAMILY HISTORY

Way back in the contacts section (see page 61), we told you there'd be a special place for your family history. You have arrived at your destination. Keep your family tree alive and healthy by sharing details and brief stories. Here's where you start planting the seeds.

PEOPLE TO INCLUDE: Maternal grandmother, maternal grandfather, paternal grandmother, paternal grandfather, mother, father, siblings, children, grandchildren, aunts, uncles, cousins, nieces, nephews, great-grandparents, friends who are practically family

FOR EACH PERSON INCLUDE THE FOLLOWING INFO:

- Name (include nicknames too)

- Birthday

- Birth location (city, state, and hospital for immediate family)

- My favorite story about this person

- My favorite memories of this person

- The most important thing I learned from this person

- Other thoughts I'd like to share about them

DITTO FOR YOUR SPOUSE: If you're married, have your spouse follow the same template for your in-laws.

It's fine to write more about the family members who had the biggest influence on your life, be it positive or negative. Not all of life's stories are happy, and what you include is up to you. Be honest and sincere, since this can possibly affect future generations. If you say Uncle Bo was a sleazeball because you didn't like him, it might not sit well with his kids. Unless they agree—then it might bring you all together. Family is funny that way.

IT'S IN YOUR DNA: If you want to expand the scope beyond your own family knowledge base, sign up for a site like Ancestry.com, FamilySearch, MyHeritage, or 23andMe, which can reveal relatives you didn't know you had. Once you create an account and add family information, it connects the dots with other accounts, linking you to possible relatives and ancestors. Most of these sites have become known for their DNA testing kits, which means you could find out you have a sibling you never knew about. (That actually happened to one of our Everplans team members. Long story short: They get along great!)

TIME FOR A STORY: Organizations like StoryCorps, the Shoah Foundation, and Geni (which is owned by MyHeritage) offer the ability to share stories and video interviews that would otherwise be lost to time.

GOING HIGH-TECH: If you want to take your family tree to the next level, and you have the technical know-how, look into creating a Genealogical Data Communication (GEDCOM) file. This is a plain-text document with metadata about your family, which you can upload to most reputable family tree sites to keep everything current and comprehensive.

If you created a family tree on one of the major services and wanted to move it to another without redoing any of the work, or if you want to cancel your membership and still have the data for future use, you can download a GEDCOM file. Then when you settle on a new service, simply reupload the file to the site of your choosing and it'll still be current and comprehensive.

Plan of Attack

FAMILY TREE

MAPPING IT OUT

TIME: Create a digital document using the template we provided on the opposite page and devote thirty minutes to writing down the basics based on what you know offhand, since much of this will require additional research. After you have the list compiled, spend fifteen minutes filling in the emotional stuff about this person. Next, call in some backup: Email or text family members and let them know you're compiling a definitive family tree and need them to fill in some blanks. Send them the questions; the technically savvy can even share the document so people can provide additional details themselves. You might find that someone in your family already did this, and you can join forces to make it even more comprehensive.

COST: If you want to fill in as many blanks as possible and discover people you never would have on your own, you can pay for a legacy site membership. These can be pricey, costing more than $100 a year—you can have other family members chip in to lessen the financial load, or get what you need and unsubscribe—but part of the fun is never knowing when you'll be connected to another relative. To take it to the DNA level, you can buy a standard test for $60–$150, or wait until they're on sale and grab a bunch for the whole family.

ROUND 4: Your Academic & Professional Life

An education or a career often defines how we spend our lives. The more you start reflecting on your academic and work history, the more you might be able to help future generations make the right decisions or avoid the wrong ones. Rather than dig too deep, focus on these aspects:

❏ Names of the schools you attended and the years

❏ Elementary | middle school | high school | college | postgrad

❏ Your major in college (and if you didn't go to college, why?)

❏ Extracurricular activities (band, sports, drama . . .)

❏ The best lesson you learned in school

❏ The best teacher you ever had

❏ Your general thoughts about education and higher learning

❏ The best job you ever had

❏ The worst job you ever had

❏ The reason you chose your profession/career

❏ Your best work advice

❏ If you had to do it over again, what would you do differently or never change?

And don't forget: Work is work. You don't have to clock in at an office or receive a regular check for your work history to be valid. Raising kids, helping care for a person with special needs, keeping a home, fostering pets, donating time or services to charity, and being on a town committee all qualify. Or maybe your high-powered career was far less fulfilling than your volunteer work? These are important things to note.

For those who did punch a clock, it's nice to look back and see if you identify any patterns or trends. Maybe the jobs you thought would be terrible turned out great, and those you thought would be dream jobs turned out to be nightmares.

ROUND 5: Your Religious & Political Beliefs and Your Charities & Causes

There's an old rule about the two topics being off-limits in mixed company (and at holidays!): religion and politics. These are lightning rods for disagreements, especially when alcohol is involved.

Discussing your faith, or lack of it, should be an exciting prospect, especially if it's very important to you, as it is for millions of people. This round gives you the chance to express your feelings on these two issues, which can comfort those closest to you and educate people who may not have shared your views. We threw in charities and causes to end on a hopeful note, since we're aware the first two topics can get quite heated. Political differences sort of melt away when you think about helping the less fortunate. Or they should.

❏ Your most fundamental beliefs

❏ Your thoughts on religion and faith

❏ Your most valued traditions

❏ Your political views can be characterized as . . .

❏ The reasons you have your political views

❏ The charities and causes that have meant the most to you

These questions can run deep, so here's a tip: Discuss only *your* religious and political beliefs. It's easy to make this about other people and what you would want them to believe, but this isn't the time or place to try to convert family and friends or dissuade them from their views. If you consider this a final opportunity to get them on your side, or at least better understand your beliefs, lower the volume and be introspective and thoughtful. If you find yourself getting upset and angrily scribbling out a rant more suitable for Facebook or Twitter, stop and think: Will this make them want to give me a hug or storm out of the room and never speak to me again? If they're reading it after you're gone, any negative sentiments might be how they remember you, so try to go easy.

While we're here, let's briefly address the elephant (and donkey) in the room: In the same way that generations have always disagreed on music and clothes, they've also disagreed on politics. The twenty-four-hour news cycle and social media have made it more overwhelming than ever, so try to put aside your beliefs and wonder: Would you let a politician you've never met come between the relationship you have with your mom or dad if they were gravely ill in the hospital?

FINAL ROUND: Your Hopes for the Future

This is the part where you get to try to steer the people you love in the right direction. If you had the chance to communicate what you want future generations to know, what would you say?

❑ These are the values I'd like to pass on.

❑ Here are my wishes for my children (or children in general if you never had any).

❑ Here are my wishes for my grandchildren.

❑ Here are my wishes for my spouse or partner.

❑ This is a mistake I made that I hope you can avoid.

❑ This is an experience I hope you get the opportunity to have.

❑ When you encounter hardship, here's the one thing I hope you remember.

You never know what advice will connect with future generations, but if the cycle of history has taught us anything, it's that they'll face basically the same struggles and triumphs you did. The best you can do is offer your wisdom and hope it comes in handy.

See how an Ethical Will isn't nearly as boring as it sounds? Maybe it just needs a new name. (OK, Spill Your Life! it is.)

Plan of Attack

ETHICAL WILL

SPILL YOUR LIFE!

TIME: One hour for a quick first pass at all the questions we presented here. Once you've completed it, add a reminder to your calendar in a week's time to reread your responses. Block out one to two hours to really dive in and get a final draft, then set a reminder for a month (these increments allow you to look at it with fresh eyes). Reread it until you're satisfied it's good to go, then store it with your other important documents, 'cause you're finished for now.

DOWNLOAD A COPY: We created a pdf worksheet you can fill out on your computer or print out so you can do it by hand. Get it here: incasethebook.com/spill-your-life.

■ ■ ■

IT'S IN THE MAIL
LEGACY LETTERS

■ ■ ■

Our ultimate goal, and it's a grand one, is to help you understand and identify the totality of your life. We know all the information we presented can be overwhelming, but this is where you get to be yourself without any laws, statutes, or other complicated aspects getting in the way. Unfortunately, not having rules doesn't always make things easier.

There's nothing more intimidating than a blank piece of paper. How can you write notes or letters meant for your friends and family after you're gone? Where do you start? What do you write? Will this even get to the right person?

Fear not! Your legacy is safe as long as you take your time, stay on track, and follow these steps.

BLURBS TO FRIENDS, ACQUAINTANCES & ASSOCIATES

Before we work our way up to the super-important letters, this is a way to affect many lives with minimal effort. It involves the contacts we helped you sort back in Level 1 (see page 59).

Every one of those people played some part in your life, so what better way to show your appreciation than by writing the one thing you liked the most about them? This can go in the Description or Notes field in the actual contact and you can instruct whoever will have access to your phone (Digital Executor, maybe?) to share these morsels of kindness either directly with the person or in a public forum. On the following page are examples of the types of things you could say.

Harris's superpower is making you feel like everything will be all right, even when you know it might not.

I always feel energized after seeing Warren, because his enthusiasm is infectious.

If I could make only one phone call in a crisis, it'd be to Tolu, because I know she'll come running from wherever she is to help out.

If I could dance as well as Yaniv, I don't think I'd ever stop.

This world would be 100 percent more honorable if everyone had the same spirit as Mary Beth.

It's perfectly cool to hand out compliments like candy, because it makes everyone feel good. You feel good being able to share something thoughtful about a person, and they feel good knowing they were recognized for something positive. It can be friends, former coworkers, professionals, your dry cleaner ("In thirty years Ben never lost one item of clothes!"), or anyone who had the slightest positive effect on you.

This is one of the reasons we can't wait for you to get your contacts sorted, because it's fun being nice. If you're not the warm, fuzzy type, all the better. It'll come as a shock to people who thought you didn't have it in you.

As for any negative blurbs, keep those to yourself. As Thumper said in *Bambi*, "If you can't say something nice, don't say nothing at all."

Public Notice

Is there anything you've always wanted to share with the world? Something you'd want posted on Facebook or printed out and put on a community or church bulletin board? Now's your chance to start preparing what you'd want to say so it can actually happen.

This isn't the same as writing your own obituary (coming up on page 213)—it's an informal way to share your thoughts, experiences, special stories, or anything you have in your soul that you want other

HOW THIS HELPS AFTER YOU'RE GONE
(Writing letters)

- You're providing a small bit of joy to any person who added assistance or joy to your life.

- The people you truly care about the most will know exactly how much you loved them.

people to know. It shouldn't be written to one specific person—it *should* be something you'd be willing to share with people who have never met you before. For this reason, keep it general and think about what you'd want to read if another person on your timeline or in your community posted something.

Do you like seeing inspirational and uplifting posts or ones that are too heavy or dark for the medium of social media? Many people skip right past those in search of the positive ones, which fill their heart with emotion and makes them want to spread the word to others in their network.

Don't feel pressured to make it a coherent story. Social media breaks the storytelling format and allows you to do whatever you want. It could be a list of lessons you learned that stuck with you your entire life (perhaps something from the "Spill Your Life!" section we just covered), a link to a song that always made you smile, a photo that provided inspiration, or a famous quote that gave you hope. Perhaps there's a saying or mantra you always repeat to close friends and family. When you're expressing your genuine emotions, there are no rules.

When the time comes for it to be posted, make sure your Digital Executor, or whoever you leave in charge of your accounts, knows where to find it, post it, and pin it to the top.

LETTERS TO THE IMPORTANT PEOPLE IN YOUR LIFE

We said there aren't any rules when it involves expressing yourself, but we never said anything about guidelines. (This is what lawyers call a loophole.)

Writing the perfect letters to your kids, grandkids, best friends, and people who had the biggest effect on your life could be more paralyzing than all the legal documents combined.

How do you encapsulate all your feelings into a page or two? We put together some guidelines to help you get focused and then offer an example to get you in the mood to put pen to paper, or fingers to keyboard if your handwriting is barely legible.

Make it brief: This is a letter, not a manifesto, so it shouldn't be too long. You should be able to slip it into an envelope that doesn't require extra postage. If you'd like to include more for a very special person, then consider buying a journal to capture as many thoughts as you desire.

Be yourself: A good creative writing class will instruct you to write the way you speak. Most people are personable in conversation, but when they write, it's about as warm as a letter from the IRS. The words on the page become too formal, which can strip away all the personality. Do you use contractions in real life? Do you say, "She is a nice person" or "She's a nice person"? "I will not do that" or "I won't do that"? Loosen up and make it so the person reading it can hear and feel your voice in their head.

Stay focused: It's easy to go off on tangents since life is often one big crazy detour after another. But if you

had to summarize your feelings in 500 words, what would you say? You can always write the letter long and cut it down. This book was almost double the length it was supposed to be before our immensely patient editor, John, cut it down, which is why you're not holding something as big as a phone book right now.

Be careful about going negative: If you're a human who has lived at all, you've probably felt slighted or poorly treated at some point. Although this is terrible, and many people can surely relate, think twice before sharing something negative. Because this is likely how you'll be remembered. If you lash out and the letter is shared (which it most certainly will be), you're not the one who will feel the repercussions— your family and friends will have to manage the backlash. Don't forget Thumper's message! We can all learn a lot from that adorable bunny with terrible grammar.

The Letter-Worthy

There are a lot of people in your life, and you don't want to accidentally exclude anyone important. Imagine how terrible someone you cared about would feel if everyone got a letter but them. A list ensures that you leave nothing to chance.

(continued on page 195)

A LETTER TO GET YOU STARTED

Dear Sydney,

The first time I held you after you were born, I never wanted to put you down. I looked into your sleepy eyes and wanted you to have the best life possible. One where you were happy, fulfilled, and had a sense of purpose that made you want to ferociously attack each day. All of those things came true, because you are perfect. Your kindness, ambition, and desire to always make things better in the world have been an inspiration to me. Oh, and you're funny too. Sometimes. (Not when you made fun of my dancing. Everyone knows I'm a great dancer.)

You gave me so many sweet memories that always picked me up when I was feeling down. Whether it was the (disastrous) breakfast in bed after I had foot surgery and couldn't walk for a few days, the time you put too much soap in the dishwasher (at least it got our kitchen floor clean too), or how you spent all your spare time with Grandma when she was sick, and kept her spirits up until the end.

I don't know if I said I love you enough or if I said it too much. All I know is I could never say it enough, because I love you more than anything in the world. You've made my life complete, and I'm thankful for every moment I had with you. OK, maybe not every moment. That time you dyed your hair greenish pink was quite startling. But that was you being you, and I love you for that too.

I don't want you to spend too much time being sad now that I'm no longer around. Find the happy memories and think of those. Like of me dancing.

I LOVE YOU!

Love,
Dad

Side Mission:
END-OF-LIFE
MEDICAL DIRECTIVES

As we near the end of our journey, it's time to tackle a heavy subject that's never easy to face, especially if it involves a person you love: creating medical directives for when the end is nigh. There's a point in many people's lives when a body simply becomes uncooperative and treatment methods in hopes of a recovery become extremely limited. To prepare for these eventualities, a POLST and DNR can help provide the softest landing possible.

THE DNR:
DO NOT RESUSCITATE
ORDER

WHAT IT IS: You fill out a Do Not Resuscitate (DNR) with your doctor when you *don't want* cardiopulmonary resuscitation (CPR) or advanced cardiac life support (ACLS) if your heart or breathing stops.

WHAT IT DOES: If you have a DNR, doctors, emergency medical service responders, and other health professionals are *legally obligated* to respect your medical decisions

and may not attempt CPR, ACLS, or other lifesaving techniques. A woman in New Mexico even sued when her DNR wasn't honored and she was resuscitated.

WHO NEEDS IT: People with terminal illnesses or serious medical ailments with no chance of recovery and for whom CPR might do more harm than good.

HOW YOU GET IT: A DNR must be completed with a doctor, who'll provide you with your state's forms and countersign it with you. Your doctor can also help you get an official DNR bracelet to alert emergency medical responders and other health professionals.

THE DIFFERENCE BETWEEN A DNR AND A LIVING WILL: A Living Will offers important guidance to your Health Care Proxy and doctors, whereas a DNR is a very specific legal document that must be honored. You can have a DNR and still receive medical treatment, medicine, procedures, and surgery. But when your heart or breathing stops, the DNR goes into effect.

DON'T GO FAR WITHOUT YOUR DNR: Keep the form with you when receiving medical treatments, and display it prominently in your home so emergency medical responders know not to attempt resuscitation. You'll want to give a copy to your Health Care Proxy, doctor, and any medical specialists or health professionals providing you care.

IT'S ALWAYS YOUR CALL: If you want every possible treatment regardless of your condition, then don't fill out a DNR. The default for doctors is to never give up; if there's no DNR, you will continue to receive treatment regardless of the cost or outcome.

ADDITIONAL OPTIONS: You can also include a Do Not Hospitalize (DNH) component if you still want treatment but don't want it to happen in a hospital. Another option could be including a Do Not Intubate (DNI), which means you don't want a breathing tube (see page 124). You should speak with your doctor or medical professional about including this with your POLST or DNR so there's no confusion about the treatments you *do* or *do not* want.

THE POLST: PHYSICIAN ORDERS FOR LIFE-SUSTAINING TREATMENT

WHAT IT IS: A POLST form is a legal document for people with an advanced progressive or terminal illness. It specifies the type of care you'd like in an emergency medical situation. A more detailed and specific DNR, it can conform to the needs of the medical condition you're managing.

WHAT IT DOES: In an emergency situation, any procedures that are *legally required* of emergency personnel will be overridden by your personal decisions indicated on your POLST.

WHO NEEDS IT: This is typically for people with less than six months to live but can also be made available for people with progressive conditions.

THE NAME OF THIS DOCUMENT IS ALL OVER THE PLACE: Unlike a DNR or Advance Directive, this document has many different names, depending on where you live, even though they're all conceptually the same. Here are some of them:

- MOST (Medical Orders for Scope of Treatment)
- MOLST (Medical Orders for Life-Sustaining Treatment)
- POST (Physician Orders for Scope of Treatment)
- TPOPP (Transportable Physician Orders for Patient Preferences)

It can be quite confusing, and looks like alphabet soup, but isn't that the way with all things medical? HIPAA doesn't exactly roll off the tongue either. Concern yourself only with the one in your state (if it's available).

HOW YOU GET IT: Like a DNR, this form is filled out with a medical professional (physician, nurse, hospice worker) and must be signed by a physician, nurse practitioner, or physician assistant. Once it's signed, all medical providers must honor the instructions no matter where you are, whether it's at a hospital, care facility, or your own home.

WHERE YOU KEEP IT: Everywhere! Just like with your DNR and Advance Directive, the people responsible for your care need to know it exists for it to be honored. As a bonus, POLST

forms are often printed on brightly colored paper so that they're easy to see and find.

DEATH-PROOF: You may have noticed this book has been devoid of dealing with the actual process of death, and we aim to keep it that way. If you're interested in learning about everything from coping with a terminal diagnosis to navigating the health care system to making the most out of one's remaining days, we suggest you check out *A Beginner's Guide to the End: Practical Advice for Living Life and Facing Death* by BJ Miller and Shoshana Berger. It makes an incredibly heavy topic practical, approachable, and at times even funny.

(continued from page 190)

Personalize the Message

This isn't a form letter being sent to everyone in a company. Each person will require a different message to help ease the grief after you're gone. Let the relationship you had with that person be your guide. If you always joked with them, why start being overly serious now? They'll probably think it was written by someone else.

Hands, Not Fingers

This is our clever way of saying handwritten letters carry more weight than typed documents. It's basic etiquette, the same way handwritten thank-you notes after a big event—wedding, baby shower, job interview—are still held in high regard. This is the final thank-you note you'll ever write, and you want it to be a memorable one.

When Handwriting Isn't an Option

There are people who, through no fault of their own, don't have the ability to write by hand. If you can type it, print it out, and sign it, great. We just don't suggest sending it as a digital document, because this should be a keepsake and not another digital file cluttering up a computer desktop.

Plan of Attack

WRITING BLURBS & LETTERS

BLURBS FOR YOUR CONTACTS

TIME: If you piggyback on the Level 1 task of organizing contacts, this won't add much time at all. Remember: one kind or thoughtful sentence that you'd like that person to know to brighten their day in the Notes or Description field of each contact.

LETTERS TO YOUR FAMILY & CLOSE FRIENDS

TIME: Thirty minutes to identify the people you think should get a letter. The writing doesn't require a time limit, but here's the process: Create a digital document and begin typing out thoughts under each name about what you want to include. From there, take out a pen and some paper and start writing. We estimate about ninety minutes per letter. When you're finished, put each in an individual envelope with the person's name, then all of them in a large envelope and include it with your other important documents.

Tell Someone About It

You probably don't want to share these letters with anyone while you're still alive. Keep them with your other important papers, and leave instructions with a person you trust so they get into the right hands. You can address them and have them dropped in the mail, but that runs the risk of them getting lost. To ensure they get to the right people, it's best if they go from human to human. Everplans has a "Letters to Loved Ones" section where you can provide details about the letters you've written with instructions on how you want them to be delivered.

READY FOR YOUR CLOSE-UP:
Videos for Loved Ones

If the camera loves you, and we're sure it does, you can leave behind a video. The result is limited only to what you want to say and how you want to say it.

If you're all about being off-the-cuff and don't concern yourself with rehearsals or having a polished final video, hit Record on your phone and go at it.

If you need more than one take—or, like in our case, dozens of takes—write out notes for what you want to cover to keep it tight and meaningful. Treat each video or audio recording like a wedding toast. People might tune it out if it rambles on too long,

and reading directly from a page might sound too rehearsed, or worse, come across like you've been taken prisoner.

Keep your notes handy for structure—as well as any props like photos you want to hold up or other items to illustrate a point—and be yourself. The purpose of this video is to provide comfort. If you find yourself getting too emotional and worry that the video may upset the person you're trying to help with their grief, take a break and come back in an hour when your thoughts are more settled.

Here's an example of how your outline could shape up—simply substitute the actual things you'd want to share for our suggested topics:

VIDEO NOTES FOR [SON]
Intro: Hi, [Name or Nickname], I wanted you to know how [much I love you/much you mean to me/ you've always been my world].

Story 1: Best first memory of him

Story 2: Something funny or endearing he did while growing up

Story 3: How proud you are of his accomplishments

Winding It Down: Final story illustrating your love and/or any lessons or advice you'd like to impart

Final Farewell: Try to hold it together and end with a message like, "You won't have to miss me, because I'll always be with you."

Script Tip

Don't overexplain why you're making the video. This isn't a spy movie where the videos often start with something like, "If you're watching this video, it means I'm dead . . ." You can do that if it fits your sense of humor, but assume the person is well aware that this is your way of saying goodbye in the best possible way.

Where to Put It

Once you're happy with the video, you'll want to be certain it gets to the right people, just like everything else you'll share with them that we've covered in this book. Unlike a letter, you can't put a video in an envelope and hand it to the person. Here are three solutions, assuming you're downloading (or uploading) it from your phone and storing it elsewhere:

A Desktop Folder: Create an easy-to-find folder on your desktop ("Videos from Me to the Family"), change the name of each video file to the name of the person who should receive it ("Joe-from-Mom.mp4"), and include instructions with the rest of your Digital Estate Plan details ("Make sure each video gets to the right place").

In the Cloud: Include the videos among the photos, documents, and other digital assets you share with your family or Digital Executor. It's just like having them on your desktop, only easier to share.

On YouTube: If you don't mind putting the videos on YouTube, you can upload them and leave instructions with direct links to be shared after you're gone. If you're high-tech, you can go into your settings and set them as private so only the people you want to see them can.

If you decide to leave the videos on your phone, mention their existence as part of your Digital Estate Plan or Letter of Instructions so they aren't ignored or accidentally deleted. Example: "I recorded a bunch of videos on my phone for everyone. Please send them to the right people."

Whatever method you choose, it doesn't have to be perfect. It just needs to be something your loved ones treasure for the rest of their lives. But, no pressure. You got this.

IT'S (REALLY) YOUR FUNERAL

■ ■ ■

Plan now, rest later. It's time for the grand finale. This last super-sized section sends you off into the sunset with all you need to know about funerals. From disposition to planning, if you're up for it, all the way to writing your own obituary, we make sure the last party you'll ever attend is one for the ages.

THE MOST IMPORTANT FUNERAL DECISION YOU'LL MAKE

What do you want done with your body? You have three options: burial, cremation, or donation. Each one takes you down a different path. To avoid confusion, you need to tell someone your ultimate preference. Even if you don't care what's done with your body, you need to make that clear so your family knows the decision will fall to them.

What needs to be done if you opt for . . .
Burial: You need a burial plot or a spot in a mausoleum at a cemetery.

Cremation: You can decide what you want done with the cremated remains, including burial, scattering, or giving them to friends and family members to be stored in an urn or other suitable container.

Donating your body to science: Your family needs to know the arrangements you made with the organization or institution of your choice. There's a chance the place you choose won't be accepting donations at the time of your passing. To be safe, you should also include one of the other options listed here as a backup plan.

It's not the method: A longtime funeral industry expert put it

HOW THIS HELPS AFTER YOU'RE GONE
(Funeral Planning)

When you make your own funeral arrangements, or let your family know what you want, you're doing the following things:

❶ Taking some of the logistical stress off your family. It's an emotional time, and there are many important (and expensive) decisions to make, so any guidance you offer will be reassuring and greatly appreciated.

❷ Alleviating the financial burden. Although you might not be able to prepay for the entire funeral, you *can* save your family from paying for things you don't want (for example, a less expensive casket or cremation instead of burial).

❸ Ensuring you get the funeral you want. It's common for each family member to have different ideas about what you would have wanted, and grief can easily manifest into bickering, so do everything you can to make it as peaceful as possible for those wishing you were still around.

❹ Don't feel you have to plan it to the last detail. Although some people are perfectly fine planning their own funeral, it's understandable if you find it too difficult. But even the most basic suggestions—like the size of the funeral, or where you'd like donations to go in lieu of flowers—can save your family a lot of unnecessary heartache and hassle.

perfectly when he told us, "A funeral isn't just about what you're doing with the body; it's about the person's life." Just because someone doesn't want to go in the ground doesn't mean they don't want their life celebrated with a service or some other form of memorial. Cremation or burial is just a means of disposition—the important thing is how your family and friends get to say goodbye.

FIVE STEPS TO PLANNING A TRADITIONAL FUNERAL AND BURIAL

This option requires the most time, effort, and money so everything goes according to plan. If you've made arrangements—perhaps you already own a plot—does your family know? Even if you've never

THE FUNERAL BU$INE$$

A standard funeral and burial can cost around $7,000–$10,000 but can easily be much more, depending on the location and products chosen. Like a wedding, you could end up spending double or triple what you thought you would.

Save all receipts for funeral-related purchases. These expenses may be deductible on estate tax returns.

considered planning, these five steps are what you need to know if you want to make it happen.

Step 1:

Find a funeral home you want to use and check it out. Here are some factors to consider before making your decision.

Whether it's a funeral home you already know well: If there's a funeral home in your city or town that family and friends have already used, this could be an easy decision.

Whether it's somewhere you've been already: You may have attended a funeral and liked the people who worked at that home and how the place was run.

Religious affiliation: These homes specialize in making arrangements for those who share your religion or beliefs.

Reasonably priced: Some homes might be more affordable compared with other places in the area.

Never feel beholden to a funeral home just because they meet one or more of those criteria. You may have a good impression of a place and feel differently after meeting with the staff. Shop around town until you're comfortable with a place, and get a price from each one you visit. The funeral industry can be very competitive, and you might be able to use information from one funeral home to get a better rate at another. A deal is a deal.

One important thing you may not be aware of is a law put in place by the Federal Trade Commission called the Funeral Rule, which guarantees your right to the funeral arrangements you want and the ability to decline any arrangements you don't want. This rule ensures a clearly itemized price list of services and products the funeral home offers, which is known as a General Price List (GPL). Funeral homes are legally obligated to provide you with it, even if you ask for pricing information over the phone.

Step 2:

Once you find a funeral home you like, start discussing the following options with their funeral director.

Type of service: There are many, many choices: Will it be a traditional, religious-based ceremony, or something more secular and personalized? Or will it be a combo, with modern or personalized aspects mixed in? Will it be open to everyone, or just to family and close friends?

Location of service: Will it take place at a house of worship, the funeral home, or another location?

Burial plot: Where will your final resting place be? This also applies if you're being cremated and want the ashes buried.

Step 3:

Discuss cemetery arrangements. Typically, the funeral director will be able to help you find a cemetery or work with a cemetery you've already chosen.

Find a cemetery: Location, religion, and the environment are factors to consider when choosing a cemetery, as are vacancy and price.

Decide if you want multiple plots: Are you buying plots for other family members as well? If you are, you'll want to find plots or mausoleum spaces that are together.

Visit the cemetery: Take a look at the grounds and see if they're well maintained. Inspect the plot you're buying, and take the opportunity to ask any and all questions before you sign the paperwork and put money down.

Step 4:

Get price quotes (and a GPL!) from the funeral director for the goods and services you'll need for the burial.

Casket: These come in a variety of styles and prices, which you can purchase from the funeral home or from a mass retailer like Amazon,

HAVE IT YOUR WAY

Not all funerals need to be conservative and traditional. For example, one man in Scotland had a Star Wars–themed funeral where the pallbearers were dressed as Stormtroopers and Darth Vader led the procession. Although this might not be your thing, you can still add little touches to have it reflect your personality and lift the spirits of the people you leave behind.

Costco, or Walmart, where they can be much cheaper.

Outer burial container: The cemetery will likely require a grave liner (less expensive) or burial vault (more expensive), which supports the soil around the casket.

Headstone or grave marker: This will have your name, and dates of birth and death, and can include personal information. There are many different types, which you can buy from a funeral home, cemetery, or retailer.

Before engraving: Cemeteries can reject headstones or markers if they violate any of their policies or guidelines, so it's best to get approval from your chosen burial site before purchasing one from somewhere else.

Green burial: If you choose a cemetery specializing in ecofriendly burials, you'll need a biodegradable (or green) casket, but you won't need an outer burial container.

Step 5:

Here are the decisions you'll want to make about the funeral service.

Choosing an officiant: If the service is held at a place of worship, the religious leader will likely lead the service or play some part. It's best to check with the house of worship first.

If you're doing something outside a place of worship, you can choose who will be in charge.

Choose participants: There are many ways for friends and family to participate, either as pallbearers, by delivering a eulogy or reading, by singing songs or playing music, or by offering other suitable tributes.

Make a guest list: You can write down the names and contact information of specific people you would like to attend so the person managing the service knows to invite them (or, if you're really thinking ahead, make a note of it in your contacts). Otherwise, let your family know if the service should be open to anyone who wants to attend or is only for close friends and family.

Design other aspects: Let your family know how you'd like the service to look and feel. Choose flowers if you want them, as well as music, prayers, poems, and other personal touches.

Photo time: You should share flattering photos of yourself— or at least ones that you approve of—to be used for memorialization purposes. If there are photos of yourself you don't like, make it clear you don't want them displayed.

A FIERY EXIT

If you want to be cremated, the first thing to decide is if you want a funeral or memorial service. As we mentioned earlier, you can still have a traditional funeral if you opt for cremation. Just follow the same funeral steps and skip the parts about burial (unless, of course, you plan to have your remains buried).

What Do You Need to Buy?

Cremation tends to be a more affordable option compared with casket burial, but there are still a few required purchases.

Cremation casket: A body being cremated has to be in a fully combustible container, which can be as simple and inexpensive as a cardboard box since it's going to be cremated along with the body. If you're having a traditional service, you can purchase a casket for the funeral (no metal allowed) or rent one and use an alternative container for the cremation.

Urn: This is what holds the remains, and it is available in many different options, depending on whether the ashes are being buried, kept, or scattered. You can shop around for one you like or leave this decision up to your family.

What to Do with Your Ashes?

There are lots of creative options—made into jewelry, embedded into an ocean reef, getting shot into space—but the three most common are burying them in a cemetery, either in a plot or urn garden, or interred in a columbarium; keeping them; or scattering them on land or at sea.

We used to think managing ashes was simple and straightforward, but our research revealed that's not always the case. The National Funeral Directors Association reports that more than half of Americans opt for cremation, a figure that is expected to rise to 80 percent by 2035 (equaling 2.8 million cremations a year). According to a survey taken in 2006 by the Cremation Association of North America, thousands of containers of ashes go unclaimed each year. Most crematoriums will keep them for as long as the law requires until burying them in a columbarium or filling a casket with urns and burying that casket. That's the upside. The downside is that they can accidentally be sold at a garage sale, which is what happened to an Australian woman's mother, as reported by Yahoo!. (Her brother didn't know the urn contained the remains and sold it for $40; luckily, they got them back.)

PAYING IT FORWARD: Funeral Finances

Paying for your funeral in advance can take the financial burden off your family, save money in the long run, and provide the exact funeral you want.

The goal of prepaying is to have an ironclad plan in place, leaving less room (or temptation) for your family to stray from the path you set. Just as you can create a Trust for a child's education, which can be spent only on tuition, you can do the same for your funeral. You're also eliminating the confusion that often comes with planning a funeral, as well as providing a thoughtful gesture from the great beyond.

To help you wrap your head around the ways to pay, we're going to focus on the five basic options: putting money aside specifically for your funeral, paying a funeral home in advance, buying Pre-Need Insurance, buying Final Expense Insurance, and setting up a Trust.

In case you're not well versed in funeral-speak, "pre-need" is when you create a plan and payment method with a funeral home when you're still alive. "At-need" is when your family plans and pays for your funeral when you're already gone. One final thing about funerals before we dive into the details: Regardless of who's paying for them, payment needs to be made up front, which has become standard to prevent people from skipping out on the bill.

Put Money Aside

A seemingly simple option to fund your funeral would be to leave money in a bank account (or envelope) and tell your family to use it for your funeral. Easy enough, right? After all, if you're following the guidance we've offered, someone in your family will have access to your bank account anyway. And remember all the stuff we wrote about probate court and how it can drag on for months or years? Funerals can't wait that long, which means that in the absence of immediate funding, someone would have to front the money and be reimbursed from your estate later.

However, if the money is accessible, are you completely sure it will be used for your funeral? And what if it's not enough? What if the person tasked with the arrangements isn't financially responsible and uses the money to go on a cruise in lieu of giving you the proper funeral you deserve? This is why you might want some more protection.

Pay a Funeral Home Directly

This can be as simple as finding a funeral home you like, working out the price, and cutting them a check. But even though this seems like a wise and simple option, it lacks protection.

What if you never share the details and paperwork with your family and they pay for a funeral all on their own? What if the funeral home goes out of business? What if they say it's not enough and your family has to pay the balance?

Some states might not allow this method of payment or might have strict regulations in place to prevent fraud. If you're putting money down, check online to see if the funeral home is in good standing. For example, do they have general positive feedback? Has anyone reviewed them negatively online, particularly in terms of being shady about pricing? That could be a red flag. If you have any concerns, ask them the questions we include later (see page 210, "Advice from the Government").

Buy Funeral Insurance

Funeral Insurance, also known as Pre-Need Insurance, is different from other types of insurance we've already mentioned in this book because it operates on a principle of not "if" but "when."

Normally you buy Funeral Insurance to make sure that money will always be waiting to cover the cost of your funeral. It's typically purchased *at* the funeral home—many homes have an insurance counselor who's also a licensed agent to help you get it into place. Let's say you already settled on a funeral home and planned out the specific details, including the type of service, the products you'll need, burial options if applicable, and anything else you want. Here's where Funeral Insurance comes into play. Instead of you paying the funeral home, you pay the same price for the policy, which also locks in those rates. If your funeral costs $6,000 today and the same one costs $7,000 years from now when you pass, your family won't be charged the difference.

When death occurs, your family doesn't have to do anything, because the insurance company pays the funeral home directly, often within a day or two. If something doesn't go as planned, like the funeral home tries to change the terms, your family can contact the insurance company for assistance.

If you choose to buy a policy, you'll want to make sure the majority of the prices are guaranteed. This typically includes body removal and transportation, embalming, the casket, the outer burial container, a viewing or wake, and services or amenities offered by the funeral director. Anything outside the funeral home's control, like death notices and obituary placements, the opening and closing of the grave, and flowers, are subject to change. You can estimate these costs in the budget, but your family will have to cover any differences. This can be upsetting if they thought everything would be covered, but the prices shouldn't be too far off. If your family feels like they're being cheated, they should get in touch with the insurance company, find out why, and ask how they can dispute the charges.

If the funeral home from which you purchased the policy goes out of business, or you move and want to choose another home, you can transfer the policy. The only reason why buying a policy wouldn't make sense is if you're opting for a direct cremation with no service or memorial, or your body is going to be donated. To be blunt: If you're not having a funeral, you don't need insurance for it.

Consider Final Expense Insurance

You've probably seen commercials about this when watching late-night TV—at least we have, especially during *Murder,*

She Wrote marathons—mainly because it's for people who can no longer qualify for Life Insurance.

As we age, or deal with complicated medical issues, we're often priced out of the insurance market. Final Expense Insurance is a way to leave your family some extra cash to deal with the things they probably won't want to pay for on their own. The payout from a Final Expense policy is given to the person you name as the beneficiary and can be used for anything, but it's supposed to be put toward funeral expenses or other things to help wind down your estate (like medical bills or outstanding debts).

There are some differences between Funeral Insurance and Final Expense Insurance. Your family isn't required to spend Final Expense Insurance on a funeral, so they could always go on a cruise and ship you off to a potter's field. The downside of Final Expense Insurance is that your family has to make all the stressful decisions and arrangements with the funeral home of their choice and pay the difference if it exceeds the Final

Expense benefit amount. Also, you need to read the fine print on the Final Expense policy before buying it to ensure that your family will be paid promptly. Funerals are time sensitive, and your family

may have to pay out of pocket until the money is available.

Although it might not seem as plush as Funeral Insurance, it's like leaving a decent-size tip to take care of the expenses that creep up on your family at the end.

Use a Trust to Pay

We covered Trusts in Level 2 (see page 86), but we didn't mention funerals. But they can certainly be used to pay for funeral expenses.

When you set up a Trust, you can name anyone as a beneficiary, including a funeral home. You stipulate that the costs of the funeral should be paid to whoever renders the service— so all the better if you know which funeral home you'd like to use—and the trustees can authorize payment. It won't lock in the price ahead of time like Funeral Insurance, but the money is waiting there safely until it's needed.

For a less-complicated method, you can get a Totten Trust, also known as a Payable on Death (POD) account. You fill out paperwork at your bank and name a beneficiary, and that person receives the funds without having to go through the courts. You can make it clear to the beneficiary that the funds should be used to pay for funeral expenses, but you'll have to trust that they'll do what you want, since the money is now theirs to do with as they please.

Aside from Trusts, there are yet other methods to fund a funeral. You can talk to your local Medicaid office to find out if you qualify for benefits. And if you served in the military, you may be due a funeral and burial, mentioned in the "Military Honors" section (see page 26).

Tell Your Family Everything

Whatever method you choose to pay for your funeral, share the arrangements you've made with your family so your thoughtful planning and any money you've already spent don't go to waste. Include the name of the funeral home, the funeral director you've worked with, and where the paperwork is (receipts, bill of sale, policy details, agreement with the home).

We can't stress this enough: One of the keys to effective funeral planning is open communication. And that applies to all the arrangements. We understand it can be very hard to talk to your children, parents, spouse, or loved ones about funeral wishes and mortality, so keep the conversation centered on practical planning—what you want done with your body, where you'd like to be buried or where you'd like your ashes to be scattered—to reduce conflict and emotionally charged disagreements.

(continued on page 210)

PLAN YOUR FUNERAL
(OR AT LEAST THINK ABOUT IT)

The most important aspect is to make your disposition decision—burial, cremation, or donation—since that determines what needs to be done. Once you know, start the Plan of Attack.

DRAFTING FUNERAL WISHES

TIME: Less than an hour to jot down the type of funeral you want based on the elements we discussed earlier (see page 199). If this is all you want to do and you have no interest in solidifying the plans with a funeral home, we suggest you take more time to craft a comprehensive plan for your family to use when it's needed.

PRE-PLANNING WITH A FUNERAL HOME

TIME: Give yourself a week to research and schedule meetings

with funeral homes to begin planning (if you already know the place, even better). Bring your funeral wishes plan when meeting with prospective funeral directors. The meetings should be around an hour if you're gathering information to compare with other homes, and around two hours if you're taking steps to start planning it for real.

PREPAYING FOR YOUR FUNERAL

TIME: If you're purchasing Funeral Insurance, it should be part of the planning process. Same goes for setting up a Trust, buying Final Expense Insurance, or leaving money in an account that is released to a family member when you pass. If you're getting an estimate and *don't* plan to pay in advance, make those instructions clear.

COST: Funeral costs can vary, depending on many factors, but on average they start at $7,000 and go up (sometimes way up) from there.

BUYING A CEMETERY PLOT

TIME: If you're being buried, you may already have a place in mind, which requires you to set up a meeting and work out the details with the cemetery. If you're unsure, take a week to do some research and set up meetings with cemeteries to see the grounds and get an estimate. Once you're set on a place, give yourself another week to work out the details.

COST: Like everything else, this varies, depending on the location and associated products and services: plot or mausoleum crypt, burial vault or grave liner, opening and closing, headstone or marker, installation of headstone or marker, endowment care. The low end is around $4,000, if you go high end across the board, it could exceed $10,000. (And now you understand why cremation is on the rise.)

DIRECT CREMATION

If you're having a funeral and then being cremated, you can factor this into planning with the funeral home. The option we describe below centers on direct cremation without a funeral.

TIME: It's oddly complicated to plan for cremation. Not to sound cavalier, but it's like a restaurant that doesn't take reservations but will always have seating available if you just show up. If you're curious, you can take two to three days to research direct cremation options and find out the details, so your family knows what to do. However, this method of disposition is mainly about costs and simplicity, which means you can leave this to your family to manage the details when you're gone.

COST: Cremation varies between $500 and $3,000 (sometimes more, of course), depending on where it takes place and any extra fees like transportation, cremation casket, and if you want the ashes in an urn as opposed to a standard plastic bag in a cardboard box.

WHOLE BODY DONATION

TIME: It can take a few weeks to research options, find out if you qualify, and complete the paperwork. Each institution that accepts whole body donations operates differently—from how they transport the body to the possibility of returning the ashes to the family after a certain period of time—so it's best to be sure of the process that must be followed after you pass. There are also professional body donation services (sometimes unfavorably referred to as "body brokers," which they hate being called) that can help facilitate the process.

COST: All services should be free of charge.

DISCLAIMER: There's a possibility the donation may fall through, in which case you should create a backup plan for your family.

(continued from page 207)

ADVICE FROM THE GOVERNMENT

In addition to enforcing the Funeral Rule, the Federal Trade Commission created a nifty booklet called *Shopping for Funeral Services* that offers helpful insight into pre-need arrangements—most notably, the questions you should ask the funeral home if you're paying them directly and not purchasing Funeral or Final Expense Insurance.

- **WHAT ARE YOU PAYING FOR?** Are you buying only merchandise, like a casket and vault, or are you purchasing funeral services as well?

- **WHAT HAPPENS TO THE MONEY YOU PAID?** States have different requirements for handling funds paid in advance for funeral services.

- **ARE YOU PROTECTED?** What if the home you dealt with goes out of business?

- **CAN YOU CANCEL THE CONTRACT AND GET A FULL REFUND?** If you change your mind about the items you bought or the arrangements you made, what steps should you take?

- **WHAT HAPPENS IF YOU MOVE OR DIE WHILE AWAY FROM HOME?** How difficult is it to transfer the policy to a different funeral home? Whom should your family contact to have your body transported, and what's the estimated cost?

If you opt for insurance, ask the agent these questions. You should also bring a member of your family or a close friend with you when scoping out possible funeral homes so they can help with any questions you may have.

If you don't feel like you can have an actual conversation with anyone about your funeral, write your decisions and wishes down and leave them in a place where a loved one can find them when they're needed. One of the most popular sections of the Everplans platform is where people can create and share their funeral wishes.

It's also important to note that not everyone in your family will necessarily agree with your decisions. Although it's nice to try to get everyone on the same page, this is your party, and it should be what you want. Give them directions, and financial assistance if you have the means, and know this is a thoughtful and loving way to say goodbye.

LAST WORDS . . . IN PRINT

It's easy to confuse a death notice and an obituary, because they're somewhat similar. A death notice is a paid announcement in a newspaper or online that gives the name of the person who died and details of the funeral or memorial service, as well as where donations can be made. An obituary is essentially a more elaborate, writerly version of a death notice. It typically appears as an article written by the staff of a media outlet that offers a detailed biography of the person who died and may include arrangements as well.

In the old days, newspapers were the only game in town. Anyone could pay to have a death notice or an obituary written by the family printed, but you had to be noteworthy or famous for a staff-written obituary. This still applies for major outlets like the *New York Times* or the *Miami Herald*. The internet leveled the playing field and changed how we announce death and celebrate life. Now anyone can get the word out about a death and include a thoughtful (and usually free) obituary on social media or a tribute site.

The goal for both of these is virtually the same: Alert the world (or the town) to your death. You can still publish them in papers for posterity reasons, and an outlet may contact the family to write an obituary, but it's not as necessary as it once was.

Read All About It: Death Notices and Obituaries in Newspapers

Newspapers almost always charge a fee for publishing a death notice, though the cost depends on the newspaper and its pricing policies. Some papers charge by word count, and others by the number of lines or inches printed. It's best to understand the pricing rules of the paper and where the death notice will appear in advance, because it can get expensive very quickly.

Including a Photograph: Many newspapers will allow you to include a photograph of the person, often for a significant charge. Papers that do allow photos will specify whether photographs must be in black-and-white or color. These days, most papers will accept only digital images—if you have only a printed version, take a high-resolution photo of it with your phone or scan it.

Filing Through a Funeral Home: If you're working with a funeral home, they may offer to write the death notice and have it published. Some funeral homes do this for free, and others charge a fee. If your family will be submitting death notices to multiple newspapers, it may be easiest to have the funeral home handle it if it's in your budget. In addition, the funeral home can collect all the bills to simplify the process.

Submitting Online: Most newspapers have links on their websites directing people to submit a paid death notice, usually under the heading "Obituaries" or "Obits." Although some newspapers manage their own obituary submission and management processes, many newspapers work with the website Legacy.com. To submit a death notice, you can go to the paper's website and follow the instructions, or you can go to Legacy.com and search for the newspaper's death notice submission page.

Lowest-Cost Option: You may also be fine with having your family post something on Facebook and link to a memorial site, since many are free or have a low one-time cost. Some sites to consider are GatheringUs (free), ForeverMissed (fee), Kudoboard (fee), MyKeeper (free),

and Never-Gone (free). For a more comprehensive and up-to-date list, check out incasethebook.com/memorial-sites.

What to Include in a Death Notice or Obituary

The amount of information included in a death notice is entirely up to you and depends on how much you want to publish and how much money you want to spend. In a standard death notice, you'll want to give the following information:

- ❏ The full name of the person who died, including maiden name or nickname

- ❏ Date and location of death

- ❏ Cause of death (optional)

- ❏ Names of surviving family members (optional)

- ❏ Details of the funeral service (public or private); if public: date, time, and location of service

- ❏ Name of charity where donations should be made

When you're looking to venture more into obituary territory, additional biographical information may be included:

- ❏ Date and place of birth

- ❏ Date and place of marriage, and name of spouse

- ❏ Educational history, including schools attended and degrees or honors received

- ❏ Military service, including any honors or awards received

- ❏ Employment history, including positions held, awards received, or special achievements

- ❏ Membership in organizations, including religious, cultural, civic, fraternal, or sororal

- ❏ Special accomplishments

- ❏ Hobbies and interests

Writing Death Notices and Obituaries for Others

Writing one of these is often a group activity, since you'll want to gather information from others and possibly get their approval if they were as close to the deceased as you were. It's also nice to get a few extra sets of eyes to eliminate mistakes that will lead to you being teased at every family gathering for the rest of your life. ("Remember the time Yariv called Grandpop 'Grandpoop' in the newspaper . . .")

Work collaboratively: A lot of information must be gathered to write a death notice or obituary. Sitting down with key family members, getting everyone on the phone together, or doing a group text can help cut down on the time it takes to secure the necessary details. In addition, having everyone participating in the process at the same time can reduce the amount of back-and-forth that often comes with writing something as a group.

Agree on the scope: Before beginning to write the death notice, figure out what information you want to include and what you want to leave out. For example, you may not want to include the details of how the death occurred. If the person had many grandchildren, it may become too long—or expensive if you're paying for it in print—to name them all.

(continued on page 218)

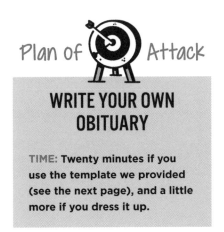

Plan of Attack

WRITE YOUR OWN OBITUARY

TIME: **Twenty minutes if you use the template we provided (see the next page), and a little more if you dress it up.**

Small.

_____ , _____ .
NAME   AGE AT DEATH

Our beloved _____ and friend passed
                                    RELATIONSHIP TO SURVIVORS

away on _____ . Memorial donations
                    DATE OF DEATH: MONTH AND DATE, YEAR

may be made in _____ 's name to
                                    DECEASED'S FIRST NAME

_____ .
                    WHERE DONATIONS SHOULD GO

Medium.

_____ , _____ , peacefully
NAME   AGE AT DEATH

passed away _____
                    DATE OF DEATH: DAY OF THE WEEK, MONTH AND DATE, YEAR

at _____ in _____ . _____ is survived
        LOCATION OF DEATH   CITY, STATE   SHE/HE/THEY

by _____ *. **
        RELATION AND FIRST NAME OF SURVIVING FAMILY MEMBERS

Funeral services will be performed by _____ at
                                                        FUNERAL OFFICIANT

the _____ at _____ on
                    FUNERAL LOCATION   TIME OF SERVICES

_____ .
        DATE OF FUNERAL: DAY OF THE WEEK, MONTH AND DATE, YEAR

*Example of how this looks: "She is survived by her husband, Matt, and their two kids, Michael and Gunderson."

**If you outlived anyone close to you (primarily a spouse or children), you can include the following after listing survivors: "and was predeceased by [NAME OF PREDECEASED FAMILY MEMBERS]." Example: ". . . and was predeceased by her first husband, Scott."

Large.

_____ , _____ , died
NAME   AGE AT DEATH

_____ * on
CAUSE OF DEATH

_____ in _____ .
DATE OF DEATH: DAY OF THE WEEK, MONTH AND DATE, YEAR   CITY, STATE

_____ was born on _____ in _____
SHE/HE/THEY   BIRTHDAY   BIRTHPLACE: CITY, STATE

to _____ . In _____ _____ married
PARENTS' NAMES   YEAR   SHE/HE/THEY

_____ , and together they raised their _____
SPOUSE   SON/DAUGHTER;

_____ . ** _____
CHILDREN'S FIRST NAMES   DECEASED'S FIRST NAME

worked as a _____ for _____ years, and was
OCCUPATION   NUMBER

particularly known for _____ .
PROFESSIONAL OR PERSONAL ACHIEVEMENT

_____ received _____ , including one
SHE/HE/THEY   AWARD OR ACKNOWLEDGMENT

for _____ . _____ is survived
SPECIFIC ACHIEVEMENT   DECEASED'S FIRST NAME

by _____ .
RELATION AND FIRST NAME OF SURVIVING FAMILY MEMBERS

Funeral services will be performed by _____ at
FUNERAL OFFICIANT

the _____ at _____ on
FUNERAL LOCATION   TIME OF SERVICES

_____ *** .
DATE OF FUNERAL: DAY OF THE WEEK, MONTH AND DATE, YEAR

Memorial donations may be made in _____ 's
DECEASED'S FIRST NAME

name to the _____ .
CHARITY DONATION INFORMATION

*Example: "died after a long struggle with [AILMENT OR DISEASE]."

**If the marriage ended in divorce, you could say, for example, "In 1980 he married Jenn Taylor; the marriage ended in divorce." If the deceased remarried, include that as well as additional children: "In 1991 he was remarried to Laura Charles, becoming a stepfather to Kayode and Atanda."

***If no service is being held, you can say, "Funeral services will be privately held."

Supersized.

_____ of _____ ,
               NAME   **CITY, STATE**

died* on _____
                DATE OF DEATH: DAY OF THE WEEK, MONTH AND DATE, YEAR

at _____ . _____ was _____ .
     LOCATION OF DEATH   **SHE/HE/THEY**   **AGE AT DEATH**

_____ was born on _____ in _____ .
  FIRST NAME   **BIRTHDAY**   **LOCATION OF BIRTH**

_____ attended _____ ,
  SHE/HE/THEY   **EARLY EDUCATION: ELEMENTARY SCHOOL**

_____ , and
            EARLY EDUCATION: HIGH SCHOOL

_____ . In _____ _____ married
    COLLEGE OR UNIVERSITY   **YEAR**   **SHE/HE/THEY**

_____ , and together they had _____
    SPOUSE'S FULL NAME   **NUMBER**

children, _____
               FIRST NAME OF EACH CHILD

_____ . **

_____ worked as a _____ at the
  FIRST NAME   **JOB TITLE**

_____ and dedicated _____
     JOB   **HERSELF/HIMSELF/THEMSELVES**

to _____ .
    PROFESSIONAL INTEREST OR PASSION

*You can include the cause of death here if you'd like. Example: "died after a long struggle with [AILMENT OR DISEASE]."

**If divorced or remarried, include it here. Example: "They divorced in 1989, and Maneesh was remarried to Simi Habib."

Supersized. (continued)

_____ served as a member of the _____ . ***
SHE/HE/THEY   *ORGANIZATION NAME*

A one-of-a-kind person, _____ was very _____
                        FIRST NAME   *PERSONAL*

_____ and enjoyed _____
CHARACTERISTIC   *SOMETHING THE DECEASED*

_____ . _____ will be greatly missed. _____
LIKED TO DO   *SHE/HE/THEY*   *FIRST NAME*

is survived by _____
                      SURVIVING FAMILY MEMBERS

_____

and was predeceased by _____
                          PREDECEASED FAMILY MEMBERS

_____ **** .

A memorial service organized by _____
                                  NAME OF FUNERAL HOME

will be held at the _____ at _____
                      FUNERAL LOCATION   *TIME OF SERVICES*

on _____ . Memorial
   DATE OF FUNERAL: DAY OF THE WEEK, MONTH AND DATE, YEAR

donations may be made in _____ 's name to the
                          DECEASED'S NAME

_____ .
CHARITY DONATION INFORMATION

***If the deceased won any awards or special achievements, include it here. Example: "He served as a member of SPECTRE and in 2010 was awarded the top prize for Diabolical Villainy."

****If there are a lot of surviving and predeceased family members, you can tighten it up this way: "Maneesh is survived by his eight daughters, three sons, and nineteen grandchildren and was predeceased by his wife, Simi."

(continued from page 213)

Proofread: Have at least two different people read it over once it's been written to avoid spelling, grammar, and informational errors. Things to look for include making sure everyone's name is spelled correctly, the names of all cities, companies, organizations, schools, and clubs are spelled correctly, the funeral service information is correct (date, time, location), and the instructions are correct for donations in the name of the deceased.

Write Your Death Notice

To help you write your own (or someone else's), we presented you with four variations, ranging from small to supersized. The bold blank spaces (with details below in brackets) are for you to fill in the information. It's like that old game *Mad Libs*. (Or *Sad Libs* if we thought this was sad, which it's not. But still a good pun, right?)

Now that you have the basic idea of how it works and what to include, you can play with the format and make it as personal as you like. Obviously, there are some parts you won't be able to fill out from the afterlife, like cause and date of death, which means you'll need to share this with someone so they can add the final touches. You can also use this template if you have to write a death notice or obituary for someone else, which is a part of life many of us may have to deal with at some point.

Don't forget to include instructions about where it should be sent or posted. If you're already working with a funeral home, they should be able to take care of it. If you want it to go to a specific outlet or site, don't hesitate to add that to your instructions.

TIERS OF MEMORIALIZATION

Would you like a tree planted in your name? An annual bike-athon? Your name on a brick in front of your favorite team's stadium? Although everyone has their own private way of remembering a loved one, there may be instances where you feel a memory isn't enough. For example, maybe your loved one was very involved in a community and you want to do more to honor their memory in the form of a public memorial. But big gestures come with big questions: What form does the memorial take? How do you get it done? How much does it cost? To get started, consider the scope of what you want to do.

Tier 1: Simple

Creating a Facebook memorial page is free, and it can even be set up beforehand as part of one's overall planning (see page 139). As a refresher, a profile page could also be retitled with the word *Remembering* above someone's name and people can post photos and stories on the timeline. You can also consider the memorial sites we mentioned earlier (see page 212).

Tier 2: Localized

If you or your loved one had a favorite park, walking spot, activity, or if one of you was active in a church or other religious organization, you may have some options for more public memorials.

Often, churches will build memorial walkways and allow people to purchase engraved bricks. These usually run anywhere from $100 to $150 or more, depending on the church. Our former coworker Ammon's late father was an avid pilot, so he added his name to the Smithsonian's National Air and Space Museum's Wall of Honor for $100, which also let him include a 500-word bio and picture on their site.

As for benches, the best thing to do is to contact the community center in the town where the desired park is and inquire about bench availability and pricing.

A memorial doesn't have to be a physical location. You can set up a memorial event in the deceased's honor. After Abby's brother died, the family set up an annual bike ride in his memory. Doug was an avid long-distance bike rider, so they created Doug's Ride, where family and friends gather annually together in Washington, DC, to honor their memories of him and show support for one another.

Tier 3: Grand

If money is no object and you want something very big, like getting-a-street-in-your-city-named-after-you big, you can always apply and see. New York City, for example, accepts applications for street naming twice a year (in October and April) and has very specific guidelines about candidates. There are similar programs in many cities and towns around the country. Research to see if the local government offers opportunities for memorialization such as park benches, street names, or even memorial statues.

You can always petition your town

or your loved one's town and see if they show interest, but it's likely only in extreme cases that your petition would be granted. Although it's extremely rare to advertise a fee associated with such petitions, it's safe to assume a generous donation to the town would need to be made in conjunction with the memorial.

The donation required to get a room or an entire wing of a hospital named after someone varies enormously—some institutions, like the Children's Center in Salt Lake City, Utah, offer memorialized rooms starting at $35,000, according to the *New York Times*. Going beyond that takes you into the multiple millions. An example is the hockey player P. K. Subban, who had the atrium of the Montreal Children's Hospital named in his honor after he donated $10 million.

■ ■ ■

Side Mission:
REMOVE SKELETONS FROM YOUR CLOSET

This entire book is about all the stuff you need to organize and share with the people you love. But what about the stuff you want to stay private forever? Whether it's personal items, correspondence, or predilections that leave a trail, we're here to help you with a two-step process: identifying said items and eliminating them from the face of the earth.

The first thing you need is a person you trust implicitly who will do exactly what you ask. We refer to this confidant as your Cleaner. They'll go through your computer, dresser drawers, medicine cabinets, and anywhere else questionable materials might be lurking. Then they'll actually delete and/or destroy whatever you desire without question, complaint, or judgment.

Even though a Cleaner isn't a legal title like executor, Health Care Proxy, or Power of Attorney, you're trusting this person with extremely sensitive information. It will also likely be a thankless job, one that requires the discretion and ability to keep everything they're asked to do a secret for the rest of their lives. Which is a very tall order.

Once you identify and get that person to agree to their solemn duty, here's the type of business you'll want them to sanitize.

THE FOUR CRITERIA FOR DISPOSAL

There are a handful of common reasons someone may want things erased from existence upon their passing.

EMBARRASSING: Apply this litmus test: Could you put this item in plain sight when the family comes over for Thanksgiving? If you answered no, then it falls into this category.

DANGEROUS: Anything that poses a safety threat, especially to kids . . . or teenagers looking to raid the medicine cabinet.

SECRET: Information, affiliations, or relationships you don't want seen by family, friends, or the general population.

ILLEGAL: Items that might have gotten you arrested if the cops searched your house while you were still alive.

When you're sorting through everything we covered in this book, particularly your digital estate, home, and personal possessions, think of this as a secret satchel where you're mentally storing anything that touches on one of these four categories.

COMPUTER, PHONE, AND TABLET

This is where the bulk of most offending material resides. You have to make sure your Cleaner has the password to your devices, along with directions if you kept things hidden especially well.

BROWSER HISTORY: This is Cleanup 101. If you've never heard of "private browsing" or "incognito," you'll probably need someone to access your computer and delete all your browsing history, along with cookies. This isn't just for adult material, even though that's usually the main culprit. It could also be searches or other pages you visited that you don't want people to know about.

If you're worried your Cleaner won't know how to delete a browser history, it's really easy and can be accomplished with a simple Google "How do I delete browser history

on . . ." search from the browser they're looking to clean. If you're logged in to a browser—the main ones being Chrome, Firefox, Safari, Microsoft Explorer, or Edge— then following the results of this search should take care of deleting browser history across all platforms (computer, phone, tablet). Still, have them check each device just to be extra safe.

HARD DRIVE: The objective is to locate and delete all offending files: photos, videos, documents, and anything else you want gone. Ideally, you should offer some guidance, since people don't keep secret items in a folder on their desktop called "Super-Secret Things Go in This Folder, Which Should Be Deleted Upon My Death." It doesn't have to be a treasure map, but it should mention folders you want deleted.

If photos and videos have been hidden or renamed, have the Cleaner search for file types (.jpg, .mov, etc.) or just delete the documents, photos, and video folders. You can also go the other route and tell them what to salvage, such as a photo folder, and then delete everything else.

After this is done, they need to remember to empty the trash or else all the work will have been for naught.

WHEN ALL ELSE FAILS . . . If you know a computer is too difficult to clean, just tell your Cleaner to either wipe it completely (factory reset) or smash the machine and throw it into the nearest volcano (or a Best Buy electronics recycling bin, which is probably closer and much more environmentally sound).

SWEEP AND CLEAR

EXTERNAL BACKUPS: People have become very adept at backing up their computers—whether it's to an external hard drive, thumb/flash drives, or even DVDs and CDs—so much so that a Cleaner could delete requested material on a computer and still have to do it all over again on backups. We covered the purpose of backups already (see page 150), explaining that the main reason they exist is to rebuild a machine after a computer meltdown. Since you're no longer around, that's not an issue. You can pick from three simple solutions: (1) Give your Cleaner specific instructions on what needs to be done with each device; (2) tell

your Cleaner to reformat the drive and use it as new; and (3) smash it and responsibly recycle the parts that shouldn't end up in the trash (mainly the battery).

> **TIP: Before making a trip to a responsible recycling facility (or a volcano), go through the rest of this Side Mission, because there's probably a lot more stuff that'll be disappearing forever.**

EMAIL: What would happen if your family, friends, or coworkers read all your emails and IMs? What if you have secret email accounts no one in your immediate life knows about? Out of context, which it would be since you can't defend yourself, it could get very ugly. Maybe you want your Cleaner to search for specific names and delete those emails, texts, and chats. Maybe you want everything deleted. You make the call; just give your Cleaner specific instructions and make sure they have access to those accounts.

PHONE/TABLET: A phone or tablet can be the ultimate source of portable secrets. You might want all your texts deleted, especially ones that could cause stress to your spouse, kids, or family. The same goes for contacts in your address book whom you'd rather keep secret.

Just like email and texts, social media has a part you share with the world (or your "friends") and a place for private messaging—think Facebook/Instagram, Google Hangouts/Voice, Twitter direct messages (DMs), and others. You could also have multiple accounts (*Catfish*, anyone?) and want all but your primary account deleted.

SITE MEMBERSHIPS AND DIGITAL SUBSCRIPTIONS

A subscription to Amazon or backups like iCloud or an external hard drive with family photos doesn't require much stealth, but what about sites or digital storage methods that require a little more discretion? Your goal is to prevent having a line in your obituary that says, "She leaves behind a husband of thirty-five years . . . and a very active dating profile he knew nothing about."

DATING PROFILES/MEMBERSHIPS AND ADULT SITES: Along the lines of deleting a browser history, a Cleaner needs to know about any online memberships that require deletion and aren't officially part of your digital estate. The most common type of paid membership would be for dating sites like Match, eHarmony, OkCupid, and so on. If you don't want

people to know you used one of these services—or if you're in a relationship but always kept your options open—send in the Cleaner.

There's also a massive slew of apps for meeting people, which are often referred to as "hookup apps." (If you don't know what this means, use your imagination.) You'll probably want these gone, especially if you're paying, still married, or want to keep this aspect of your life completely private.

A Cleaner might also have to cancel subscription payments for adult sites. If you happen to be active on these types of sites, and uploaded photos or videos, you might want to give instructions for these to be deleted or else they might stay up forever and become the opposite type of video we suggested leaving behind ("Videos for Loved Ones," see page 196).

DIGITAL HELP FOR PERSONAL ISSUES: Although "cleaning" might be centered on hiding secret relationships and adult content, there are other types of subscriptions and memberships that require discretion.

For example, if a person is a member of a support group for abuse, addiction, or a mental disorder and kept it private throughout their life, why should it be revealed in death? It might be common in society for people to talk about their problems, but many people still prefer to keep their personal struggles to themselves. If this is the case, leave instructions for what your Cleaner needs to do. This doesn't have to be a negative thing. For example, perhaps you want to write a special message to a group for all the help they provided.

CLOUD-BASED STORAGE: We grouped services like Dropbox, iCloud, Google Drive, and others that allow you to back up files to a virtual hard drive earlier (see page 11) but left this part out. Something you think was deleted on a phone, computer, and external drive could still be hanging out in the cloud. Treat these accounts the same way you would files on a computer and have your Cleaner review them for anything possibly upsetting to others.

PHYSICAL MEDIA AND OTHER MATERIAL

Let's ease into this section, because it can get uncomfortable very fast.

DO YOU WANT ANYONE READING NAUGHTY LOVE LETTERS YOU EXCHANGED WITH A HIGH SCHOOL CRUSH?

Sometimes, people hide things around their homes. They might be odd trinkets or memories that have no apparent meaning, but others are painfully obvious upon discovery. Younger generations might not have the number of physical items older generations do (example: a stack of adult magazines), but there's always something somewhere you might not want on display. The item could even be something that was given to you as a joke and was later thrown in the back of a drawer. (Or at least that's what you'd say if anyone ever found it.)

Apart from "professionally" produced material, there could be copies of amateur footage, either video or photographs, or even something homemade. (Again, no judgments!) If your Cleaner already deleted the digital stuff, this should be a breeze. Just shred and toss.

After your Cleaner has done a full sweep, they should put everything into a black garbage bag and discard it in a dumpster behind a superstore or some other anonymous location. Have them do it off-hours and it'll make them feel like a spy!

> **TIP: A good Cleaner will always have some rubber gloves and hand sanitizer at the ready.**

BOOKS AND OTHER ITEMS: Self-help books or pamphlets might seem harmless, but some could reveal a problem of yours that you don't want known. Example: Most men don't go around bragging about impotence. The same goes for books or relics centering on what may be viewed as radical ideology (anarchism, communism, terrorism . . .). If there's something you worry might have people question your beliefs or how you lived your life, add it to the list.

PERSONAL CORRESPONDENCE, HIDDEN ASSETS, WEAPONS, AND . . .

This part starts off quite romantic but then escalates quickly. It can be embarrassing for your heirs to find a private diary with your innermost desires, but it can be extremely dangerous if they find a cache of unregistered weapons in a secret compartment in the closet.

LOVE LETTERS AND NOTES: Books and movies like *Bridges of Madison County* and *The Notebook* have made finding old love letters and journals the height of romance. And although it might be sweet to see how your parents corresponded when they first met, do you really want your son or daughter reading naughty letters you may have exchanged with a high school crush? Or give them definitive proof of an affair?

Perhaps you kept these missives because of sentimentality or maybe you never got around to throwing them away. But if you don't want them passed around at the next family reunion, tell your Cleaner to shred them.

JOURNALS AND DIARIES: Private diaries and journals aren't usually meant to be shared. Personal thoughts can be shocking, especially if the person who wrote them was going through a tumultuous time in their life.

If you wake up in a cold sweat worried that a sibling, child, spouse, or friend might one day read these private thoughts, let your Cleaner know where you keep them so they can be tossed into a fireplace. (We'd suggest the volcano, but that's getting awfully crowded with all the other stuff and, well, polluting.)

HIDDEN ASSETS: There's a seemingly endless number of stories where someone buys a couch or painting at a garage sale or thrift store and finds thousands of dollars stashed inside. Usually because the person who generously donated the couch or painting forgot or didn't know there was money in it.

We already covered how estate distribution works, and how all your cash and valuable assets need to be accounted for by your executor and go through probate (see pages 79–85). But what if you have a lot of money hidden somewhere that you don't want to be part of your estate? Do you want the $50,000 hidden in the basement going to the mother of your most recent child or to the children from another marriage? Unreported money or assets over a certain limit are illegal, so although we can't condone having a Cleaner take these assets and give them to the person you want to have them, it's your life (and death). Just know that if a Cleaner is caught with these funds, they can get in trouble, so the best (legal) way to do this is to create a Trust (see page 86).

MEDICATION: From a safety perspective, it's always smart to dispose of all medication after a death. However, if you've secretly lived with a condition, like a mental disorder (example: manic depression), or a persistent sexually transmitted disease (like herpes), your Cleaner should do a sweep of your medicine cabinet and throw away anything and everything that's stronger than Advil or Tylenol.

Another issue may arise if you were on painkillers (Percocet, Oxycodone, Vicodin) and are worried someone close may steal them for personal use. The Partnership for Drug-Free Kids reports that one in five teens misuses prescription drugs, and often shares them with friends. Maybe you also want to keep them out of the hands of a family member suffering from addiction. Rather than have the temptation around, have your Cleaner toss these as well. We also suggest taking off the labels, since they may contain personal information.

NARCOTICS: Even though prescription drugs can be just as deadly and addictive as illegal drugs, there's now the "legalization" factor to consider. Unless your family is the type that passes bongs down from generation to generation, you probably don't want your stash being discovered while people are cleaning out your stuff.

Even though marijuana is legal in some states, and becoming decriminalized in others, it might still technically be illegal. Have your Cleaner do with that as you see fit, and don't forget to include all the related paraphernalia. And although the stigma of pot has lessened, the harder stuff (cocaine, crack, heroin, methamphetamines) often indicates a bigger problem and can cause a lot of heartache to friends and family after a death.

Keep in mind that, regardless of the circumstances of a death, afterward it's about the surviving loved ones. And they will have to deal with the judgment that comes with a secret addiction going public, especially among families or social circles that feed off of negative drama.

Granted, most people in the midst of a serious addiction have bigger issues than posthumously preserving their reputation. Naming a Cleaner might not be a factor for this person, but a thoughtful and understanding close friend or family member can help tremendously. The same can be said for removing alcohol from the house of a deceased alcoholic out of respect for the family.

Unless the deceased publicly struggled and wanted to be used as an example for future generations, discretion as opposed to sanctimonious morality goes a long way in these situations.

UNREGISTERED WEAPONS: There's a protocol for properly transferring or getting rid of registered guns, rifles, and other firearms. Call up local law enforcement, and they'll come over and remove them. But that's not what we're talking about here. What if you have unregistered firearms and explosives?

This is where things can get very dangerous, because the person caught with weapons will suffer the consequences. If your Cleaner gets pulled over with illegal weapons in their trunk, then they're the ones going to jail. So please be responsible.

FIREARMS AND EXPLOSIVES: This is one of the few areas where a Cleaner should not remove the items from the house. Instead, the Cleaner should treat these the same way they would any firearm that they didn't know existed beforehand. In some cases, gun owners may have created a Gun Trust or accounted for these weapons as part of their estate, especially if they're worth a lot of money. (If you're interested in this route, speak with an estate attorney to learn more.) If the deceased didn't make any plans for the weapons, let local law enforcement know the situation and have them safely removed. Unless it's a box of firecrackers, the Cleaner should not, under any circumstances, be handling them if they don't know what they're doing.

BUT WHAT IF . . . the weapon a Cleaner is asked to dispose of was used in a crime? OK, Columbo, we'll play along.

If you're asking someone to get rid of, let's say, a gun you used in an unsolved crime, we have this question for you: Why are you still keeping that gun?! Unless you want the gun to be a posthumous confession (example: "Cleaner, I want you to tell the police the location of this weapon along with this letter explaining what I did"), either turn yourself in and face the consequences or get rid of it right now. Otherwise your Cleaner might take the rap.

FINAL
Break Time

What Happens If . . .
You Don't Plan Ahead?

I f you choose to not follow the great majority of the stuff we included in this book, there's a plan waiting for your family. It's called "the default." And one of the main purposes of this book is to help you avoid the default.

Even if you *did* some (or most) of the planning we laid out for you, the reality is that everything can revert to a default if the right people don't know what plans you've put into place, or what your decisions and wishes are. This concept was brought to our attention by Dr. Jeff Belkora, a professor at University of California, San Francisco, and author of the book *DEAL! Discovery, Engagement, and Leverage for Professionals*. When it comes to planning in general, he champions "changing the default so people have to opt out rather than opt in." For example, some countries are working toward making organ donation the default, which means everyone's a donor unless they say otherwise. Unfortunately, most of the situations covered in this book require planning in advance,

otherwise you better be OK with . . . the default. We're not using this as a scare tactic—you simply need to know the repercussions of avoiding a plan until it's too late.

THE END-OF-LIFE DEFAULT

Most lives end with a series of decisions about which treatments to pursue and which to avoid. Then comes the ultimate decision: when to completely discontinue *all* medical interventions. There are also decisions about whether you want to spend your final days at home, in a hospital, or at a hospice facility. Frequently, a person reaches a moment where they're unable to communicate or advocate for themselves, and all these decisions need to be made by a loved one or family member.

If you haven't created an Advance Directive, named a Health Care Proxy, or discussed how you want your end to go, here's the default.

Doctors won't give up: They'll keep fighting whatever medical hardship you're up against, even if it means difficult medical procedures that will erode the quality of your life. They might schedule you for surgeries from which you'll never recover. They might hook you up to machines to keep your body going. It's not because they're bad people—they're trained to never give up, and without clear input from you or someone in charge of making medical decisions on your behalf, they won't. If given the choice, this isn't how most people want to go out.

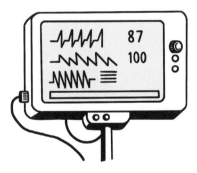

Emergency interventions will lead to cascading outcomes: If something relatively minor happens that requires a visit to the emergency room or a visit from an EMT, you may have to be admitted to a hospital and you might never get out.

An emotionally taxed family will make decisions they aren't prepared to make: At some point a hospital or hospice worker will turn to someone in your family and ask them to decide on next steps, or ask them if they want to execute a POLST (see page 193) to help direct subsequent medical intervention (or nonintervention). Not only is this an incredible burden to place on someone you love, but it often leads to disagreements within families that can have disastrous ramifications, even leading to court battles over who should be making the decisions. When someone doesn't know what you want, it's human nature to err on the side of "keep them alive at any cost," leading back to our first point about doctors never giving up.

HOW TO CHANGE THE END-OF-LIFE DEFAULT

Have a conversation: Just letting someone in your family know your wishes can make a huge difference.

Record your decisions: Take the time and fill out an Advance Directive (again, a combo of your Living Will and naming a Health Care Proxy), like we explained in Level 2 (see page 120).

Reveal the location: Your family needs to know how to access your Advance Directive and any other medical directives (DNR or POLST) when they need it.

THE FROZEN BANK ACCOUNT DEFAULT

When you die, the default is that anything that isn't *explicitly* jointly owned with someone else becomes part of your estate. Anything that's part of your estate essentially becomes "locked" until it clears probate, which can make it inaccessible to your family for months. This can be a huge problem for paying end-of-life and funeral expenses, as well as continuity on day-to-day expenses like mortgage payments or even keeping the lights on.

How to Change the Default:

First, organize all your major assets (see page 16) and debts (see page 96) so your family has a clear lay of the financial landscape. Next, your primary spending accounts should be set up as joint tenants with rights of survivorship (or JTWROS for you initialism lovers). This allows the surviving member to continue to access that account and pay bills until the estate is settled.

If you have separate accounts and your partner has a terminal illness, speak to your bank or financial advisor about shifting some cash out of joint accounts into your own to guarantee it's available. If your partner has a fatal accident, and you have access to their accounts because they were shared in advance, use the time before the death is reported to transfer money into your account to pay for things like the funeral and other required expenses. This may seem like you're painting outside the lines (because you are), but if you keep track of all the money transferred, where it was spent, and proof it was for a legitimate purpose, you can deal with it later when going through probate.

THE CHILD CUSTODY DEFAULT

If you die without naming guardians for your minor children or other dependents in your Will, a court will decide who gets custody. By default, this is the other parent. This could be a disaster if the other biological parent is out of the mix and the children consider the stepparent their "real" parent.

If both parents die together, by default the court will have to choose someone else (see page 77). This could be any member of your family who asks for custody, which means your kids could end up with someone completely unsuitable to raise them and almost always results in epic family disagreements.

How to Change the Default:

If you're looking for a complicated solution, there isn't one: Create a Will and name a guardian! This is especially beneficial to people with a complicated family structure, be it a blended family or a situation where the other biological parent should not, under any circumstances, gain custody.

The same goes for naming an executor (see page 79), which helps you avoid a different, but still extremely maddening, default. Recap: It requires that someone be named an administrator by the court and might require that an expensive bond be posted against the estate.

THE LOCKED PHONE DEFAULT

We started this book with passwords and codes, so that's how we'll end it. Having access to a phone paves the way to a smoother process of unwinding an estate and dealing with nagging issues that can haunt a family for months. This includes letting important contacts know

the person has died, accessing digital accounts to transfer or close them, and much more. Think about the panic you feel when you think you've misplaced your phone because you put it in a different pocket. Now imagine it being gone forever, because if someone dies without providing its password, there's no way a phone provider or manufacturer will grant you access.

How to Change the Default:

Share the unlock code to your phone. See, sometimes the most obvious solution is the right one. If you don't want to share it today, put it in a place where it can be found, as well as instructions for how it will be useful for the person to start unraveling your estate. While you're sharing your phone code, share all your passwords. This is probably the 12,000th time we've written this, and we have no regrets for the repetition. It's that important.

There are other defaults involving property, taxes, lost benefits, and paying way too much for a funeral. This book has been basically one massive tip sheet to avoid defaults. Keep that in mind when you start doing all this stuff, because then you'll realize that getting a plan in place is *really* giving your family and loved ones a gift they don't even know they need.

AFTERWORD

One last thing before we meet again: When we began this planning quest, we told you to constantly visualize your purpose for doing all this work. For those who didn't identify a purpose at the outset, we said it would eventually be revealed. By now, after absorbing all the information here into your mind, something has struck a chord (we hope!). When things get tough and you want to put this off till later (knowing later may never come), visualize that purpose. Sear it into your brain so that when you're frustrated at all the photos you have to sort or concerned about sharing this much information about your life, the people who will benefit from all your hard work will one day be grateful. That day could be many years from now (again, we hope!) or tomorrow. We never know when, and it's always too soon, but at least you can rest easy, knowing everyone you care about will be prepared.

Enough about us. We've said plenty. What about you? Tell us your stories, planning progress, biggest worries, and anything else. This isn't just a book. It's our mission, and it's always evolving. You're a part of it now, so please contact us at **us@incasethebook.com** and we'll be in touch.

—Abby, Adam, and Gene

PLAN OF ATTACK CHECKLIST

You made it to the end! Here's a parting gift, which should be especially helpful for those who may have nodded off during some sections of this book. We get it. Trusts aren't thrilling for us either.

LEVEL 1 ----------------------------------➤ 1

❏ Organize Passwords & Codes

❏ Compile All the Money You Have

❏ Create a Home Operating System

❏ Organize Contacts

⟼➔

ACKNOWLEDGMENTS

Everplans has been on a mission since day one to get people organized through critical life moments, and there are so many people who helped (and continue to help) along the way.

To Warren Habib, Atanda Abdulsemiu, Kayode Adeniyi, Yariv Alpher, Sarah Bunnell, Peter Bogart Johnson, Bernard Kravitz, Yoko Nakano, and Harris Scher, we want to thank you for everything you do. A special mention to Sarah Whitman-Salkin for being the first official Everplans employee, who sat in a tiny room (and at coffee shops) with Adam and Abby laying the foundation for our numerous planning resources, and our PR and communications guru Jennifer Newman for being there with us from the start.

Throughout this book we stealthily used the names of almost everyone who has worked at Everplans. Apologies if we left anyone out: Adan, Adebayo, Alvin, Ammon, Bart, Brandon, Caitlin, Casey, Charles, Dan, Dania, Dina, Elizabeth, Geoff, Hugh, Jade, Jamie, Jordan, Julio, Keith, Kevin, Laura, Mary Beth, Maneesh, Matt, Mike, Ryan, Scott, Simi, Stan, Taylor, Tolu, Yaniv, and Zeina.

To our incredible board members, investors, advisors, partners, consultants, and friends in the business who've helped us turn our vision into reality, including: William Charnock, Joe Landy, Anil Arora, Carolyn Balfany, Mark Showers, Stephanie Grass, Chris Murumets, Ray DiDonna, Tim Rozar, Dennis Barnes and everyone on the RGAX team, Knut Olson, Tim Schaefer, Dave Anderson and NGL, Dave McCabe, Brad Harrison, Brendan Syron and Scout Ventures, Parker Hayden, Paul Yun, Adam Dawson, Ed Zysik, Georg Schwegler, Andrew Pitz and Transamerica Ventures, Lior Yahalomi, Steve Schlesinger, Andy Schwartz, Mark Seelig, Jon Cherins, Merrill Dubrow, Chad Comiteau, Michael Luftman, Archie Gottesman, Gary DeBode, Greg Blank, Henlopen Group (Dana Warren, Josh Warren, Whitney Horton Leberman, Dan Leberman, Wendy Reiners, Kendall Hochman, Lauren Mason), Katy Fike, Stephen Johnston and Aging 2.0, Art Chang, Heather Myers, Ariel Aberg-Riger and Spark No. 9, Steve Pressler, Steve Gross, Shara Mendelson, Jeremy Johnson and Andela, Adam Reuben, David Sharrow, Matthew Smallcomb, Ken McVay and everyone at Gunderson, DXagency, Scott Grand and Narrative, Catherine Frey, Mark Palmer and James Frey, Brandon Ellison, Casey Watkins, Brian Pope, Doug Zeh and the SFG team, Mark Figart and Digett, Tim Maguire, Brian McLaughlin and Redtail, the Orion team, Matt Berman, Gary Freilich, Frank McAleer, Amanda Stahl and the Longevity Planning team at Raymond James, The Advice Center team at Transamerica, Adam Holt and Asset-Map, Neil Ash, Brian Williams, Jeffrey Marrazzo, David Glitzer and Jill Fishman, Archelle Georgiou, Brad Hargreaves, Marie Swift, Will Schwalbe, John Whitman, Jeff Belkora, Lisa Olender, Joe Ziemer, Andrew Ross Sorkin, Ann Sardini, Michael Civello, and Deb Korb Maizner. We have certainly left important contributors off this list and we thank you all.

Thanks to the millions of visitors

to our site and tens of thousands of users of our platform, including financial professionals and employers and other organizations. This includes all the people who shared their personal experiences and stories with us, some of which were used in this book.

We can't praise Workman Publishing enough. From the first meeting we knew we were in the perfect hands. Workman understood us immediately, sharing stories of their own and helping us distill everything we knew into book form. Special thanks to Suzie Bolotin for helping us keep focus, John Meils for his thoughtful and extremely patient editing (packing this much information into a 256-page book was no easy task), their design team of Vaughn Andrews and Lisa Hollander for bringing it to life, and a deft marketing team (Cindy Lee, Diana Griffin, Lathea Mondesir, Ilana Gold, Rebecca Carlisle) and so many more for being there every step of the way, including Hillary Leary, Barbara Peragine, and Emily Krasner. And of course, to Katie Workman and our agent Pilar Queen, who shepherded this book from the earliest stages through the entire process.

Adam and Abby need to begin by thanking Gene, who really led the way in getting this book written.

Abby would like to thank her incredible family and friends for putting up with her for the past ten years as she ignored their texts, missed a lot of bedtimes, and showed up late to countless events because she was on a mission trying to make Everplans—and now this book— happen. But in particular to her parents Karen and Milton, her sisters Jessie, Lisa P., and Lisa S., who have been so supportive at every step along the way and who allowed her to share their family's very personal story with the world—in order to help as many people as possible. "To Ben, Wynne, and Dani, nothing in the world is more important than you are to me. You are my reason for everything. And lastly, to my brother Doug. The person who I brought to kindergarten for show and tell as my hero. And the person I think about every day and who has inspired so much of this Everplans journey. I miss you so much."

Adam would like to thank his parents (Joan and Bob) for being good test subjects for a lot of the planning advice in this book and his family (Carrie, Milo, Casey, and Wally) for giving him a healthy dose of motivation for getting his own plans in place. And a shout out to his siblings Eric, Merin, and Jason for working through a lot of these "adulting" situations together.

Gene would like to thank his mom and dad (Judy, Jeff), siblings (Julie, Jill), sibling-in-law (Larry), niece and nephew (Sydney, Riley), and dogs (Dollar, Plissken) for putting up with how weird he can be, even though they're mostly responsible for it. Finally, Abby and Adam for having the courage, foresight, and tenacity to create Everplans, a natural default toward empathy and compassion, and not forcing him to eat all the strange things they like to eat (but still find ways to expand his palate beyond sad salads).

■ ■ ■

RESOURCES

DIGITAL:

PASSWORD MANAGERS:
Dashlane, 1Password, and LastPass

DIGITAL FINANCIAL TOOLS:
Mint, Clarity Money, Personal Capital, Trim, You Need A Budget (YNAB), Quicken, eMoney, Asset-Map, TurboTax

CLOUD STORAGE:
Amazon Photos, Dropbox, Google Photos, iCloud, Microsoft OneDrive

RECIPE APPS: Paprika, BigOven, Cookpad

GENEALOGY/FAMILY HISTORY:
Ancestry, FamilySearch, MyHeritage, 23andMe, StoryCorps, the USC Shoah Foundation, Geni, Genealogical Data Communication (GEDCOM) file

ORGANIZATIONS AND INSTITUTIONS:

Pew Research Center
(pewresearch.org)

National Association of Unclaimed Property Administrators
(unclaimed.org)

National Cemetery Administration
(cem.va.gov)

National Suicide Prevention Lifeline
(suicidepreventionlifeline.org)

HelpWithMyBank.gov

National Fire Protection Association
(nfpa.org)

Electrical Safety Foundation International (esfi.org)

American Pet Products Association
(americanpetproducts.org/)

SpareFoot (sparefoot.com)

Nolo (nolo.com)

Consumer Action
(consumer-action.org)

West Health Institute
(westhealth.org)

NORC at the University of Chicago
(norc.org)

Administration for Community Living
(acl.gov)

LongTermCare.gov

Council for Disability Awareness
(disabilitycanhappen.org)

Organ Procurement and Transplantation Network
(optn.transplant.hrsa.gov)

United Network for Organ Sharing
(unos.org)

US Department of Health and Human Services (hhs.gov)

National Heart, Lung, and Blood Institute (nhlbi.nih.gov)

National Center for Biotechnology Information (ncbi.nlm.nih.gov)

World Journal of Gastroenterology
(wjgnet.com/1007-9327/index.htm)

American Heart Association
(heart.org)

Centers for Disease Control and Prevention (cdc.gov)

Mayo Clinic (mayoclinic.org)

OrganDonor.gov

Uniform Law Commission
(uniformlaws.org)

Wells Fargo Financial Health Survey

Federal Trade Commission: The FTC Funeral Rule (consumer.ftc.gov /articles/0300-ftc-funeral-rule), Shopping for Funeral Services (consumer.ftc.gov/articles/0070 -shopping-funeral-services), and Funeral Costs and Pricing Checklist (consumer.ftc.gov/articles/0301 -funeral-costs-and-pricing-checklist)

National Funeral Directors
Association (nfda.org)

Cremation Association of North
America (cremationassociation.org/)

Legacy.com

Smithsonian National Air and Space
Museum (airandspace.si.edu/)

Partnership to End Addiction
(drugfree.org)

BOOKS

***The Gentle Art of Swedish Death
Cleaning:*** *How to Free Yourself
and Your Family from a Lifetime of
Clutter,* **by Margareta Magnusson**

The Conversation: *A Revolutionary
Plan for End-of-Life Care,* **by Dr.
Angelo Volandes**

A Beginner's Guide to the End:
*Practical Advice for Living Life and
Facing Death,* **by Dr. BJ Miller and
Shoshana Berger**

***DEAL! Discovery, Engagement,
and Leverage for Professionals,***
by Jeff Belkora

Nudge: *Improving Decisions About
Health, Wealth, and Happiness,*
**by Richard H. Thaler and Cass R.
Sunstein**

MEDIA OUTLETS

New York Times

Kaiser Health News

Washington Post

InfoTrends

TechJury

Yahoo!

Yahoo! Finance

Statista

Albuquerque Journal

Chicago Tribune

NHL

Everplans

LINKS

incasethebook.com/password
-manager

incasethebook.com/financial-tools

incasethebook.com/advance
-directive-forms

incasethebook.com/digital-account
-matrix

incasethebook.com/spill-your-life

incasethebook.com/memorial-sites

CONTACT US

us@incasethebook.com

■ ■ ■

INDEX

. . .